Sound Change

Edinburgh Historical Linguistics Series
Series Editors: Joseph Salmons and David Willis

The series provides a comprehensive introduction to this broad and increasingly complex field. Aimed at advanced undergraduates in linguistics, as well as beginning postgraduates who are looking for an entry point, volumes are discursive, accessible and responsive to critical developments in the field.

Individual volumes show historical linguistics as a field anchored in two centuries of research, with a rich empirical base and theoretical perspectives, and one tied tightly to all areas of linguistics. Fundamentally, though, the series shows how historical linguists approach language change. Every volume contains pedagogical features such as recommendations for further reading, but the tone of each volume is discursive, explanatory and critically engaged, rather than 'activity-based'.

Series Editors

Joseph Salmons is Professor of Language Sciences at the University of Wisconsin

David Willis is Professor of Celtic at Jesus College, University of Oxford

Titles available in the series:

Analogy and Morphological Change
David Fertig

Analysing Syntax through Texts: Old, Middle, and Early Modern English
Elly van Gelderen

Sound Change
Joseph Salmons

Sound Change

Joseph Salmons

EDINBURGH
University Press

Edinburgh University Press is one of the leading university presses in the UK. We publish academic books and journals in our selected subject areas across the humanities and social sciences, combining cutting-edge scholarship with high editorial and production values to produce academic works of lasting importance. For more information visit our website: edinburghuniversitypress.com

Edinburgh University Press Ltd
The Tun – Holyrood Road, 12(2f) Jackson's Entry, Edinburgh EH8 8PJ

Typeset in10/12 Times New Roman by
Servis Filmsetting Ltd, Stockport, Cheshire

A CIP record for this book is available from the British Library

ISBN 978 1 4744 6172 6 (hardback)
ISBN 978 1 4744 6174 0 (webready PDF)
ISBN 978 1 4744 6173 3 (paperback)
ISBN 978 1 4744 6175 7 (epub)

Contents

Figures and Tables

Map

Figures

Tables

Series Editors' Preface

We are delighted to present this new volume in the Edinburgh University Press *Historical Linguistics* series of advanced textbooks on language change and comparative linguistics. Each individual volume provides in-depth coverage of a key subfield within historical linguistics. As a whole, the series provides a comprehensive introduction to this broad and increasingly complex field.

The present volume exemplifies the kind of content, tone and format we aim for in the series, and the volumes that are coming down the pike do as well. The series is aimed at advanced undergraduates in linguistics and students in language departments as well as beginning postgraduates who are looking for an entry point. Volumes in the series are serious and scholarly university textbooks, theoretically informed and substantive in content. Every volume contains pedagogical features such as recommendations for further reading, but the tone of the volumes is discursive, explanatory and critically engaged, rather than 'activity-based.'

Authors interested in writing for the series should contact us.

Joseph Salmons (jsalmons@wisc.edu)
David Willis (david.willis@ling-phil.ox.ac.uk)

Preface: What We're Doing Here and Why

Most speakers of North American English a couple of generations ago distinguished words like *which* versus *witch* and *whether* versus *weather* (/ʍ ~ w/) or *cot* versus *caught* and *Don* versus *Dawn* (/ɔ ~ a/). Young speakers today have overwhelmingly, if not entirely, lost the first distinction and are rapidly losing the second. The /æ/ vowel in words like *bad* and *sad* or *bag* and *flag* has changed, usually raised toward [ɛ] or something similar, but varying regionally and socially. The distinction between word-final /s/ and /z/ (*bus* versus *buzz*) seems imperiled for many in communities where it was once robust. Throughout the South and much of the East, the vowel in *boot* has moved to the front of the mouth and the one in *coat* is following a parallel path, giving something like [bʉt] and now [kʰɵt]. In various parts of the country and in various social groups, words like *struggle* and *strong* are increasingly pronounced with [ʃ] rather than [s], with some extending the pattern to words without an /r/ in there. North American English is hardly unusual in this way: In Scotland, /ɔ ~ a/ merger is happening and British varieties are undergoing similar kinds of back vowel fronting and a very noticeable change is spreading rapidly, 'fronting' of *th*-sounds [ð, θ] to [v, f], such that *smooth* and *throat* are pronounced *smoove* and *froat*.

All these changes are away from what we think of as 'standard' pronunciation. Whatever the pressures of schooling, broadcast and social media and general attitudes about 'correct' language, many (though by no means all!) innovations are moving speakers away from prescribed norms, something hardly restricted to uneducated or marginalized populations.

These are only a few examples of changes underway at present in English – treating only consonants and vowels, for instance, leaving aside intonation ('uptalk'), stress and other prosodic changes (creaky voice or vocal fry). (In North America, both of these have been discussed in the popular media, and a quick web search will give you plenty of examples.) But this rate of change is utterly normal: How people pronounce particular sounds, patterns of sounds and particular words changes constantly, over generations and even to an extent over the lifespan of individuals. You do not pronounce things the way your grandparents do or did. By the time you are sixty, you won't pronounce everything the way you did at twenty. Changes in pronunciation are the focus of the field of sound change or historical phonology and understanding them is our mission.

Sound change is both one of the oldest areas of linguistic inquiry and today one of the areas of most vibrant and most rapid progress. Patrick Honeybone and others are starting to talk about a field of 'sound change studies,' reflecting the connections people are making over various approaches, theories and methods. Yet no modern introduction to the field is available in monograph form (though there are excellent brief overviews, like Bermúdez-Otero 2007 or Hualde 2011, from different perspectives, and a major handbook, Honeybone and Salmons 2015). Beyond a need for such a book among students, a broad and growing set of scholars from outside the specialization are doing work today that directly bears on sound change, including in phonetics, phonology, sociolinguistics, historical linguistics, computational linguistics and far beyond. I've written this book for all those people.

Before we get to business, I should say something about the background I'm assuming. If you've had an introduction to historical linguistics and some kind of course on speech sounds (phonetics and/or phonology), you should have an easy read in front of you. But you don't need that much: You should have some modest background knowledge here, familiarity with the International Phonetic Alphabet is helpful and having had an introduction to linguistics course would be good, but willingness to engage and do an occasional web search on some points should be enough for most readers. To make sure there's enough background for students with only an introductory course in linguistics or something similar, like a history of a language, I have checked many concepts and terms against two widely used textbooks, *Language Files* (2016) and Yule's *The Study of Language* (2017), plus my own *A History of German* (2018). If something is not clearly introduced in those textbooks, in the kind of depth that would make for a good test question, I dedicate some space to that. For concepts you would know from reading one of those, I'll review basic points (like the vowel space at the beginning of the first chapter) or focus on going deeper with something than introductory textbooks would. If you haven't had at least an introduction to linguistics, you might want to have a textbook at hand. You will find some passages challenging, but I trust you can get through them with some patience.

Getting to our topic, the theoretical stance I adopt – or more precisely the ecumenical but theoretically informed approach that I strive for – is important to understand from the beginning: While linguistics is riven by a number of deep differences in theory, method and data, many current approaches provide indispensable insights into sound change if we can take a more holistic view. Some research traditions look to understand language, including sound change, in terms of 'usage' or exemplars, while others look primarily to formal analyses of language. My views about the foundations of grammar are not exemplar based, but such views make important contributions and I want to understand how to integrate an approach like that into a fuller understanding of language and language change. As part of this, I sometimes give relatively extensive quotes from other scholars, to let them speak for themselves. And you'll notice that this book has an unusual amount of cross-referencing to related discussions in other chapters. This reflects the tightly interconnected nature of the material.

At worst, the shortcoming of some scholarship reflects a kind of misguided parsimony, where proponents claim that their theories and methodological tools can do more than they can, occasionally arguing against utilizing a full set of tools. Better but still suboptimal, many scholars take one slice of the huge field of sound change studies and declare the rest Somebody Else's Problem (from the *Hitchhiker's Guide*, Adams 1982), about which I'll say more in the next chapter. While not every current view about sound change is right, in the end there is more of value out there today than any one framework is capturing. This calls for a synthesis, like on the roles of phonetics versus phonology (and morphology, and beyond), the roles of traditional formal models versus recent usage-based work, and the roles of structural versus social factors in sound change. And philology, once derided as a butterfly-collecting *Hilfswissenschaft* (literally 'helping discipline,' often translated as 'ancillary science'), plays an important role in the progress of our field. (That characterization came from a senior historical linguist in conversation when I was still a young scholar, and the complex position of philology in language studies is laid out in Ziolkowski 1990.) This book aims to provide a coherent overview of the range of facets of the study of sound change. Many students need an introduction to this range of areas and I trust that many working specialists will find the synthesis and the new perspectives useful. Some primary literature does explore relationships across approaches and theories and subfields, but in limited ways, and the relationships have not been well addressed at all for student audiences in historical linguistics.

For many scholars, the most fundamental issue about sound change is whether it is regular, whether it precedes sound by sound or word by word, essentially the Neogrammarian position versus a lexical diffusionist one. For instance, if speakers in a community begin to pronounce the vowel /æ/ in *bad* more like *bed* or even *bid*, does that change affect all /æ/s (*flattening, fantastical, understandable*) or all /æ/s in single syllable words (*fan, scan, stamp*), or single syllables ending in /d/ (*bad, sad, had, glad*)? Or does it happen in everyday words but not more learned ones (*bad, spam* but not *climatological, nanosyntactic*)? Or does this change involve frequent words like *mad* and *dad* to the same extent it does less common ones like *Vlad* and *shad*? Recent work has made advances by distinguishing more clearly and with better data where sound change appears to be a 'regular' phenomenon and where we see effects in particular words or types of words before others (Labov 2020).

Another central issue is the extent to which change is motivated by 'internal' versus 'external' factors. If people change their /æ/ vowels, are they following the speech patterns of other people (peers or prestigious people) or doing it because /æ/ is somehow harder to pronounce or hear? I take as settled today that understanding sound change always involves both structural and social aspects. I have argued this point for years, but it's better known from Dorian 1993, Mufwene and Gilman 1987 or Rickford 1986. Tthe issue clearly concerned scholars in the nineteenth century, such as Hermann Paul (1920 [1880]; Auer et al. 2015). Structural motivations often introduce variants into the pool of speech in a community, while social motivations often promote their successful spread through a community.

The point of all this bears stressing: We have the Blind Men and the Elephant problem, where in the parable, a group of blind men are trying to figure out what an elephant is by touching it. Each comes to a dramatically different conclusion depending on whether they had felt the trunk, a tusk, the side or a foot, etc., but in many versions of the story, they fail to pool their knowledge and end up with a wildly incorrect and incomplete understanding of what the animal is. (The metaphor was applied to language variation and change by Tagliamonte 2012.) In studying sound change, each school of thought understands and provides an analysis of some part of sound change, but we have not yet pooled our knowledge to understand the whole. There are original contributions in this ecumenical approach.

Throughout, I generally lead with data, often detailed examples of some phenomenon. After presenting sound changes, typically with related evidence from other subfields, we can put the data into the context of the technical or theoretical issues at hand. My approach is to prompt you to engage actively with concrete material and start thinking about it for yourself, rather than giving you an abstract notion and then exemplifying it. In line with the format for this book series, I've given some suggestions for further work and such at the end of each chapter. These are not ordinary homework assignments but are aimed at being more engaging and far more challenging than your standard discussion questions, including suggestions for original research. They are less daily homework assignments and more semester projects ... if not dissertations or books. More is available at www.edinburghuniversitypress.com.

My case studies often begin with examples from languages you are more likely to be familiar with, like English, other Germanic languages and various Romance languages. The chapters move from there to examples giving broad cross-linguistic coverage from the world's languages, so that you see that what happens in Spanish or Norwegian isn't different from what happens in Mixtec or Jumjum. The organization of the book and the individual chapters reflects a simple strategy of starting with material that less experienced readers will be more likely to be familiar with and then moving on to show how the same patterns hold across the world's languages. A reviewer was concerned that this was somehow exoticizing less familiar languages, but the intent is precisely the opposite: You may not know anything about Arapaho or Hmong, but you will see that sound change works exactly the same in those languages as it does in English and French. Along another parameter, we'll discuss a few issues repeatedly over the course of the volume. For instance, umlaut illustrates some issues that serve as bookends to open and close the book. And the palatalization of stops provides close parallels across the world's languages, while the development of distinctive (lexical) tone may look superficially different but reveals a lot about how phonologization in particular takes place.

By this point in my career, I've learned so much from so many people that it's odd and slightly uncomfortable to have my name as sole author on a publication, especially for this manuscript. This book has been surprisingly hard to write, but all the support has made it vastly easier. It has been profoundly shaped by undergraduate and graduate students over the last decades, some whose work is cited here and many more whose influence is harder to document so directly.

I have been unspeakably lucky in the set of students I've worked with over the decades and I thank you all. The students in my introductory class on Sound Change in the fall of 2018 provided key input on primitive or partial drafts of many chapters. Many co-authors and collaborators have taught me a vast amount about sound change, especially the full context in which it happens. I'm grateful for how David Willis and Laura Williamson handled the submission to Edinburgh University Press and the tremendous amount of constructive feedback they got from reviewers and editorial board members. The process has yielded a vastly better book and every single one of the imperfections is all mine, but there are far fewer of them thanks to feedback on early drafts from Monica Macaulay and Marc Pierce. James Kirby, David Natvig and Patrick Honeybone all provided incredibly helpful comments on that early draft. Sarah Holmstrom provided a really valuable last read and helped finalize the manuscript.

With that, let's get to work.

Beyond this book

At the end of each chapter, you'll find a section called 'Beyond this book.' After this one – it's for the preface, after all – they all have three sections, one on looking at more data, one on learning a little more from the specialist literature and one to get you thinking about possible original research on sound change. I'll sometimes suggest specific readings but we're now at a point where I simply assume readers will be able to easily find relevant work using web searches, especially those that focus on published scholarship. On the EUP website (edinburghuniversitypress.com/soundchange) you'll find all these 'Beyond this book' sections in expanded form, including some references to get you started or additional specific suggestions for possible projects, etc. Most importantly, I'll update this regularly. I include all the links mentioned in the book. 'Link rot' is pervasive and this should allow us to mitigate that. I hope people will send suggestions for additions to these sections, and I'll happily include them, with credit to the people who make suggestions. Finally, the field is changing so fast and there is surely so much relevant material I've missed that this is a place to call attention to new work or, sigh, make corrections.

Two suggestions to get you started:

First, get a couple of textbooks or handbooks on historical linguistics and look at the chapter(s) on sound change. Compare the topics and examples and basic line of argument there to the table of contents of this book. Where and how do they differ?

Second, most readers of this book will have knowledge of and interest in some language(s). This is a chance to get a history of such a language, or much better, a handful of them. For now, look at some sections on sound change and related material in those resources just to gauge how they are approaching things:

- To what extent is the presentation descriptively versus theoretically motivated?

- Is the work situated in a cross-linguistic context or is discussion restricted to the language at hand?
- To what extent is the presentation of structure and social history integrated versus segregated, assuming both are present?

If you've got some experience in the field, take some of your favorite papers and maybe some of your least favorite papers on sound change and do the same.

I'm not suggesting being critical of any particular approach – a wide range of approaches will be appropriate depending on audience and goals of a language history – but I am urging you to start thinking about how sound change is being presented and why.

Part 1

The background

1

Introduction: What is Sound Change and How Do We Understand It?

In the last section of this chapter, I'll discuss some usual introductory chapter matters, including exactly what 'sound change' is, but to set that up, we need some data on the table. Let's dive in with some data from English and related languages. The example is umlaut and I'm going to give you a lot of detail about how it developed to set up later discussions. If you're new to the field, take some time to digest what's in here; it will pay off.

1.1 An example of sound change over the long span

For our first example, dealing with vowels, I'll introduce things from the foundations up. Two dimensions of vowels are height and backness. Height (or 'open' versus 'close') indicates how raised or lowered the tongue and jaw are (say *beet* and then *bod* and you can feel the lowering) and how far front or back the body of your tongue is (say *boot* and then *beet* and you should feel some movement toward the front). For a simple vowel system like the one below, we can characterize things with a few features (though we'll refine the notion of 'feature' soon enough), with English examples (since our spelling system is so far from the pronunciation, for reasons we'll also soon enough discuss):

TABLE 1.1. Table Simple vowel space [American English]

	Vowels			Examples		
	front		*back*	*front*		*back*
high	i		u	beet		boot
mid	e		o	bait		boat
low		a			bod	

In (1) you can see some word forms in various West Germanic languages, singular versus plural nouns. In each case, the form on the left has a different vowel from the one on the right, usually (but not always) a back vowel or diphthong (like /u, o, au/) versus a front one (like /i, y, ø/). The front ones are innovations, new developments where the vowels were historically the same in both forms.[1]

(1)   Vowel differences in related word forms

English	*foot ~ feet*	/fot, fi:t/
German	*Gast ~ Gäste*	<ä> = [ɛ], 'guest ~ guests'
Std Yiddish	*noz ~ nezər*	'nose ~ noses' (Jacobs 2005: 163)
Dialectal Yiddish	*nez ~ nozn*	'nose ~ noses' (Jacobs 2005: 163)

You may recognize these, at least some of them, as examples of 'umlaut' (also called 'mutations,' or described by movements like 'fronting' or 'raising'). This is not only the name for the two dots over certain German vowels (and in the names of metal bands, like Mötley Crüe, see https://en.wikipedia.org/wiki/Metal_umlaut), but also the name of a historical process that created vowel patterns and vowels. In modern Germanic languages, these are not 'active' processes in most senses, that is, they aren't automatic phonetic processes that occur whenever the relevant sounds appear in the relevant environments. But it's clear that these were once active and the traces of that history are readily visible in different ways across the family. On one end, there are a few scattered remnants in English (most often and most visibly in a few noun plurals) and somewhat more in Dutch. In German, umlaut marks large numbers of plurals (*Mantel ~ Mäntel* 'coat ~ coats'), many subjunctive verb forms (*wir waren ~ wir wären* 'we were ~ we would be'), comparative and superlative adjectives (*stark ~ stärker* 'strong ~ stronger') and many more categories, as we'll see momentarily. One type is in some sense active, u-umlaut in Modern Icelandic, that applies to new words, *Mazda ~ Mözdum*, the brand of car showing the umlauted form in the dative plural.

In part of early Germanic, an unattested but reconstructible ancestor of English – let's call that language West Germanic – the word for 'mouse' was *mu:s. In some inflected forms of the word, like in the nominative plural, an *i* was part of the suffix, so that the word form was *mu:siz (see the first column of (2) below and note that the *z was lost early). Over time, back vowels (u, o, a) followed by such an *i* (or a glide, *j*, using *i* as a cover symbol) became front but retained their roundedness, in this case, the original *mu:si became *my:si, pronounced with a front rounded vowel, IPA [y], like German <ü> in *Blüte* or French <u> in *vu*. This is a 'complementary distribution' of allophones: Wherever *i* appeared in a following syllable, the fronted variant appeared; wherever it did not, the original back vowel surfaced, as in the second column. A chapter in the history of the English language, and Germanic languages more broadly, is that

---

1   // indicates phonemes, sounds that contrast like /æ/ versus /e/, which yield different words, like *bat* versus *bait*. <> indicates spelling and [] reflects phonetic, non-contrastive, differences. ':' means a sound is long. An IPA chart is provided here, and you can click on symbols to hear them pronounced: http://linguistics. ucla.edu/people/keating/IPA/inter_chart_2018/IPA_2018.html. I use '*' to signal reconstructed rather than actually attested forms; I don't italicize such forms because they aren't real data in the relevant sense, even farther from 'real' than written representations.

unstressed vowels – including lots of them in word-final position – weakened and were eventually lost. When this final *i* went, the fronted form of the vowel remained, so that the paradigm for 'mouse' now included alternates like in the third column of (2).

(2)   Old English i-umlaut

	I	**II**	**III**	
	West Germanic	**Pre-Old English**	**Old English**	**Gloss**
Singular	*mu:s	mu:s	mu:s	'mouse'
Plural	*mu:siz	my:si	my:s	'mice'

Clearly, over time, these vowels have changed. The development of /y:/ was a conditioned change; it happened only in certain contexts, here before a high front vowel or glide in the next syllable. As long as the /i/, the conditioning sound or 'trigger,' was present, umlaut did not change the contrasts of the language – these were two alternative forms of the vowel, used in clear contexts, not two different vowels. But once the final vowel reduced sufficiently and then was lost, it changed the sound inventory of the language, introducing new vowels (/y:/ in our example, but several others). Below are the inventories of West Germanic and early Old English vowels, leaving aside the length distinction (streamlined from Purnell and Raimy 2015: 537; Purnell et al. 2019). We'll talk more about this approach in Chapter 9; for now just consider the West Germanic system compared to the early Old English one.

(3)   West Germanic vowels

	i	e	u	o	a
Low					✓
Front	✓	✓			
High	✓		✓		

(4)   Early Old English vowels

	i	**y**	e	**ø**	**æ**	u	o	a
Round		✓		✓		✓	✓	
Front	✓	✓	✓	✓	✓			
High	✓	✓				✓		
Low					✓			

The three new sounds, highlighted in bold, made the featural description of the system more complex: In our first stage, front vowels were unrounded and back ones were rounded. Take the high vowels for the moment – the mid vowels behave basically parallel, though the long and short and high and mid vowels differ in their chronologies and more (Minkova 2014: chapter 7). In the early stage, you could capture the front-back part of the system with one feature, front versus back or rounded versus unrounded. Once these front rounded vowels are contrastive, you need both, since the set of /i/, /y/ and /u/ requires reference to two features, like this in one traditional form:

(5)   Vowel specifications
      West Gmc.   Old English
      /i/ [+front]   /i/   [+front, -round]
      /u/ [-front]   /u/   [-front, +round]
                     /y/   [+front, +round]

Later, mostly by Middle English, the high front rounded Early English /y:/ unrounded to *i:*, yielding singular *mu:s* versus plural *mi:s*. At this point, the grammar of English contained various sets of forms that alternated between /u:/ and /i:/ and other back/front pairs, more like Modern German than contemporary English.

A few of these still exist in English, as shown in (6), examples from Greenbaum (1996: 101, 106):

(6)   Reflexes of umlaut plurals in English

      Singular   **Plural**
      man   men
      woman   women
      tooth   teeth
      goose   geese
      foot   feet
      mouse   mice
      louse   lice
      cow   kye   [dialect form, related to the old plural, *kine*]

In Middle English, the vowels in *mu:s* versus *mi:s* may still be recognizably related (both have high, long vowels) but the connections are no longer directly phonetic (that is, automatic assimilations). With time, I argue that these patterns become more generalizations about word forms than sounds. They are, for example, prone to more exceptions and wrinkles than prototypical sound patterns. As we'll discuss in a moment, some people still see later stages as phonological rather than morphological, because they involve identifiable alternations of sounds, though others argue that the analysis of such pairs in contemporary English and other languages rests on generalizations about particular word classes, not sounds per se.

As noted, while those classes were once large in English and remain large in German, we eventually reduced umlaut to a handful of exceptional lexical forms in English, as just given. Much later again, the Great Vowel Shift (don't worry if you don't know about this – we'll talk about it later) changed these vowels into our modern forms *mouse* versus *mice* [maʊs] and [maɪs].

The bigger point is that today it is difficult to see these as involving any regular process. For the moment, I'll just stipulate that people don't learn a general pattern of vowel alternations but rather that certain nouns have odd plurals, like those given in (6), also including *ox ~ oxen* or *child ~ children*. But as already noted above, the fate of these old vowel assimilations differs tremendously across the family. Two examples give you an idea of the diversity of roles – German and Icelandic.

For German, Wiese (2000: 181) states, 'The rule named *Umlaut* is the central rule in the Modern Standard German vowel system.' Unlike the position I have just taken for English (where the patterns are less obviously phonological), Wiese sees contemporary German umlaut as phonological rather than morphological (1996, 2000). Consider the complexity of the data given in (7), drawn from Lieber (1987: 100ff.) and reproduced in Wiese (1996). I have expanded the set to give more examples and to include examples where umlaut does not occur, mostly from Wiese. Umlaut is involved in a broad set of inflectional and derivational processes and for each one it occurs for some but not all of the members of the set, with only a couple of apparent exceptions. (I leave aside many further, often fine-grained patterns, e.g. differences in behavior of nouns by gender or causative verb formation like *fallen ~ fällen* 'to fall ~ to fell', where the second means 'to cause to fall', and <ä> = [ε].)

(7)　Variability and morphological roles of German umlaut (¨ marks frontness)
　　(a)　Derivational affixes regularly conditioning umlaut (umlaut-conditioning):
　　　　•　-e forming abstract nouns from adjectives: gut ~ Güte 'good ~ goodness', klagen ~ Klage 'to complain ~ complaint'
　　　　•　Ge ... e forming nouns from verbs: bauen ~ Gebäude 'to build ~ building', tun ~ Getue 'to do ~ ado'
　　　　•　-chen forming diminutives: Hund ~ Hündchen 'dog ~ doggie', Mutter ~ Muttchen 'mother ~ mom'
　　　　•　-lein forming diminutives: Vogel- Vögelein 'bird ~ birdie', **no known umlautless forms**
　　　　•　-ling forming masculine (often pejorative) nouns: dumm- Dümmling 'dumb ~ dummy', roh ~ Rohling 'raw ~ brute'
　　(b)　Derivational affixes sometimes conditioning umlaut (umlaut-variable):
　　　　•　-in forming feminine nouns: Hund ~ Hündin 'dog ~ female dog', Gatte ~ Gattin 'male spouse ~ female spouse'
　　　　•　-er forming agentive nouns: backen ~ Bäcker 'to bake ~ baker', fahren ~ Fahrer 'to drive ~ driver'
　　　　•　-lich forming adjectives: Arzt ~ ärztlich 'medical doctor ~ medical', Amt ~ amtlich 'office ~ official'
　　　　•　-ig forming adjectives: Bart ~ bärtig 'beard ~ bearded', Wolke ~ wolkig 'cloud ~ cloudy'
　　(c)　Inflectional categories in which umlaut appears:
　　　　•　Plurals in -er: Mann ~ Männer 'man ~ men', **no known umlautless forms**
　　　　•　Some noun plurals ending in -e: Fuchs ~ Füchse 'fox ~ foxes', Tag ~ Tage 'day ~ days'
　　　　•　Subjunctive II (used for hypotheticals, etc.) of strong verbs: kam ~ käme 'came ~ would come', **no known umlautless forms**
　　　　•　Some subjunctive forms of weak verbs: brauchen ~ bräuchtest 'to need ~ you [sg.] would need', sagen ~ sagst 'to say ~ you [sg.] say' (variable and not standard)

- Some comparative and superlative forms of adjectives: groß ~ größer 'big ~ bigger', froh ~ froher 'happy ~ happier' (with some words varying between the two groups)
- 2nd and 3rd person singular of strong verbs: schlagen ~ schlägst 'to hit ~ you [sg.] hit', laden ~ ladest 'to load ~ you [sg.] load' (with much variation between the two groups, as strong verbs regularize)

These patterns, as should be becoming clear, have historical explanations, phonological and morphological, and where there is variability it can but doesn't necessarily reflect change in progress. Note how different this historical outcome is from the same basic process we find in English: English has eliminated almost all umlaut alternations, while German has woven them throughout the morphology. Still, there's an important generalization: In the morphologically more basic forms, we don't have umlaut; the umlauted forms are derived or inflected. This naturally reflects history, with some connection (not always a simple or direct one) to where suffixal -*i* occurred 1,200 or more years ago.

Turning to Icelandic, consider this small dataset, showing only forms where umlaut appears. The broad picture looks similar to those for German, like in (8a), but with differences in (8b) (data from Árnason 2011, especially pp. 240–1).

(8)   Icelandic i-umlaut
   (a)   Umlaut in derived or inflected form:
   - Comparative and superlative adjective forms: stuttur ~ styttri 'short ~ shorter'
   - Verb derivation: fagur ~ fegra 'beautiful ~ beautify'
   - Noun plurals: nótt ~ nætur 'night ~ nights'
   - Present tense verb inflection: koma ~ kemur 'to come ~ comes'
   - Preterit subjunctive of verbs: buðu ~ bjóði ~ byði 'offered, 3.pl. ~ would offer ~ would have offered'
   (b)   Umlaut in basic form:
   - Present versus preterit verb forms: telja ~ taldi 'to count ~ counted'

Here, too, history is reflected in today's language, though facts like those in (8b) are poorly understood. The puzzling thing is that umlaut shows up in the more basic form of the verb (the infinitive) while it otherwise almost always appears in inflected or derived forms.

Lest they seem really exotic to you, these kinds of assimilations – regressive, where a feature spreads from a vowel or glide late in a word leftward, and involving frontness – exist around the world, like in Svan (a South Caucasian or Kartvelian language spoken in Georgia) and Rotuman (an Austronesian language on the Rotuma Islands in the South Pacific). Consider a little Svan data from Schmidt (1962: 30–48, keeping his orthography), showing both Svan historical developments and loanwords from Georgian:

(9)   Svan umlaut
      i-gwända   < *i-gwanida 'he cried'
      ašxünda   < *ašxunida 'that he saw'
      sädil   < Georgian sadili 'lunch'
      buleḳi   < Georgian boloḳi 'radish'

As Tuite shows (1997: 12), Svan umlaut shows variation, dialectal and phono-logical. For instance, /a/ is most likely to umlaut, /u/ least, and short vowels are more and long vowels less likely to. Those patterns closely parallel our under-standing of the history of German umlaut (though Svan differs in other ways, for example that non-high front vowels can trigger umlaut). Howell and Salmons (1997, building on Iverson and Salmons 1996) understand this in terms of the phonetic origins of umlaut: If assimilation drives umlaut, the greatest distance across the vowel space from /i/ would have been /a/, with /u/ the closest. This is how we represented that graphically (1997: 93), where heavy lines show stronger tendencies to assimilate:

(10)   Variable umlaut targets, by distance from /i/

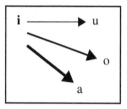

Like early Germanic, Svan shows some vowel-to-vowel raising and lowering effects across intervening consonants, what we've called 'height harmony,' though the details are different.

The bigger point is that we see strong similarities across many languages, related or not, with relatively minor variations on a theme. Umlaut is complex but profoundly systematic.

1.2   Understanding sound change

Umlaut sets up the question driving this book: Why and how do speech sounds change over time? People have offered remarkably different analyses of such changes. It's worth taking a little time now to introduce part of that range of views as they apply to this example. We'll go into detail on all these theories and approaches and more in coming chapters. And we'll return to umlaut as well.

The answers I develop involve virtually all of these theories and approaches. I hope to convince you that most of the specific approaches have a place and contribute to our understanding but that none tells the whole story. In that way, the focus now comes to fall on determining what role each of these plays in a bigger understanding of sound change. This, in turn, has large implications for how we understand human language generally, for linguistic theory. Let us now explore some attempts to answer how and why umlaut arose. I'll sketch, in varying degrees of detail, six major positions using umlaut and supplementing it as needed. These are hardly all the perspectives on sound change but they should set you up to start thinking about the range of views we'll encounter and that I'll work to integrate in this volume.

(i) Ease of articulation. Maybe the most traditional way to motivate sound change is by appealing to ease of articulation, often connected to a view that

certain patterns are more 'natural' or 'easier' than others: Sound change, it is claimed, allows us to reduce effort. For umlaut, the assimilation involved in making a back vowel front before a following front vowel actually saves you a lot of work. In going from [mu:si] to [my:si] you no longer have to move the body of the tongue forward from the time of the /u:/ (with the tongue far back in the mouth, for early Germanic speakers), to the position of /i/. As the speech organs go, moving the tongue that way is a lot of physical work. In my pronunciation, an /s/ lasts about a tenth of a second, not much time to move the tongue.

Defining ease of articulation rigorously and showing that speakers actually really gain something has proven maddeningly difficult. One issue is that making things easier has to be balanced against being understood … if we reduce everything to /da/ (a prototypically 'simple' consonant, vowel and syllable type), communication doesn't work. Jespersen (1969: 15) writes: 'In linguistic changes we see the constant interplay of two opposite tendencies, one of an individual, and the other of a social character, one towards ease and the other towards distinctness.' Still, there's something to economizing as a motivation, it seems. It appears to be a universal that we all do some vowel-to-vowel assimilation of this type to some extent whatever language we speak. That is, the first vowel in English *poppy* is more front than the first vowel in *papa* and the same pattern seems to hold across languages. This anticipatory coarticulation in sequences of vowel + consonant + vowel – usually written as VCV – has been recognized since at least Öhman (1966).

Consider now a very different example. If you're reading this book, I assume that you understand that sign languages are complete human languages, with full phonetics, phonology, morphology, syntax, as well as dialectal and social variation. They also change over time. In early experimental work on American Sign Language, Rimor et al. (1984) compared signs produced at different speeds of signing and also citation forms (reciting words from a list) versus use of the same signs in conversation. In their first experiment, they asked signers to sign at three different speeds: Normal, twice that, and as fast as possible. They looked at five specific signs which are attested in old films, including the sign for the question word WHO, historically produced this way: '1. Pass the index finger around the face. 2. Look left and right a little.' In both the experiment and comparing old attestations to contemporary usage, they found that the circle of the index finger around the face was smaller. In the second study, they found that signs were produced far faster in conversation than in citation, along with reductions in other kinds of articulations, such as fewer hand movements and head tilts.

They conclude (1984: 116) that 'insofar as diachronic change and synchronic variation in signs are characterized by reductions[,] they stem from the same origin, natural phonetic processes reflecting ease of articulation and ease of perception.' This does indeed look like a good case for ease of articulation driving change. Much work since has pursued phonetic and phonological change in many sign languages with various methods and kinds of data, reviewed by Brentari (2019: chapter 8) and Wilcox and Occhino (2016).

(ii) Perception. One way people motivate the shift from an automatic, low-level process like vowel-to-vowel assimilations to full-on sound umlaut is by

appealing not to how we speak but to how we listen. Ohala (1981 and elsewhere) developed a movement dedicated to giving the listener a central role in sound change. (Marc Pierce notes that this is foreshadowed in Hockett 1958: 442ff.) Humans have tremendously nuanced understanding of how sounds behave in context – we know at some level to expect the differences in the first vowels of *poppy* and *papa*, so that we readily hear the intended vowel in *poppy*, basically filtering out the frontness by recognizing it as an effect of the following vowel. Ohala calls this 'reconstructing,' since what we're doing is untangling the complex acoustic signal in an effort to get back to what the speaker was saying. For a variety of reasons, we may fail to do that, something that Ohala calls hypocorrection. For example, if the final /i/ isn't fully and clearly produced, as often happens historically in Germanic languages, we may not pick up on the pattern. For our /mu:si/ case, that could trigger a reinterpretation by the listener … what was a low-level phonetic effect comes to be heard as a different vowel.

Ohala sketches a process from what a speaker intends to how they produce a form to how a listener hears it and then how the listener interprets that acoustic signal. In (11a), you see his model applied to our umlaut example; it's the typical situation where the listener hears what the speaker intended. In (11b), the listener fails to decode the signal and that triggers a change in their speech.

(11) Listener-driven umlaut (after Ohala)

    (a)   Successful reconstruction

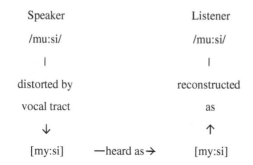

    (b)   Hypocorrection

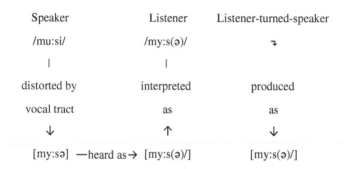

In (11a), the /u:/ sound gets distorted by the following /i/ and the listener picks this up, but gets that it's distortion and essentially 'fixes' it in interpretation. This yields a stable situation, where everything works as planned and leads to no change. In (11b), though, for whatever reason, the listener doesn't filter out the distortion and takes [y:] to be the intended pronunciation and they then reproduce that [y:]. This under-correction leads to a new pronunciation. (Soon, we'll talk about the reasons why listeners might not recognize the distortion.) Ohala has pursued this experimentally, manipulating vowels and pasting them into different consonantal contexts. The results show that listeners actively take consonantal effects into account to decide what vowel they are hearing.

(iii) Contrast. The approaches to sound change just noted – one focused on production and one on perception – are both profoundly phonetically oriented, focused on how sounds are produced and interpreted. Much of the twentieth century was dominated by equally profoundly phonologically-oriented theories. In structuralist perspectives, like American Structuralism, what matters is when the new umlaut vowels become contrastive, come to carry differences in meaning. As long as [y:] is 'conditioned' by the following /i/ sound, it's just a form of /u:/. The frontness of [y:] in [my:si] is there, but the [i] is enough to signal the plural form to listeners. Like the common comparison in introductory phonology, the alternation between [u:] and [y:] while the [i] is still there is a case of Clark Kent and Superman … you never see them in the same place because they are the same person (or sound), but they appear in different environments. When /i/ is reduced and lost, they split and /y:/ and /u:/ can appear in the same environment. Frontness becomes the only thing that signals plural as opposed to singular.

On this view – where it is not something about the sounds themselves but how they fit into a system of contrast – Bloomfield (1933: 347) could write that 'The process of linguistic change has never been directly observed … such observation, with our present facilities, is inconceivable.' In a moment, we'll turn to the role of variation in sound change, as a way to get beyond this conundrum. Later, I'll show how modern work makes considerably more hay with how contrast itself works.

(iv) Language acquisition. Since Paul's seminal *Prinzipien der Sprachgeschichte* (*Principles of Language History*, 1880), linguists have argued that language change is tightly connected to how children acquire language. In some work, including early generative work, this was framed in terms of 'imperfect learning.' That is, children didn't master the exact grammar of adults around them. Children have to build their own grammars (including sound systems) from the input they hear. Our cognitive capacity plays some role in what we can (not) acquire and how the system functions, but under any mainstream view the input the learner gets shapes their language. Variability in that input has long been recognized as important (Locke 1983).

Recall the Ohala model just introduced. In theory, it would be possible that children somehow don't learn to 'reconstruct' or repair the signal they hear. Another possibility, one that has some good support, is that when children are getting diverse input, like being surrounded by people with different regional accents, they have a harder time building a model like that of, say, their parents.

But in general, as a leading specialist in language acquisition and change responded when I asked her a basic question about whether we should expect children to really acquire a particular phenomenon, 'Joe, kids are really amazing little language learners.' We need, in other words, a story with considerable nuance.

I see a real role for acquisition in sound change. With umlaut, it wasn't just the change to the stem vowel that mattered but also the reduction of the final vowel. Where we see it today, that kind of reduction is highly variable and reflects something about actual (phonetic) production and not our abstract (phonological) mental representation of the word. English speakers, for instance, seem to have a vowel, typically schwa ([ə]), in the first syllable of words like *photography*, but if you listen in ordinary conversation, it's utterly unsurprising to hear it pronounced as [ft], without any vowel. Variable patterns easily change over the lifespan; they don't involve learning structure, just changing how often you deploy what form. In academic environments, you may say *talking* and *working* more often than *talkin'* and *workin'*. You already knew both variants, [ŋ] and [n], but learned to adjust the frequency of use by context.

This helps us resolve the infamous 'paradox of phonologization' with regard to umlaut: The new umlaut vowels only become phonemic with the loss of triggers, but the loss of triggers is expected to mean the loss of the fronted vowel. One typical response is to claim that the new vowels must be phonemic before loss of the triggers and Kiparsky in various works has posited 'quasiphonemes' to address the problem. That rests on distinguishing two steps in the phonologization process: '(I)n the first stage, some redundant features become quasi-distinctive, and in the second stage, quasi-distinctive features become distinctive when their conditioning is lost' (2003: 329). This goes in the right direction, but not yet far enough.

A change like this, I assume, unfolds over more than one generation, each with its own phonological representations and phonetic realizations. Imagine a generation that has umlaut as a phonetic pattern (Generation X-1 in (12) below). These people have an /a/ vowel in their minds (like in *calm*, for many English speakers) but automatically produce an [ε] vowel (like in *bet*) when it's followed by [i]. They may reduce the final vowel sometimes but they produce it often enough for the next generation to acquire what they have – learners hear a range of final vowels from [i] to [ə], maybe even nothing at all on occasion, but learn /i/ as the basic form with others being reduced in particular contexts. A later generation, here Generation X, continues to consistently produce [ε] but reduces the /i/ often enough that children learning the language from them interpret it as [ə] – this is a tipping point, where learners can no longer recover the /i/ in the suffix but they consistently hear, and acquire, /ε/ as the stem vowel. That breaks the automatic assimilation, so that Generation X+1 learns /ε/ as the basic vowel.

(12) Transgenerational transmission of umlaut, inflected form of Old High German *gasti* 'guests'

	Phonology	Phonetics	
1. Generation X–1	/gasti/	[gεsti]	Phonetic umlaut
2. Generation X	/gasti/	[gεstə]	Reduction
3. Generation X+1	/gεstə/		Restructuring

Generation X+1 learners don't recover the underlying full /i/ vowel of the earlier generation that was subject to reduction, but they do acquire the umlauted form of the old /a/ vowel. This is oversimplified – for instance, 'generations' aren't clear and distinct entities in this way – and we don't have direct evidence for it – these changes are already reflected in the earliest German writing, before 800 CE – but it's a story that works without invoking any kind of magic, as many accounts of umlaut have had to. This may account for why the fronted vowels didn't revert to back when the conditioning was lost. This is only one way this kind of phonologization can happen (see Iverson and Salmons 2012 on paradigms where there are morphophonemic alternations). The failure to revert with loss of conditioning is often treated as remarkable and problematic, but I'll note other examples of non-reversion in §4.6.

Most generally, this shows how I'll argue in this book. Sound change, from all we know, unfolds gradually and in discrete steps. Low-level phonetic effects become phonological and then morphological, and, with the vestiges of umlaut in English, restricted to a few forms. This suggests a coherent path of development of sound change, a 'life cycle' of change. We'll build the pieces of such a story and then assemble them in Chapter 11, which directly addresses the life cycle and argues for it as a possibility, but I stress now that there is no necessity of any particular change going through a cycle.

(v) Variation. The account of umlaut just sketched rests crucially on the role of variation. Putting variation on center stage is only a half-century old now, the insight of Weinreich et al. (1968). They maintain that 'structural theories of language, so fruitful in synchronic investigation, have saddled historical linguistics with a cluster of paradoxes which have not been fully overcome.' They argue that 'The key to a rational conception of language change – indeed, of language itself – is the possibility of describing orderly differentiation in a language serving a community.' I adopt that perspective and you'll see that it consistently bears fruit.

(vi) Social factors. From the snippets above, we can piece together parts of an account of how some person or group of people might initiate or advance a sound change. Not everybody in a broader community will experience those same particular patterns and certainly not at one time. Somehow, changes have to spread or diffuse through a community. Traditional accounts often appeal to 'prestige' – assuming that you adapt your speech to that of influential people. Modern work focuses more on peers – that you come to talk like those in the group(s) you belong to. (I'll argue against 'prestige' having much role at all in language change.)

Social factors can also play smaller, more local roles. Some Americans, for instance, pronounce the word *wash* as *warsh*, inserting an r-sound that wasn't there historically. A major difference across varieties of English is between those who pronounce *r* at the end of syllables and those who don't, of the *park the car in Harvard yard* stereotype of a Boston accent or 'Received Pronunciation'. One proposal for *warsh* is that it arose along the border between *r*-less and *r*-ful speech patterns, the idea being that people were unsure of where there was an *r* and inserted it where historically it wasn't. For some reason, people imagined that they should be pronouncing this r and inserted it where it was not historically present. Other factors may have supported this, like acoustic effects of the [ʃ] sound that resemble those of /r/. This is known as 'hypercorrection', a process where a speaker aims for something they've recognized in speech – 'oh, those folks pronounce r's at the ends of syllables and words' – but overdo it, applying a pattern in the speech when those who have it naturally would not, so adding it to *wash*. (Ohala uses the same word in a very different sense discussed elsewhere in this book.)

In the history of German, many central and southern dialects unrounded umlaut vowels, like we saw in the history of English. With this, words like *schön* and *grün* ('beautiful' and 'green') came to be pronounced with /i:/ and /e:/, respectively. In a border area for unrounding, a whole set of words that historically lacked umlaut come to show front rounded vowels. Our words *swear* and *hell* reflect the unrounded vowels we expect historically, going back to forms like *swerian* and *hellia*. Yet, Modern German has *schwören* and *Hölle*, with front rounded vowels. Hypercorrection appears to have driven this, a process we'll discuss in Chapter 7.

1.3 What it means

In something widely attributed to Mark Twain (though not actually found in his writing, apparently), 'To somebody with a hammer, everything looks like a nail.' Phoneticians naturally look to understand sound change in terms of speech production and perception, while sociolinguists look to understand it in terms of social behavior, and so on. This has two flavors: Where people declare that what they can do with a hammer is all there is to be done and where others declare everything you can't do with a hammer to be Somebody Else's Problem. I'm arguing that we need the fullest set of perspectives to 'get the goodie out' on sound change, as my father used to say about getting all of the meat out of pecans.

As someone who loves to play sports but is catastrophically bad at them, it's tempting to think about this in terms of sports: The most gifted midfielder on the pitch, the quickest power forward on the court or the best puck-handling centerman on the ice has no chance of actually winning a match or game alone. They may play the central role at central junctures, but in every case and on almost all plays it takes a set of team-mates to make things happen. Understanding sound change requires teamwork, and profound breadth of perspective.

This is not merely a question of theory and method, but just as importantly it is an empirical question. One of the most quoted pieces in recent historical linguistics is surely Labov's comment that historical linguistics is about 'making the best of bad data' (for example, 1972: 100, 1994: 11). I have to push back a little on that and stress that we actually have a lot of data for a lot of issues in sound change and that if we use them effectively, we learn a lot. This has been captured in the notion of 'informational maximalism' (Janda and Joseph 2003: 37), which they define as 'the utilization of all reasonable means to extend our knowledge.' In a similar spirit, the historical sociolinguist Mark Lauersdorf implores us to 'use ALL the data,' including not only linguistic data but also the socio-historical data about language and language use. (See Lauersdorf 2018: 211–12.) I dub this the Lauersdorf Principle, and this is how we'll work.

FIGURE 1.1. Hammer hunting trophies

1.4   What IS sound change?

What is sound change and what is not? Bowern (2018: 284) writes that 'some linguists believe that change should be defined as the spontaneous creation of a novel variant in the mind of a single speaker,' but goes on to add that 'this focus on the creation of innovations belies the fact that the bulk of change in linguistics comes from shifts in the relative frequency of variables, not from innovation in a single speaker de novo.' The opposite end of this spectrum would be to restrict the notion of change to utterly complete changes, like the absolute loss of old front rounded vowels in English. Ultimately, our goal is to understand each piece of the picture, from true innovation to absolute completion, changing frequencies of variables and conditioning of variables, and different social meanings of variables. These are different creatures structurally and socially, as we will see throughout this book.

I understand sound change broadly as speech sounds becoming different over time for some groups of speakers. In other words, we'll think about sound change from tiny variation to massive completed changes. This includes low-level phonetic changes that don't (yet) change the phonological system, like the raising of /æ/ or the change of /s/ to [ʃ] in some contexts, as mentioned in the Preface, or the earliest stage of umlaut. Perception is a piece of this, in terms of who hears what sound how. It also includes changes to phonological systems, like the /ʍ ~ w/ or /ɔ ~ a/ mergers from the Preface or the split of back vowels with umlaut. You haven't seen an example of it yet, but language contact can lead to borrowing of sounds, which is how English got the /ʒ/ in *pleasure* and how German got nasalized vowels like in *Bonbon* 'piece of candy'. That too might be counted as sound change, since it definitely changes the set of sounds in the language. When umlaut has become largely or entirely morphologized, like in German, this may no longer be directly about sounds, but we cannot understand the patterns and processes fully without understanding the sound changes underlying them. The same holds for the lexical remnants of umlaut in English. In practice, most people focus on some piece of this complex landscape, phonological change or phonetic change (in terms of acoustics, articulation or perception) or the social setting of sound change. A goal of this book is to connect those dots.

At the same time, Milroy (1992a) stresses that in studying language change, we cannot ignore that most of language is overwhelmingly stable. That's true for the amount of change over generations – only in catastrophic circumstances does a whole sound system get rebuilt in a generation or two – but some parts of sound systems remain stable as far back as we can reconstruct. Somehow, from pre-Indo-European to many languages spoken today, word-initial /p/ was consistently transmitted from one generation to the next. Hundreds of sets of children across vast spaces and times have continued to pronounce this sound essentially like their forebears had.

The label 'sound change' for this topic is firmly established, but it's unfortunate, since sign languages, languages that rely on visual rather than auditory communication, have phonetics and phonology and so there is phonetic and phonological change, as we've already seen with American Sign Language.

A less obvious but equally important issue is this: What changes in sound change? Bloomfield famously wrote, in discussing the regularity of sound change, that 'phonemes change' (1933: 354, and see Labov 1981). A competing view is that words change, a view called 'lexical diffusion' (e.g. Phillips 2006). We'll discuss both in the coming chapter. On a Bloomfieldian view, changes like the merger of /ʍ ~ w/ or /ɔ ~ a/ are about changes to sound systems, the loss of a phoneme in each case. On a diffusionist view, the sound is not simply lost from the system but rather on a word-by-word basis. The vast tradition of work on 'language variation and change' is overwhelmingly focused on yet another facet, phonetic changes, such as often subtle differences in the pronunciation of a particular vowel.

1.5   A roadmap to the rest of the book

This book's organization is fairly simple. This '**Background**' section (Part 1) continues with some history of the field. '**Starting points**' (Part 2) introduces issues to orient you to the rest of the book. Chapters 3 and 4 provide overviews of kinds of sound changes, a basic typology, with segmental issues in Chapter 3 and everything 'above' the segment in Chapter 4. Chapter 5 surveys the sources of evidence we have for sound change.

'**Where sound changes**' (Part 3) turns to the loci of sound change: Scholars have long seen language learners as central to how sounds change (Chapter 6). Chapter 7 looks beyond the individual to how changes do or don't spread through a community.

'**Sound change in grammar**' (Part 4) pursues the details of the modular view of grammar already hinted at, with a focus on phonetics in Chapter 8, phonological theory in Chapter 9 and sound change in the rest of grammar in Chapter 10.

We close out the book by stepping back to look at the '**Bigger picture**' (Part 5) constructed over the course of the book, with a synthetic discussion organized around the notion of a 'life cycle' of sound change or, in some ways, of language change (Chapter 11).

Beyond this book

1. Digging deeper: Data

Umlaut occurs in any number of languages around the world and vowel harmony in many more. Beyond Germanic, Svan and Rotuman, processes called umlaut are found in Chamorro, Korean, Tocharian and some Australian languages, for example. The Arabic process called *imala* (Owens 2006: chapter 7) looks like umlaut as well. Search for language names and 'umlaut' in research-oriented search engines to find literature. Look at a couple of such cases and see whether they allow the same kind of story I've told about Germanic for how umlaut has developed and changed in those languages.

2. Digging deeper: Theory

I defined 'sound change' in this chapter, but definitions vary across the field. Starting from books on historical linguistics (modern handbooks, for example) and classic works in the field (Saussure, Bloomfield, among others), look at how other people define the field and how those definitions are underpinned in terms of their theories of sounds and language generally.

3. Moving beyond what we know

- Assuming you have language histories at hand (see 'Beyond this book' in the Preface), take some major example of sound change in language histories and look at the range of approaches considered and what approaches are not considered. You might even look into some specialist literature (starting with a web search for recent articles) to see what range of accounts are out there. A few suggestions:
  - English: the Great Vowel Shift
  - Any Germanic language: Grimm's Law, aka the First Consonant Shift, or spirantizations in any family
  - French and other languages that have them: the rise of nasalized vowels
  - Spanish and many other languages: weakening of stop consonants

- Russian: palatalization
- Chinese and any tone language: the rise of distinctive tones
- The example of Svan umlaut is one of many places where earlier work feels like an invitation to do a full analysis. We have descriptions of Svan umlaut, but essentially no broader theoretical interpretation of the story, e.g. how it compares to and might inform our analysis of umlaut in Germanic and other languages. Umlaut in Rotuman has been discussed more often in the theoretical literature, but warrants further work as well. Do the analysis.
- I have tried hard to give fair assessments of various approaches to sound change, but the nuance and complexity of current views go far beyond what I can convey. If you find any of these ideas promising, you should dig into the primary literature, like Pouplier (2012), for instance, on 'ease of articulation' or Oxford (2015) on how contrast does or doesn't inform our understanding of sound change.

2

The History of the Field and Why You Need to Understand It

2.1 Introduction[1]

The nineteenth-century study of sound change was central to the rise of linguistic science. We've made huge strides in many ways, but to paraphrase Isaac Newton, if we have seen farther, it is by standing on the shoulders of giants. Just as striking is how often we have failed to grasp the lessons learned by our forebears.

This chapter introduces the basic history of the field, concentrating on a couple of central issues, especially whether sound change is regular and what 'regularity' means (§2.3). This includes introducing an opposing view (more or less), known today as 'lexical diffusion' (§2.4). I'll briefly discuss some historical views on the relationship between synchrony and diachrony, in particular how variation plays into that (§2.5). Finally, I introduce the notion of 'uniformitarianism' and the controversies surrounding it (§2.6). This sketch keeps a close eye on recent perspectives and we will follow through: The questions raised will be pursued throughout the rest of the book.

2.2 Early days

A fair bit was understood about historical and comparative linguistics long before the nineteenth century, for instance in terms of relatedness of languages; not just Indo-European but families like Algonquian and Finno-Ugric were recognized. But as Murray (2015: 12–13) shows, sound change in a modern sense didn't really play a role. Sounds were talked about as 'letters' and these letters were just matched in comparisons that lacked any clear sense of phonetic similarity, so that in Mayans y Siscar's eighteenth-century history of Spanish (Murray 2015), Latin *gypso* 'gypsum' corresponds to Spanish *yeso*, where p is seen as permutating into e, with the loss of g, as direct correspondences:

---

1 Parts of this chapter draw on Salmons (forthcoming a) but deployed in a very different context. I leave aside developments before the nineteenth century to focus on strands of work leading to current views. For the rich history of earlier work, see for instance Allan (2013).

(1)   Pre-modern 'correspondences': Letter-by-letter matching

g   y   p   s   o

| | | | |

Ø   y   e   s   o

These matches are spurious: From a modern perspective, *p* has been lost, the g has weakened into a glide and the old <y> is now /e/.

Key early innovations come from Rasmus Rask (1818), an early person to recognize the changes known now as Grimm's Law. Rask and later scholars talked about 'letters' but, Murray argues, this was terminological and they fully understood that the action was in the sounds and not the graphic representations of them. Rask drew correspondences that begin to look more like modern phonetic and phonological descriptions. Here are some of his examples, where the unshifted forms are like forms in Latin or Greek and shifted ones from Old Norse:

(2)   Rask's correspondences for the Germanic consonant shift

Correspondence	Examples
p to f:	platus 'broad' ~ flatur 'flat' patēr ~ fadir 'father'
t to þ:	treis ~ þrír 'three' tego ~ þek 'cover, roof' tu ~ þu 'you'
k to h:	kreas 'meat' ~ hræ 'dead body' cornu ~ horn 'horn' cutis ~ hud 'skin'

In Grimm's Law what we have is particular sounds (like *p*) generally turning into another sound (like *f*), in ways that reflect phonetic and phonological similarity. In the examples in (2), three voiceless stops (*p, t, k*) all become voiceless fricatives (f, þ, h, as he writes them, in IPA /f, θ, x/). Also important is that these aren't patterns in isolated words but ones that hold across large sets of the vocabulary of the languages (see §3.1 for details).

Early researchers saw sound change in terms of tendencies. Even Jacob Grimm's own understanding of the relationship between sounds like /p, t, k/ in many Indo-European languages and /f, θ, x/ in Germanic was a tendency, not a law. As Murray puts it (2015: 16), 'Grimm believes that some words can resist the general changes,' though he clearly believes that the generalizations at hand are far-reaching.

There was once an impression in much of the historiography of linguistics that the world began with the Neogrammarians (§2.3), but you should see here a point that is underscored in much modern work, that even before the revolution we're about to discuss serious work was going on. These scholars, today sometimes known as Paleogrammarians (see Cser 2016), laid important foundations for later work. They anticipate later developments in having recognized systematicity in sound change in ways that require abstractness. (In addition to the almost universally discussed example of Grimm's Law, Cser (2016) shows how early discussions of Indo-European vowels presaged in some aspects how an analysis would look in modern phonological theories like Particle Phonology or Government Phonology, for readers who know about them.) But comparative linguistics by no means started first or only with the Indo-European. Roughly by the time Sir William Jones declared in 1786 that a whole set of Indo-European languages were 'sprung from some common source,' Sajonvics showed the relatedness of some languages we know today as Uralic and Jonathan Edwards Jr did the same for Algonquian. See Campbell and Poser (2008) for good arguments that Sajonvics and Edwards were using more sophisticated methods and data than Jones.

2.3   The Neogrammarians

The 1870s saw a scientific revolution. Late nineteenth-century theorists who helped establish the scientific study of language were part a group called (dismissively) the *Junggrammatiker* (the Neogrammarians or Young Grammarians), associated with the University of Leipzig. They defined sound change as a regular process, one without exception. This is often called the Regularity Principle or the exceptionlessness of sound change (German *Ausnahmslosigkeit der Lautgesetze*). The principle is widely cited in this formulation from Osthoff and Brugmann (1878: vii, in the translation of Lehmann 1967: 204):

> … every sound change, inasmuch as it occurs mechanically, takes place according to laws that admit no exception. [… aller Lautwandel, so weit er mechanisch vor sich geht, vollzieht sich nach ausnahmslosen gesetzten.]

An early formulation of the importance of regularity comes from Leskien (1876: xxviii):

> If we allow arbitrary, random deviations that cannot be connected to one another, then we therewith declare that the object of study, language, is not accessible to scientific understanding. [Lässt man … beliebige zufällige, unter einander in keinen Zusammenhang zu bringende Abweichungen zu, so erklärt man im Grunde damit, dass das Object der Untersuchung, die Sprache, der wissenschaftlichen Erkenntniss nicht zugänglich ist.]

Osthoff and Brugmann's statement is often understood today as a DEFINITION of sound change rather than a general claim about how speech sounds change. They and their colleagues were fully aware of changes involving sounds that were not regular, and these simply are not classified as sound change in this sense. Certain kinds of changes like metathesis – changing the order of sounds in a word, like the alternation between *ask* and *aks* that goes back to Old English, or the variant *purty* of 'pretty' – are typically irregular, for example. And languages borrow sounds in language contact, like English did with /ʒ/ from French, as in *pleasure* and *measure*, though that story has some complexity to it that I'll mention in Chapter 7. (We'll talk more about irregular changes in the next chapter.)

Sound change, on this view, behaves in the way that natural phenomena do, in accordance with laws, so that we can predict that certain things will occur when particular conditions are met. This allows us to posit laws, just as we do in physics or geology. In other words, this puts linguistics among the sciences. As Labov puts it (1981: 272), following Hoenigswald 1978, this declares sound change to be 'a certain kind of object.' As a reviewer on my forthcoming paper (cited above) argued in a comment, it is central to much (but by no means all) linguistic theorizing that …

> language is not an artifact (created by humans for the purpose of communication) but a biological/natural object produced by regular evolution. This was the foundational statement of the neogrammarians, applying Darwin to language at that time. The whole purpose of sound laws is that they can only be laws because we are talking about a natural object, rather than about an artifact. Only natural objects have absolute regularities, and explicit parallels to physics/chemistry/biology are often drawn by the neogrammarians.

Whether that is right or not, it captures how powerful the Neogrammarian position was. In short order, a set of 'laws' was established, involving sound changes in Indo-European languages. The year 1876 has been labeled the *annus mirabilis* for the publication of many key works. But like many revolutions, as we'll see, not everybody made the change. Leaving aside metathesis or dissimilation for the moment (see §3.5), the Neogrammarians acknowledged three kinds of change: Sound change, borrowing and analogy. Borrowing naturally deals with material from another language, most commonly of words but also of sounds, as in the fricative in the middle of the words *measure* and *pleasure*, both borrowed from Norman French and retaining a /ʒ/ not native to English. Analogy is a more complex notion but generally can mean any change that brings some structure into line with others. This is most familiar in morphology, where irregular plurals or past tense forms yield to regular -*s* and -*ed*, respectively, but we will see more on this in the next section when we come to lexical diffusion.

2.4 Opposition to the Neogrammarians

From early on, there was skepticism about and opposition to the notion of regular sound change. Schuchardt (1972 [1885]) provides a famous critique, in *Über die Lautgesetze–Gegen die Junggrammatiker* (On sound laws: Against the Neogrammarians). Schuchardt saw sound change as inherently sporadic, starting in some words and spreading potentially to others (Murray 2015). Changes can also generalize phonologically, spread from one type of sound to related ones. Finally, he sees sound change as based on imitation and inherently conscious. For these reasons, he is often considered a forerunner of modern exemplar and lexical diffusionist approaches (see below). The Neogrammarians see sound change hitting all words at once, as being 'lexically abrupt', but often phonetically gradual. Lexical diffusionists see sound changes as lexically gradual, but often phonetically abrupt (Wang 1969).

Modern narratives about the history of the field overwhelmingly present a kind of intellectual battle between this view and a sharply contrasting one, built on the motto *Chaque mot a son histoire*, 'every word has its own history.' This is attributed to the French dialectologist Gilliéron – Labov (1994: 16) cites his 1918 book and Janda and Joseph (2003: 115) cite his 1912 volume, though I am unable to find it in his major works. The great Romance historical linguist Yakov Malkiel calls the 'widespread belief in Gilliéron's authorship' of the quip a simplification and gives no citation from Gilliéron (1983: 218).

Certainly some sound changes do not end up looking regular. Words spelled with <oo> in English, for instance, once all had /o:/ and then after the Great Vowel Shift /u:/ but today are split between /u:/, /ʊ/ and /ʌ/, as with *food* versus *stood* versus *blood* with considerable variation remaining today between /u:/ and /ʊ/ in some words (*hoof, root, roof, room, whoops*) but not others (*gloom, soon, moon*) (Minkova 2014: 273ff.). These may well reflect dialect differences.

Wang argues, with a set of examples of this type, that 'the "regularity hypothesis" must be modified to allow for residue caused by competing sound changes which intersect in time' (1969: 24). The argument is that sound change is, or at least can be, lexically gradual, not affecting all words in the lexicon at once but eating its way through. This launches modern work into lexical diffusion, often aimed at discarding Neogrammarian regularity.

Chen and Wang (1975) review a set of such examples, including a case of tone split, where Middle Chinese tone 3 yields two different tones (2b and 3b) in modern Chaozhou without any apparent phonetic or other conditioning (drawing on their earlier work, summarized also by Labov 1994). The splits are remarkably even overall by the main conditioning factor, the initial consonant in Middle Chinese, as in (3).

(3) Chaozhou tone splits as lexical diffusion, from Middle Chinese tone 3

	Cháozhōu tones	
MC initial	**2b**	**3b**
b	6	7
v	1	3
d	11	14
dz	6	2
z	3	3
ḍ	3	4
dẓ	1	3
dʒ	2	1
g	6	4
ɣ	14	15
Total	**56**	**61**

Examples of exceptional processes exist all around us. As noted in the Preface, the old distinction between /ʍ/ and /w/ (as in *whether* versus *weather*) is dying rapidly in English and it has largely been lost, with /w/ winning out. Some older speakers of conservative dialects – like me – maintain the distinction, and others have a few word pairs but have largely lost the contrast. Blevins (2006b, see also 2008) gives this as an example of an 'unnatural' history of a sound where factors like literacy, language standardization, and prescriptivism lead to the survival of a sound that otherwise would be lost.

This can happen with single lexical items. In much Southern US English and in some non-Southern African American varieties, a set of words have initial stress that, for many other speakers, begin with unstressed syllables:

(4) Regional stress differences in US English

Southern	Other
ínsurance	insúrance
pólice	políce
úmbrella	umbrélla

In talking about sports, some non-Southerners have adopted this for the word *defense*. Such people, and I live among them, may talk about the 'Department of Defénse' but a sports team's 'défense.' This could be a move toward initial stress, but it may also reflect that sports such as American football are often associated with Southern and/or African American speech. We have an example of borrowing, dialect borrowing of a word in a particular pronunciation, showing how lexical diffusion is similar to analogy. Kiparsky (2003: 316) provides the comparison below of sound change, borrowing, and analogy with lexical diffusion. The last two look identical.

(5) Sound change, borrowing, lexical analogy and lexical diffusion

	Sound change	Borrowing	Lexical analogy	Lexical diffusion
Generality	Across the board	Item by item	Context by context, item by item	Context by context, item by item
Gradience	Gradient	Quantal	Quantal	Quantal
Origin	Endogenous	Contact	Endogenous	Endogenous
Rate	Rapid	Rapid	Slow	Slow
Effect on: Rule system	New rules	No change	Rules generalized	Rules generalized
Sound/phoneme inventory	New inventory	Peripheral	No change	No change
Vocabulary	No change	New words	No change	No change

The conflict is, though, precisely about the regularity of sound change itself and Labov is right that the *chaque mot* tradition is rich in examples of apparent irregularities even in the geographical distributions of a single sound change. But as we'll see throughout this book, examples like these are often something other than 'sound change' in a technical sense.

This difference of perspective about the basic 'unit' of sound change is called the Neogrammarian Controversy (Labov 1994: 16, also Labov 1981): 'while the practice of historical linguists assumes the regularity of change, it is generally agreed that the massive data of dialect geography supports the contrary view, that "each word has its own history".' In many ways, regardless of the regularity question, each word can and does have its own history. As Malkiel points out (1983: 219):

At first glance there seems to be no serious incompatibility between individual word history and the postulate of regular sound change. No scholar, not even one of the most austere 'regularist' persuasion, has denied the possibility of non-phonological changes (say, those controlled by analogy) being superadded to the normal 'expected' transformations. It is further generally conceded that the agency of dialect mixture may add extra ingredients to the composite whole; the dialects involved may, in turn, be either regional or social (if the latter situation prevails, some scholars would favor the metaphor of different levels, channels, or conduits of transmission – vernacular, learnéd, partially learnéd). The existence and importance of semantic change has, in principle, never been disputed, though there has been no unanimity of opinion on the wisdom or even the possibility of dealing with this phenomenon in terms germane to linguistic analysis.

In historical linguistics and beyond, the Neogrammarian position has continued to play an important role. Among American Structuralists, for instance, Bloomfield (1933: 354), who studied under some Neogrammarians, stressed the value of their position.

> The real point at issue is the scope of the phonetic correspondence classes and the significance of the residues. The neo-grammarians claimed that the results of study justified us … in seeking a complete analysis of the residues.

Apparent exceptions may reflect finer conditioning than we have recognized, as we'll see with Verner's Law (Chapter 4), dialect borrowing, stylistic or related differences. Bloomfield is exactly right that it is our job as historical phonologists to account fully for all those forms, 'a complete analysis of the residues.'

We will eventually discuss efforts to reconcile evidence for lexical diffusion with regularity. The point for now is that this is an old battle with high stakes, for the nature of phonology and for the scientific status of the study of sound change.

2.5   Synchrony, diachrony and variation

A common narrative about the history of linguistics is that the nineteenth century was diachronically oriented, while work since Saussure became increasingly synchronic, even to the exclusion of historical work. There are grains of truth and buckets of imprecision in that story, but important to us is how current work moves beyond this perceived state of affairs.

A moment in the field, to an extent not yet fully appreciated, was the publication of Weinreich et al. 1968, 'Empirical foundations for a theory of language change.' I mentioned the work in the previous chapter. Their long chapter lays the groundwork for modern 'variationist' work, the field of 'language variation and change.' One way that they changed linguistics generally is by putting real and direct focus on variation, 'orderly heterogeneity,' something picked up on most recently in Sonderegger et al. (2020). Another was the effort to situate language in the community rather than the individual, including sharp critiques of searches for homogeneity.

In their view, linguistic theory has pursued linguistic homogeneity – often by looking at idiolects (how better to minimize variation than by looking only at a single speaker?) or in an 'ideal speaker-hearer' (maybe by idealizing from the single speaker's actual speech) – and this has been treated as a 'prerequisite for analysis.' For them, 'a model of language which accommodates the facts of variable usage and its social and stylistic determinants not only leads to more adequate descriptions of linguistic competence, but also naturally yields a theory of language change that bypasses the fruitless paradoxes with which historical linguistics has been struggling for over half a century' (1968: 99), and they trace the roots of this problem back to the Neogrammarians.

Weinreich et al. place variation at the center of language, language use and change. Here are their conclusions (1968: 187–8), proposing a profound reorientation of linguistic thinking, moving variation and variability to center stage, and bringing language structure and social context together.

1. Linguistic change is not to be identified with random drift proceeding from inherent variation in speech. Linguistic change begins when the generalization of a particular alternation in a given subgroup of the speech community assumes direction and takes on the character of orderly differentiation.
2. The association between structure and homogeneity is an illusion. Linguistic structure includes the orderly differentiation of speakers and styles through rules that govern variation in the speech community; native command of the language includes the control of such heterogeneous structures.
3. Not all variability and heterogeneity in language structure involves change; but all change involves variability and heterogeneity.
4. The generalization of linguistic change throughout linguistic structure is neither uniform nor instantaneous; it involves the covariation of associated changes over substantial periods of time, and is reflected in the diffusion of isoglosses over areas of geographical space.
5. The grammars in which linguistic change occurs are grammars of the speech community. Because the variable structures contained in language are determined by social functions, idiolects do not provide the basis for self-contained or internally consistent grammars.
6. Linguistic change is transmitted within the community as a whole; it is not confined to discrete steps within the family. Whatever discontinuities are found in linguistic change are the products of specific discontinuities within the community, rather than inevitable products of the generational gap between parent and child.
7. Linguistic and social factors are closely interrelated in the development of language change. Explanations which are confined to one or the other aspect, no matter how well constructed, will fail to account for the rich body of regularities that can be observed in empirical studies of language behavior.

It's hard to imagine a more forceful commitment to the study of language variation. Many young scholars today are growing up with this mindset, but this was a revolutionary manifesto when it appeared. And like many revolutions, the seeds of this one can be found in earlier work. People often quote Bloomfield: 'The process of linguistic change has never been directly observed; we shall see that such observation, with our present facilities, is inconceivable' (1933: 347, cited above). Bloomfield focuses on change in phonemes: 'We can speak of sound-change only when the displacement of habit has led to alteration in the structure of the language' (1933: 367). Still, he is thoroughly aware of phonetic variation, 'deviant forms' as he often writes, as well as differences due to (language or dialect) borrowing and analogy, and part of his concern is empirical (1933: 365):

> Historically, we picture phonetic change as a gradual favoring of some non-distinctive variants and a disfavoring of others. It could be observed only by means of an enormous mass of mechanical records, reaching through several generations of speakers. The hypothesis supposes that such a collection – provided that we could rule out the effects of borrowing and analogic change – would show a progressive favoring of variants in some one direction, coupled with the obsolescence of variants at the other extreme.

A cornerstone of Labov's work has been to establish methods and techniques for assembling and analyzing massive records of change in progress, the 'empirical foundations;' Weinreich et al. – keeping in mind that Labov was one of the authors – distinguish actuation and implementation. Actuation, the beginnings of change, tends to be sought in low-level phonetics. Implementation looks at how changes spread through a community and how they become structurally integrated into the sound system, broader grammar, and carry social meaning. This involves social but also phonological factors, as we'll see throughout the book.

In some parts of the world, Coșeriu's *Sincronía, diacronía e historia*, originally published in 1957, is rightly cited as an earlier attempt to deal with variation, in the context of rejecting Saussure's dichotomy between synchronic and diachronic linguistics. Coșeriu shifts from the traditional static comparison of two different historical stages, like Old English versus Middle English, to a more dynamic perspective, looking at changes themselves. He sees language as an activity rather than as an object and argues for a focus on the historicity (*historicidad*) of language (1978: 239). This work is seldom cited in the English-speaking tradition.

We will later unpack this discussion, but note for the moment how far this moves us away from the one-toolism of a person with only a hammer.

2.6 Uniformitarianism

When we talk about sound change in the past we make assumptions, including that the processes at work are the same as those at work today. That is, to understand the past requires that the structure of language, human cognition and even the basic dynamics of society were the same. This is known broadly as the uniformitarian hypothesis or principle and it is not uncontroversial on various grounds (Janda and Joseph 2003: 23ff.). Walkden (2019) provides a set of cautions as to what uniformitarianism actually means and how to constrain it. But on any view, as Campbell and Poser point out (2008: 390–2), uniformitarianism has to break down at some point in the past, as human language as we understand it today was emerging. Uniformitarianism assumes a set of what they call 'design features known from today's languages' and it cannot work before those features emerged. We know vanishingly little about when human language as we know it emerged; Hurford (2014: 15) suggests that it is 'only half a million years old at most, and perhaps much younger.'

While battles on this topic have been waged often over the history and philosophy of science (Janda and Joseph) or evolution (Poser and Campbell), I see more modest and less speculative issues with uniformitarianism. Consider two examples where changes in the relatively recent past could compromise a uniformitarian position while our cognitive facilities may have remained completely constant.

First, how language change is embedded in society is understood today mostly in ways that are tied to specific social structures and cultural practices. I'll give examples involving socio-economic class, social practices among pre-adolescents, how adults speak to young children, and so on. How those and other social factors map to human societies from a couple of thousand years ago is hard to gauge. Other issues include things like community size and mobility, and how many people you interact with and how often. In recent years, scholars have looked for correlations between such factors and sounds. Hay and Bauer (2007) argue that the more speakers a language has, the more consonants and vowels it is likely to have. Atkinson (2011) proposes that the number of phonemes a language has decreases with distance from Africa, which he interprets as supporting a 'serial founder effect' as the earliest human languages spoken in Africa spread around the world. Both these proposals have, however, been vigorously questioned, by Moran et al. (2012) for the former and contributions in Bybee (2011) for the latter.

A vast amount of research comes from urban areas and little from communities of low population density. Do robust contemporary generalizations such as that women lead in sound change hold for the kind of social structure that Proto-Germanic speakers had in Northern Europe two millennia ago? While we do have some evidence from hunter-gatherer communities and other traditional societies, much of our evidence is from settings that clearly differ profoundly from those of not long ago.

Second, there is a recent claim that our diets may have shaped one aspect of our sound systems. In 1985, Charles Hockett published a paper exploring something he had observed about the world's sound systems: The sounds /f/ and /v/ were surprisingly rare. He shows a geographical distribution of these sounds and suggests that this is connected to how people have traditionally gotten their food: 'language spoken by crop-raising people may or may not have f-sounds. But, as our data and maps show, where there is no agriculture f-sounds are exceedingly rare' (1985: 268). Hockett does a broad survey of languages, showing that areas less associated with early agriculture are less likely to have /f, v/, like most of Canada, Australia and western South Africa.

When I read that article early in my career, I was puzzled by the correlation and supposed that there had to be something else going on. Recently, Blasi et al. (2019) followed up on Hockett, arguing that, indeed, these sounds were likely innovations after the Neolithic and they attributed the rise of these sounds to how 'food-processing technologies modified the human bite from an edge-to-edge configuration to one that preserves adolescent overbite and overjet into adulthood.' They trace in particular the history of f-sounds in Indo-European. If they are right, it puts a small dent in uniformitarianism, with one specific kind of change to our sound inventories in the relatively recent past. Whether they are right or not, the collaboration between specialists in paleoanthropology, speech biomechanics, ethnography, and historical linguistics points to one way to make progress.

These kinds of points make clear the need for caution in extrapolating from contemporary evidence to the relatively recent past, certainly in terms of social structure – how sound change works its way through communities – and possibly in terms of linguistic structure.

2.7   Conclusion

This chapter has set up the history of a fundamental issue in sound change, whether it is 'regular' or whether lexically diffuse. We can define sound change as regular and be done with things: Anything that is not regular – whether particular types of change like metathesis or dialect borrowings like initially stressed *defense* or whatever – is simply something else.

That sound changes in progress show lexical exceptions is beyond doubt, and completed sound changes also show exceptions. Many of these are readily interpretable as borrowing or analogy, others not. This is Bloomfield's challenge to seek 'a complete analysis of the residues.' All that aside, the tremendous value of positing regularity – it makes linguistic reconstruction possible, in a pretty basic sense – has limited the number of people who abandon the principle.

This is part of the bigger story of this book: People with different perspectives on this question draw on different kinds of data, choose to give central roles to certain kinds of data and choose to ignore certain kinds of data. This is a pervasive problem in academia and in linguistics. I'm pushing for inclusion and integration of the widest range of data and approaches. For the moment, I suggest we assume that change is ultimately regular and that we are obligated to account for apparent irregularities. A crucial piece of this is variation, a lack of regularity in language in use in a community.

Beyond this book

1.   Digging deeper: Data

Starting from your language histories, look for examples of sound change and what wrinkles or 'exceptions' are discussed, looking especially for things labeled 'sporadic' or 'irregular.' Do you think they could be accounted for in terms of borrowing, social differentiation, etc., or do they represent challenges to Neogrammarian regularity that you can see?

2. Digging deeper: Theory

Start reading your way into the regularity debate. An excellent place to start is Labov's 2020 paper. You might want to read one or two of the pieces he critiques that argue for lexical diffusion. Based on what you see, is sound change 'regular' in the relevant sense? What kind of evidence would you want to see to increase your confidence in your answer?

3. Moving beyond what we know

It's valuable to know the history of research on any question. Compare language histories from two or three different periods and how they present some sound change like those discussed so far.

- How do theoretical notions inform discussion?
- Are there changes in the data presented and how data get presented?
- Is the context of the change – how it connects to morphology, regional variation, social variation – static or does it change over time?

Part 2

Starting points

3

Segmental Sound Change

3.1 Introduction

This chapter and the next conduct an ostensibly mundane piece of business, introducing types of sound change. We'll divide these into changes involving particular sounds, changes that affect larger units of sounds, like syllables or feet, as well as tones, and then finally some kinds of changes that appear to often be irregular. But this isn't a simple catalogue of change types. This survey allows us to flesh out part of a point from the Introduction, that we need to understand different motivations for and theories of sound change.

I'll review some types of segmental change together with classic ways of accounting for them. I begin with assimilation, a kind of change often seen as making articulation easier (§3.2), and then how segmental changes are shaped by larger chunks of speech, like syllables or words; segmental change is sometimes seen as 'improving' syllable structure (§3.3). Section 3.4 deals with the related issue of coda neutralization, which has been argued to reflect universal constraints on change. For each type of change, I'll sketch ways that linguists have sought to account for them. Certain tools work better for certain jobs than others. This underscores again that a bigger theoretical and methodological toolbox allows us to account better for more kinds of change. If you've had an introductory phonology class, many changes in this section may be familiar: The alternations you look at in basic phonology problems often have roots in sound change.[1]

Let's start with the best-known sound change in linguistics, Grimm's Law, already mentioned earlier. Grimm's Law – known by other names, including the Germanic Consonant Shift and the First Consonant Shift – is built on systematic correspondences between Germanic and many other Indo-European languages. With reconstructed IE, those correspondences are particularly clear. Here are some forms in (1), with the relevant sounds highlighted, in data from Kapović (2017: 15ff.). The Indo-European forms on the left are reconstructed, not attested (recall from Chapter 1 that '*' means reconstructed). The picture is simplified in some ways, such as leaving aside labiovelar stops (which show complications)

---

1 This chapter draws in places on Salmons (2010), with considerable reworking.

and palatal stops (whose existence is controversial), but I've given only word-initial forms. (H or h with a subscript indicates an IE 'laryngeal,' which is still poorly understood today and not connected to the laryngeal features we'll discuss several times.)

(1)   Some basic Indo-European-Germanic consonant correspondences (Kapović 2017: 15ff.)

	Indo-European	Germanic
p	*pods 'foot'	Gothic *fotus* 'foot'
t	*tod 'that'	Gothic *þata* 'that'
k	*krewh$_2$s 'raw, meat'	Old English *hrēaw* 'raw'
b	*bel- 'strong'	Low German *pall* 'unmovable'
d	*doru 'tree'	Gothic *triu* 'tree trunk'
g	*gerh$_2$n- 'crane'	Old English *cran* 'crane'
bh	*bhewH- 'be, become, grow'	Gothic *bauan* 'dwell, inhabit'
dh	*dhuh$_2$mos- 'smoke'	Old High German *doum* 'smoke'
gh	*ghl(e)h$_2$dh- 'smooth'	Old High German *glat* 'clear'

If the reconstructions on the left are correct – and that is uncertain – we have a clear set of changes into Germanic.

1. The first three examples, **voiceless stops**, all become **voiceless fricatives**.
2. The second three, **voiced stops**, all become **voiceless**.
3. The last three, '**voiced aspirates**' (murmured or breathy in modern terms), all become **voiced**.[2]

These correlations were recognized in the 1700s and better described in the nineteenth century, first by Rasmus Rask and then by Jakob Grimm. In the early days, people like Grimm saw these as broad trends but their regularity and the importance of regularity only became apparent later (recall Chapter 2). But the regularity is not the only striking thing – every single *p becomes an *f*, and so on – these three changes are interlocking, in a chain-like fashion. One way of representing this would be, using the labials as an example: *bh > *b > *p > *f. The effect, as illustrated in (1) above, is a complete reorganization of the obstruent system from Indo-European to Germanic. While these changes involve phonetics, they are profoundly phonological – about the consonant system as a system (Chapter 9).

Generally, such changes have usually been named by features that change – fricativization or spirantization, devoicing and deaspiration for these. I won't rehearse a full list of such terms; Campbell and Mixco's 2007 *Glossary* is reliable and readily available online. Cser (2015) notes a few important types in pairs:

• **Assimilation versus dissimilation.** Sounds often become more like each other – as with umlaut (assimilation). Sometimes they become less like

---

2   You can hear examples of voiced aspirate stops from Sindhi, an Indo-European language with four manners of stops, at the UCLA Phonetics site: http://www.phonetics. ucla.edu/course/chapter6/sindhi/sinhi.html

each other, often as irregular or sporadic change, and sometimes at a distance. In the Indo-European rule called Grassmann's Law, roots with two aspirated stops lose the aspiration on the first, so *C^hVC^h > *CVC^h (Collinge 1985) (dissimilation).

- **Deletion versus insertion.** Sounds can be lost entirely (deletion) – like the *i/j* sounds that triggered Germanic umlaut. They can also be inserted, for example to break up clusters (insertion or epenthesis). Some kinds of English, Dutch and other Germanic languages seem to disprefer sequences of *l+m*, so that words like *elm* and *film* have a second (schwa-like) vowel in them, or /θl/ so that *athlete* is often pronounced with a third vowel, *athəlete*. We'll see examples of consonant epenthesis below.
- **Merger versus split.** Before final vowels were lost in the history of English and German, they generally merged into a single sound, schwa, the vowel we often see in modern German. The spreading loss of a distinction in pairs like *cot* versus *caught* is a merger in progress today. This reduces the number of sounds in a language, but the number of sounds can increase as well. When the umlaut vowels (Chapter 1) become contrastive with their back counterparts (/y/ versus /u/, etc.), we have splits. In many cases, mergers are conditioned, like loss of various distinctions in word-final position, often talked about as 'neutralizations.'
- **Lenition versus fortition.** Sounds can become 'weaker' (more vowel-like, lenition) or stronger (more consonant-like, fortition), usually described in terms of 'sonority.' This is a complex and controversial notion but it involves an effort to characterize speech sounds on a scale from more consonantal (less sonorous) to more vocalic (more sonorous), generally connected with how much constriction of the airstream there is in a sound's production. English speakers like me who produce vowel-like sounds for /l/ at the ends of syllables are weakening the /l/.

The first and last pairs can vary along a continuum, as we'll discuss for the 'lenition hierarchy' in §3.3. While processes like deletion or merger might seem binary – something's been deleted or not – these are complex. Labov et al. (2006) and others have investigated the low back merger, where some speakers are merged in production but not perception (pronouncing *cot/caught* the same but able to hear the difference), merged in perception but not production, and so on. Deletion may seem like an even clearer yes/no difference, like when English speakers delete /t, d/ in clusters, of the type *perfect memory*. Recent work by Purse (2019) shows that even deletion is gradient: In words without an audible stop, speakers tend to raise their tongue tip, the gesture associated with producing /t/.

Let's turn to some examples and how particular approaches help us understand them.

3.2 Assimilation and ease of articulation

We find assimilation in both synchronic alternations and historical change. Consider the sharing of laryngeal features within obstruent clusters. Laryngeal features are those that refer to states of the glottis – most notably voicing and aspiration. In Indo-European, a *-t suffix triggered a laryngeal assimilation of the final stop in the root *nég^w-'become dark' yielding Indo-European *nék^{w}t-, ancestor of *night*. Voiced *g^w loses its voicing, adopting the voicelessness of *t, a process which created many daughter-language alternations. This pattern and many others – such as assimilation of /n/ to the place of articulation of following obstruents with /in+/ of *impossible* versus *i*[ŋ]*credible* – represent partial assimilation, where segments come to share some feature(s) but remain distinct. This is a persistent rule (see §4.6) rather than a sound change: It has happened historically but remains 'active' today, so that if we create a new adjective beginning in *p*, adding the prefix would yield an [m]. Total assimilation can be illustrated with that same cluster of *k^{w}t in other Indo-European daughters: In Italian it yields *notte* 'night', full assimilation where the old cluster has become a single long stop /t:/.

These examples illustrate regressive assimilation, where features spread to the left, but progressive assimilation is also well attested. Historically, Germanic languages had /x/ with a relatively unrestricted distribution (Robinson 2001). Some modern dialects, like Alemannic (southwestern German-speaking areas, including almost all of Swiss German), retain the original velar fricative pronunciation [x] in codas regardless of the preceding segment. In most varieties, though, a progressive assimilatory process arose so that after front vowels, the fricative is realized as palatal [ç]. For example, while in Old High German *ih* 'I' and *buoh* 'book' the orthographic <h> was realized as [x], Standard German today has [ɪç] and [buːx], with alternations in paradigms involving umlaut such as the plural *Bücher*, [byːçɐ]. Speakers are aware of these differences and some minimal pairs, if marginal ones, have been debated in the literature – such as *Kuchen* 'cake' with [x] versus *Kuhchen* 'little cow' with [ç], taken by many as evidence that we now have two phonemes.

These examples also reflect contact or 'adjacent' assimilation. 'Distant' assimilation favors certain features over others, with laryngeal and manner but not place features in consonant harmony (Rose and Walker 2004). As we've already seen with our umlaut examples, distant place assimilations happen with vowels, over intervening consonants. For example, Old High German formed adverbs in *-o* from adjectives, including from forms in *-i*. Back stem vowels like /oː/ took on the frontness of following *i* (or *j*), informally illustrated in (2) below.

(2)   Old High German i-umlaut

     OHG   German

     skōni   schön 'beautiful'

     skōno   schon 'already'

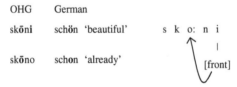

These assimilations created new distinctive front rounded vowels, and new alternations (Chapter 1).

The changes just described illustrate another central dimension of sound change, that is its impact on contrast, changes to the phonological system. Hoenigswald (1960) reviews such impacts on overall sound systems, both inventory and the distribution of elements. For instance, merger and loss remove elements from the system. This can be 'conditioned,' where a segment no longer appears in a particular position but still exists in the system overall. The [ç] ~ [x] alternation just described is conditioned by place of preceding vowel (or consonant). Hoenigswald (1960: 91) gives an example of unconditioned change with Old Latin *h*, which was lost entirely from the language.

When sounds split, Hoenigswald distinguishes primary from secondary split. In primary split, a new sound merges with an existing sound, creating a redistribution of contrast. With our example of *in* + *possible* yielding *impossible*, there's already an *m* in the language so that it's the distribution of *m*s that changes, not their presence in the system. In secondary split, the new sound expands the phonemic inventory, as we've seen with Germanic umlaut when the conditioning final vowels are lost (adapted from Hoenigswald 1960: 77):

(3) Primary versus secondary split

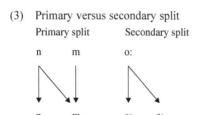

One way that people have long tried to explain sound change is 'ease of articulation,' an idea that many students seem to come up with independently when they start thinking about change. All of the above changes have sometimes been regarded as lessening articulatory effort: A reduction in differences between sounds often correlates with less movement of the relevant articulators. Instead of producing one consonant with vocal fold vibration and the next without, the same setting is used for both. Instead of producing a nasal with a coronal occlusion and an adjacent obstruent with a labial one, both are produced with the lips. Following generations of others (e.g. Paul 1920 [1880]: 56), Hoenigswald wrote (1960: 73):

> A phonetic comparison between earlier and later forms in sound change very often, perhaps generally, suggests a rationale: simplification in the articulatory movements. A given phone is replaced by one which resembles the phones that precede or follow (not necessarily immediately) or which for some anatomical reason combine more easily with surrounding phones or represent a less taxing combination of distinctive features.

Measuring effort has proven difficult. Even then, not all change involves reduction of articulatory effort. In the early days of historical phonology, Sievers (1881: 196–7) concluded that ease of articulation, if it is of any value at all, must be constrained. For instance, reduction of articulatory effort in one realm (V-to-V articulation) may lead to greater complexity elsewhere (the creation of vowels produced with both frontness and lip rounding). Historical processes that lead to new synchronic alternations by definition increase the complexity of the phonology, and they can obscure connections among words in paradigms or derivation. Old English nominal classes showed alternations like the following between singular and plural in two cases, where the final -*s* was 'voiceless' or fortis.[3]

(4) English plural alternations

Old English		Modern English	
NOM/ACC.SG	NOM/ACC.PL	SG	PL
stān	stānas	stone	stone[z]
enġel	enġlas	angel	angel[z]
ġiest	ġiestas	guest	guest[s]
sċip	sċipu	ship	ship[s]

The unstressed vowels of the plural were lost, and the *s*-plural spread to words like *ship*. Agreement in adjacent laryngeal specifications leads to clusters that are all fortis or lenis, creating plural alternations we know today and as illustrated in the last column. The phonetically simple assimilations create a new rule in the phonology, alternations between /s, z/ for plurals and possessives and between /t, d/ in past tense forms like *jogged* versus *walked*.

Ease of articulation accounts are often built on intuitions and assumptions about speech production, while phonetic data show complexity. For example, in the American Upper Midwest, a recent change has raised /æ/ specifically before /g/, so that words like *bag, lag, tag* are pronounced with vowels in or near the range of [ɛ] or even [eː]. The last line of Labov et al.'s *Atlas of North American English* (2006) declares prevelar raising (as it is known) 'unexpected' and a pattern that demands 'a further accounting' (p. 305, §7). This has informally been reckoned to be assimilation, where the low front vowel was drawn upward by the following velar stop. But Purnell (2008) uses X-ray microbeam data to show that prevelar raisers use more lip rounding in producing /g/ compared to /k/. This gesture lengthens the vocal tract and helps contribute to an acoustic impression of raising (with raised F2 and lowered F1 in acoustic terms), and it also correlates with a more forward tongue position. He summarizes acoustic effects associated with prevelar raising in (5) below.

---

3 You may have learned that English /p/ versus /b/ is a contrast based on the feature [voice]. Throughout this book, I'll follow the view of 'Laryngeal Realism' developed in works like Iverson and Salmons (1995) and Honeybone (2005), and §3.4. For now, on this view, languages like French and Polish have [voice] as the active feature in this contrast (specifying /b/ as voiced), while languages like English employ [spread glottis] or a similar feature on /p/ that correlates with aspiration. 'Fortis' is often used for this series in such systems and 'lenis' for consonants such as /b/.

(5) Articulation of prevelar raising (Purnell 2008)

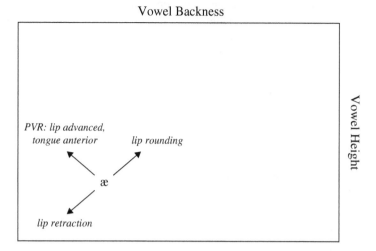

Bauer (2009) further shows, using ultrasound data, that the larynx is lower in the production of /g/ than /k/, which also lengthens the vocal tract. In short, a whole set of articulatory gestures, sometimes quite effortful and certainly different from the simple articulatory account, are used by prevelar raising speakers to create the acoustic cues of a raised /æ/ before /g/. Such application of speech science tools to problems in sound change provides one of the most promising avenues for progress in this field. But there's a serious warning to us in this example: Even where a seemingly obvious, simple explanation for a change presents itself (such as, moving the dorsum in anticipation of a low front /æ/ raises the vowel), we may be using other, sometimes very effortful, ways of producing a sound or enhancing it.

3.3 Syllable-based change: Lenition, fortition and 'preference laws'

Many changes discussed so far are conditioned – not every /æ/ changes, only those before /g/, for example – and the conditioning is often very 'local,' a following or preceding sound. In the next chapter we will turn to changes in larger stretches of speech, but let's first look at how those can serve as an environment for sound change. Sound structures 'above,' or longer than, the segment are referred to as 'prosody' (or 'suprasegmentals') and include syllables and groups of syllables called feet.

I've already mentioned lenition (weakening) and its counterpart, fortition (strengthening) (see Holsinger 2000, 2008; Honeybone 2001, 2005). Lenition tends to follow a restricted number of paths, and Hock (1991: 80–6) proposes a lenition hierarchy, a few trajectories running from voiceless geminate stops, the 'strongest' segments, to [h], [ʔ] or Ø, including loss of occlusion (spirantization), voicing, loss of frication (sonorization), where sounds weaken stepwise, often feature by feature, as illustrated below in (6) (Hock 1991: 83). This movement along the 'sonority hierarchy' runs to ever more sonorous forms. Such hierarchies are not without controversy – some have a simple hierarchy, like vowels > sonorant consonants > obstruents, while others make fine distinctions, like whether /r/ is more sonorous than /l/. Hock's network aims to capture the different paths we find in lenition, for example that /t/ can weaken into any of at least the three links shown.

(6)　Hock's lenition hierarchy

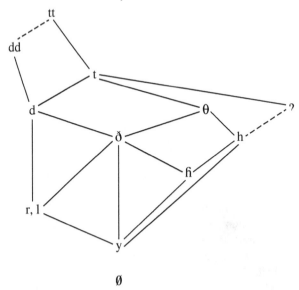

A somewhat different view of lenition comes from Lass in (7), where stronger forms are higher and weaker forms are lower on the chart:

(7)　Lass's lenition hierarchy (1994: 178)

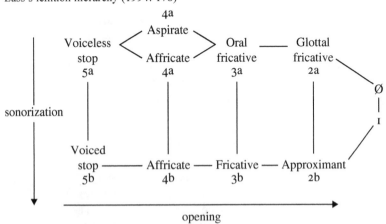

Linguists have long recognized that lenition correlates with prosody. Syllable structure shows asymmetries: Onsets tend to strengthen, codas tend to weaken, and similar patterns hold at levels higher on the prosodic hierarchy as well, especially the foot and the phonological word. One representation of the prosodic hierarchy is shown in (8), ranging from the 'prosodic word' (where phonological behavior rather than orthography or morphology is central) through the 'foot' (one or more syllables with the most prominent typically on the left or right edge) to the mora (a measure of syllable weight where one mora = a 'light' syllable and two = a 'heavy' syllable):

(8) The prosodic hierarchy

> Prosodic Word
>
> |
>
> Foot
>
> |
>
> Syllable
>
> |
>
> Mora

Vennemann (1988) builds this into a theory in which fortition is associated with 'strong' syllable positions and lenition with 'weak' ones.

Syllables are traditionally divided into onset, nucleus and coda, with the last two often grouped as the 'rhyme.' The nucleus is the most sonorous part, usually a vowel, and the onset and coda are less sonorous, coming before and after the nucleus, respectively. Ends of strings of sound often seem prone to weakening and loss, as we've already seen. In Spanish, for example, new restrictions appeared vis-à-vis Latin on word-final consonants (Penny 1991: 74–5).

(9) Coda loss in Spanish (Penny 1991: 74–5)

Latin	Spanish	
illīc	allí	'there'
dīc	di	'say IMPER.'
nec	ni	'neither'
ad	a	'to'
aliquod	algo	'something'

The forms illustrate loss of coda /k/ and /d/, but there were broader, more complex developments. In the history of French, codas have likewise disappeared, often leaving contrastive segmental traces, such as phonemic nasalization on vowels (Gess 1999).

While lenition tends to target codas, languages sometimes strengthen syllable onsets; this strengthening process is called fortition. Vennemann (1988: 50–3) illustrates this with word-initial glide strengthening (see (10)), to fricatives in German and sometimes to stops or affricates in Italian (mostly in words of Germanic origin):

(10) Glide strengthening

German	/jaːr/	>	/jɑr/ *Jahr* 'year'
	/wal/	>	/val/ *Wall* 'bulwark'
Italian	januarius	>	gennaio [dʒ] 'January'
	wadan	>	guad(are) [gʷ] 'to wade through'
	triuwa	>	trégua 'truce'

In German, glides or approximants have hardened into fricatives, while in Italian they have gone farther to become stops or affricates. This is about syllable structure and not just position within the word: In syllable onsets within words, we find Latin *dol.eō* 'I hurt' realized in Italian as *dol.go* (via a stage with a glide onset) and Middle High German *var.we* 'color' becoming Modern German *Far.be.*

Syllable structure is in a sense subordinate to foot structure, lower down the prosodic hierarchy, and that can lead to parallel asymmetries at the foot rather than syllable level. Some Highland Mixtec languages show regular foot-initial development of glides into fricatives – *j > /ž/ – and into stops – *w > /b/ – while syllable-initial but foot-medial sounds weaken (Macken and Salmons 1997). In (11), a more conservative dialect, San Miguel el Grande, is compared to a more progressive one, Chalcatongo. In (11a), you see a loss of medial consonants (illustrated with and without a glottal stop medially), and (11b) shows strengthening of *w and *y (= /j/) compared to what is reconstructed for Proto-Mixtec.

(11) Foot-based strengthening and weakening in Mixtec

    a. Foot-medial consonant loss in Chalcatongo (Macken and Salmons 1997)

San Miguel	Chalcatongo	Gloss
ndivì	ndiù	'egg'
kivì	kiù	'day'
si?vi	si?u	'name'
ti?vi	ti?u	'to suck'

    b. Foot-initial strengthening (data from Josserand 1983; Macaulay 1996)

Proto-Mixtec	Chalcatongo	Gloss
*wexi	bèi	'come'
*wa?a	bà?à	'good'
*we?yi	be?e	'house'
*yuku?	žúkú	'hill'
*yu?u?	žu?u	'mouth'

Vennemann (1988) proposes 'preference laws' to account for syllable patterns. He conceives of sound change as 'improvement,' where the above changes improve syllable structure and bring it more closely into line with the familiar CV template, a simple low sonority onset and a simple high sonority nucleus without a coda. As noted, however, these represent tendencies, not absolutes and Vennemann (1988: 1–2) is aware that changes can also worsen syllable structure, in a formulation that may risk circularity:

> Every change in a language system is a local improvement, specifically an improvement relative to a certain parameter. For instance, every syllable structure change is an improvement of syllable structure as defined by some preference law for syllable structure. If a change worsens syllable structure, it is not a syllable structure change, by which I mean a change motivated by syllable structure, but a change on some other parameter which merely happens also to affect syllable structure.

Syllable-worsening changes lie, then, beyond the scope of Vennemann's theory, but they occur widely. Stops can emerge from or following vowels or glides, even in codas. Mortensen (2012: 445) assembles a set of such cases and they are more widespread and systematic than previously recognized, exemplified in (12), with new stops in bold:

(12) Reflexes of Proto-Tibeto-Burman *-əy and *-əw in Burmish languages

Proto-T-B	Written Burmese	Zaiwa	Maru$_1$	Maru$_2$	
*səy	se	šî	šì**t**	sì**k**	'die'
*krəy	khre	khyí	khyì**t**	khyì**k**	'leg/foot'
*rəy	re	—	ɣì**t**	ɣə**k**	'water'
*gyəy	kyê	jì	jì**t**	—	'parrot'
*kləy	khyê	khyì	khyí**t**	khyí**k**	'dung'
*krəw	khrui	khyúi	khyù**k**	khyù**k**	'horn'

Some Written Burmese forms follow the preference laws, losing coda glides to yield open syllables. The two varieties of Maru shown, though, have created voiceless stop codas. We do not need to go to the Himalayas to find parallels. In various German dialects obstruents have arisen in word-final position, as in these Thuringian (East Central German) forms, where Standard German continues the historical forms:

(13) Excrescent word-final -*b*, Buttelstedt (Kürsten and Bremer 1910)

Buttelstedt	Standard German	
khāmn̥ ~ khām**b**	kamen ~ kam	'they came, he/she/it came'
khīm**b**	käme	'he/she/it would come'
nāmɛ ~ nīm**b**	nehmen ~ nähme	'to take, he/she/it would take'

In these forms, historically nasal-final words have developed final obstruents, again counter to claimed universal preferences for syllable or word structure. Some Westphalian examples from Hall (2014) are given in (14).

(14) a. Soest German [ɪɣ] < Old Westphalian [iː]

    [sxrɪɣə]   *schreie*   'scream, 1 sg' [OS, OHG *scrīan*; OF *skrīa*]
    [frɪɣən]   *freien*   'court, 1 sg' [OS *frīehann*]
    [klɪɣə]   *Kleie*   'bran' [OHG *klī(w)a*, MLG *klī(g)e*]
    [nɪɣə]   *neu*   'new' [OS *nīgi*; OE *nīwe*; OF *nīe*]

  b. Soest German [ʊɣ] < Old Westphalian [uː]

    [bʊɣən]   *bauen*   'build' [OS *būan*]
    [trʊɣən]   *trauen*   'trust' [OS *trūon*]

In these forms, historical glides have hardened into obstruents, strengthening a medial onset, suggesting a syllable-based and not a foot-based pattern.

Mortensen proposes a perceptual account of the Tibeto-Burman facts, arguing (2012: 435) that the obstruents:

originate in the context of high vowels and that high vowels engender this type of change because of their aerodynamic properties. Since high vowels and their homorganic glides entail a constriction of the vocal tract – resulting in a

relatively high oral air pressure and a relatively small difference in the supra-
glottal and subglottal pressures – there is variable devoicing of the terminus
or terminal off-glides of high vowels. The resulting whisper or 'glottal catch'
is mistakenly reanalyzed by learners as an obstruent coda.

Speakers use various means to signal to listeners where important boundaries
occur, and Smith and Salmons (2008: 425) argue that Thuringian epenthetic
stops mark right edges of words: 'fortition characterizes many prosodic edges
and lenition characterizes non-edge positions.' In those analyses, while these
changes may violate syllable-level preferences, they may serve to satisfy other,
higher-level prosodic structures. All these prosodic structures – the syllable, the
foot, edges and non-edges of those domains – exist and are available locations
for lenition or fortition.

Even more interesting, weakening can occur in strong prosodic positions.
Most notable is perhaps the 'complete loss of all initial consonants' in the
Arandic languages (Australia; Koch 2004: 138), illustrated here with pronouns
(Koch 2004: 139). Similar changes are found elsewhere in Australia (Koch
2004: 135).

(15) Arandic initial consonant loss (Koch 2004: 139)

	Pre-Arandic	Aranda
1st singular ergative	*ngathu	*athe, the*
3rd dual	*pula	*ale-*
2nd plural	*nhurra	*are-*

While left edges of words are in some sense inherently prominent positions,
these languages have shifted from initial to second position stress (Koch 2004:
137). If initial syllables were unstressed when this happened, it would help
account for the change – those consonants would be in a prominent position at
the word level, but still unstressed. Nonetheless, stress shift is not found in other
languages with limited loss, so there's more going on. In the Plains Algonquian
languages, Arapaho, Atsina and Cheyenne, we see the perhaps even more
remarkable pattern of loss of initial *k, one of three oral stops in the language,
completely in Arapaho and Atsina and partially in Cheyenne (Goddard 1994:
193, and next chapter).

Once again, similar examples can be found in languages of Europe. In the
history of Spanish, Latin /f/ in onsets weakened in most contexts to /h/ and was
then lost (though it is still written): Latin *filiu* 'son' and *farīna* 'flour' are reflected
in Spanish *hijo* [ixo] and *harina* [arina] (Penny 1991: 79ff., and elsewhere). This
process is yet further from the predictions of the preference laws. Onsets of a
single segment are preferred in Vennemann's Head Law over complex onsets
(1988: 13–21), but while simple onsets are lost, as in the examples just given, /f/
in clusters is maintained, so that Spanish *frío* 'cold' and *fuerte* 'strong' retain the
fricative with following /r/ and /w/ (which arose in a different development). The
pattern, by the way, is obscured in the modern language by the reintroduction of
Latin terms with *f*, like *forma* 'shape' and *falso* 'false'.

Other examples include the Goidelic branch of Celtic, where old *p was lost,
including initially, in a language with initial stress. In Germanic, the reflexes

of Indo-European *k were originally presumably voiced velar fricatives, which weaken to [h], including in stressed syllables. Some varieties of English have deleted even that, again including in stressed initial position, so that *house* is vowel initial.

Vennemann builds his approach on what he sees as universals – though this is far from Neogrammarian regularity. He anchors these 'preferences' in function and phonetics rather than generative Universal Grammar, the innate, genetic component of human language.[4] Syllable preference laws 'have their basis in the human productive and perceptive phonetic endowment. They ... would be derivable – and thus explained – in a sufficiently rich phonetic theory' (1988: 4). Like 'ease of articulation,' preference laws are grounded in phonetics. In generative views, Universal Grammar constrains sound change. In a moment, we'll consider another syllable-related process, laryngeal neutralization, and how it is interpreted within that framework.

Lenition is an area of new progress, with work like that of Cohen Priva and Gleason (2020) arguing that lenition is driven by reduced duration of the relevant segment(s). From a different perspective, Katz (2016) is developing increasingly sophisticated typologies of lenition. He sees duration as having a central role – shortening drives lenition – and focuses on the role of perception. He distinguishes two types. One is 'loss lenition,' that triggers neutralization of contrasts where the formerly contrasting forms were 'perceptually indistinct.' The other, 'continuity lenition,' 'can target segments in perceptually robust positions, increases the intensity and/or decreases the duration of those segments, and rarely results in positional neutralisation of contrasts' (2016: 43). While Katz is most interested in the challenges continuity lenition poses for phonological theory, it offers opportunities for historical phonology.

Lenition and fortition are among the best-studied and probably most common types of sound change. They usually show conditioning by position in the syllable or foot, leading some to argue that these changes 'improve' prosodic structure.

3.4 Coda neutralization and universal constraints on change

Sound change not only eliminates segments from certain positions but also eliminates particular features. Many languages neutralize laryngeal distinctions in codas or word-final position, prototypically in 'final devoicing.' In the classic situation, voiced and voiceless obstruents contrast in syllable onsets but not in codas, where only the latter can appear. Consider these West Frisian examples in (16):

(16) West Frisian final devoicing
Contrast in initial position: **d**ei 'day'   ≠ **t**ei 'thaw'
Neutralization finally: grae**t** 'fishbone' = grae**d** 'degree', both [graːt]

---

4   Preference laws in some ways anticipate the 'violable constraint ranking' at the heart of Optimality Theory; see §9.5.

We have good evidence that this is a recent process, by the way. Tiersma (1985: 30) writes that:

> [R]ecords indicate that final devoicing in Frisian is a phenomenon of recent origin. In the phonetic study of the language of Grou by Eijkman (1907: 19), *b* and *d* are said to be largely voiced at the end of a word. But in Sipma's grammar (1913), there are signs that devoicing has started to set in. His transcriptions, although not entirely consistent, suggest that devoicing had taken place following long vowels, falling diphthongs, and liquids, but not after short vowels or rising diphthongs.

Stop devoicing correlates early on with heavier syllables – syllables with more material in them.

Such changes are common across the world's languages (Blevins 2004, 2006a), including where the process is limited to phrase- or word-final position, which suggests a path along which neutralization develops. That is, devoicing may begin at the end of a phrase or utterance and generalize to smaller prosodic units.

Kiparsky (2008: 46) argues that 'universals constrain change' in such cases. He sees the kind of neutralizations just mentioned in the context of 'the robust phonological generalization that marked feature values [those that are specified as discussed just below] tend to be suppressed in certain prosodic positions,' which he sees as covering 'coda neutralizations' overall (2008: 45). His understanding ...

> locates the neutralization constraint in the design of language. This does not mean that coda neutralization applies in all languages; it just means that, whenever it does apply, it always imposes the unmarked feature value. It can be decomposed into two separate constraints. One says that onsets have at least as many place and manner contrasts as codas, which is really a special case of a family of constraints which differentiate between strong and weak positions. The second constraint says that neutralized features assume their unmarked value (voicelessness, in the case at hand).

Kiparsky understands our endowment for language as licensing contrasts in onsets over codas and mandating that coda neutralization between contrasts in codas must go to the unmarked. This may be anchored in the relative economy of articulation: 'More effortful articulations would be used in positions where a contrast must be marked.' Kiparsky argues that 'the learner ... selectively intervenes in the data, favoring those variants which best conform to the language's system. Variants which contravene language-specific structural principles will be hard to learn, and so will have less chance of being incorporated into the system' (2003: 328). Other work treats transmission as 'vernacular reorganization' (Labov 2001: 415), how 'children learn to talk differently from' their primary caregivers. This gives a more prominent role to social identity (see Chapter 8), well beyond the initial phase of language acquisition, and indeed other work explores changes that can occur over the lifespan (Sankoff and Blondeau 2007, and Chapter 6).

Returning to the empirical question at hand, consider a fuller typology, illustrated with synchronic reflections of historical change. I'm again drawing on

Laryngeal Realism (Iverson and Salmons 2006a: 210, 2011; Salmons 2020, and using 'spread' for [spread glottis] or 'aspiration'). One element of this view – if not a necessary one – is 'privativity.' I'll say more about this in Chapter 9, but here's the basic point: On some views, phonological contrasts are 'binary,' so that a consonant might be [+voice] (/b/) or [−voice] (/p/). Laryngeal Realism treats two-way systems as having a single active feature, [voice] (like /b/ for French) or [spread] (like /p/ for English). The other pair of the contrast (French /p/ or English /b/) is not marked or specified phonologically. This is represented with empty square brackets, [   ], while ']σ' indicates the right edge of a syllable and the bars through a vertical line indicate deletion.

(17) Typology of final laryngeal neutralization, after Iverson and Salmons 2011

Featural contrast	**Neutralization**

a. Final **devoicing**: /d, t/ → [t] (Dutch, Polish, Turkish, Maltese)

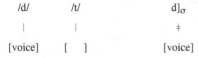

/d/	/t/	d]σ
|	|	ǂ
[voice]	[ ]	[voice]

b. Final **voicing**: /d, t/ → [d] (probably Lakota, possibly Lezgian)

/d/	/t/	t]σ
|	|	↑
[voice]	[ ]	[voice]

c. Final **lenition**: /tʰ, t~d̥/ → [t] (Korean; combined with final devoicing as well in Sanskrit, Thai)

/tʰ/	/t/, /d̥/	tʰ]σ
|	|	ǂ
[spread]	[ ]	[spread]

d. Final **fortition**: /tʰ, t~d̥/ → [tʰ] (German, Kashmiri, Washo)

/tʰ/	/t/, /d̥/	t]σ
|	|	↑
[spread]	[ ]	[spread]

What Kiparsky predicts, neutralization by feature removal, is well-attested in (a) and (c). The pattern in (b), insertion of the feature [voice], is still controversial (Blevins et al. 2020), but (d), insertion of the feature [spread], is widely and securely attested. Rules like 'coda aspiration' in Kashaya (Pomo) are common (Buckley 1994: 87–8):

(18) Kashaya coda aspiration
      /s'uwac-i/   →   s'uwaci   'dry it!, SG'
      /s'uwac-me-ʔ/   →   s'uwacʰmeʔ   'dry it!, FORMAL'

An underlying 'plain' (laryngeally unmarked) stop becomes 'aspirated phono-logically, and not simply subject to some rule of obligatory final release at the phonetic level' (Buckley 1994: 88). This means that Kiparsky's second con-straint, mandating neutralization specifically to unmarked members of contrasts, is incorrect empirically.

I strongly agree with Kiparsky that human cognition and 'the design of lan-guage' are central to understanding synchronic and historical phonology. At the same time, history shapes a sometimes surprising amount of synchronic sound patterning (as we'll discuss with Evolutionary Phonology) and the role played by society is huge (as in the Labovian and allied traditions). This kind of integrated and broad view of grammar – in the sense that includes phonology – leads me to the view that synchronic grammar's role is 'managing, not micro-managing' (Macaulay and Salmons 2017: 208). Our focus remains on figuring out what is driving particular parts of sound change and sound structure. 'Big t' linguistic theory has moved in this direction as well, especially since Chomsky (2005), where three factors are proposed for 'language design': our genetic endowment (Universal Grammar), our linguistic experience (data) and 'third factors,' which are not specific to language, including general cognition. Much recent attention in syntax and elsewhere has gone to these third factors.[5]

3.5   Conclusion

This chapter has surveyed a range of types of sound change, highlighting how some particular approaches understand them. You should see the utility of this range of theories and approaches but also appreciate the limits of any single perspective.

I have not given you anything like the full taxonomy of types of sound change – if you encounter terms like aphaeresis or anaptyxis in reading, checking Campbell and Mixco or doing a web search will give you simple explanations and examples. (Aphaeresis is loss of an unstressed initial vowel, like *lectric* for *electric*, and anaptyxis is insertion of a vowel between two consonants, like our example of *athəlete*.) The terminological tangle is considerable and our focus is on understanding sound change in a deeper sense than being able to recite a catalog of types of change.

A major limit on the typology of sound change is empirical, a solid empirical basis for what does and does not happen, as well as claims about what is more or less common. There seem to be apparent differences of frequency, like *p* becom-ing *f* often but apparently more seldom *f* becoming *p*.

To the first point, the question comes up of whether there are impossible sound changes. It seems clear that certain changes have to involve multiple leaps and are extraordinarily unlikely if not impossible in single steps. I cannot easily imagine /p/ becoming /i/ directly, without some steps like those in the lenition

---

5 The widespread belief that language is uniquely human is usually discussed in terms of syntax, but there is work on whether there is 'animal phonology,' see Yip (2006a, 2006b).

hierarchy. Honeybone (2016) argues that there are impossible changes, namely that θ > f but f ⇸ θ, in his formulation (Chapter 4).

To the second point, claims may reflect biases of histories of familiar languages, so that Romance coda loss is 'normal,' while Tibeto-Burman excrescent stops are 'exotic.' We will eventually be able to address this, for example with the Sound Comparisons project at the Max Planck Institute in Leipzig: https://soundcomparisons.com/

The stakes are high in terms of motivations and causes of change, but immediate for reconstruction, where we would automatically posit a proto-form with *p if we find both /p/ and /f/ in attested languages. That case seems relatively clear, but many others just are not.

Beyond this book

1. Digging deeper: Data

Most language histories note some changes and types of changes that are seen as less common: dissimilation, fortition, addition of new codas. Try to find some examples: Do they change how you think about the notion of 'common' sound changes?

2. Digging deeper: Theory

I've mentioned a couple of interesting recent studies of lenition above, like Katz (2016) and Cohen Priva and Gleason (2020). Take some example of lenition and look for ways to test their views.

3. Moving beyond what we know

Take one or more of your language histories and skim through sound changes.

1. How easy is it to classify them along the lines developed in this chapter? How many involve multiple types of change (like umlaut does with assimilation, deletion, phonemic split)?
2. Does the overall picture line up with what this chapter describes from previous research, for example in terms of frequency of particular types of changes, regularity or irregularity of particular types, and so on?
3. Are there any broader patterns that emerge, for example that the language shows repeated changes of the same type or changes that seem to 'conspire,' where different changes all seem to yield some general outcome, like creating open syllables or other prosody?

4

—

Sound Change Beyond the Segment

—

4.1 Introduction

The last chapter covered some traditional types of segmental sound change and some traditional ways that people have approached them. In this chapter, I introduce two different issues, moving 'beyond' the segment, that is, changes involving longer strings of sounds and units higher on the prosodic hierarchy than the segment. The first is the set of 'stress,' 'accent' and 'tone,' that is, how we use loudness, duration and pitch in speech, and how those change: change in prosodic systems (§4.2), the rise of distinctive tone (§4.3), then the rise of and change in prosodic templates (§4.4). Second, I turn to two issues that people might call 'meta,' issues more abstract than concrete types of sound change, changes thought to be prone to irregularity (§4.5) and issues of common and 'persistent' changes and why that matters (§4.6).

Let's start with examples to bridge from the last chapter to this one. First, the role of prosody in sound changes was recognized in the nineteenth-century debates over regularity. Grimm's Law showed amazing regularity, and led people to identify sets of apparent exceptions. One set involved voicing: IE *p, *t, *k normally yielded Germanic *f, *θ, *x, but in some words, including in basic vocabulary, we find voiced fricatives – *β, *ð, *ɣ. Indo-European also had an *s sound and we find some cases of that as *z as well. Examples in (1) illustrate (data from Salmons 2018: 51–4, recalling that H indicates one of the IE 'laryngeals'):

(1) Verner alternations

	Indo-European	**Germanic**	**gloss**
*t	*bhréH$_2$ter	*brōθar	'brother'
	*pH$_2$ter	*faðar	'father'
*k	*swekrúh	*swéɣur	'mother-in-law'
	*swékuros	*swéxur	'father-in-law'

These alternations extend to different forms of the same word, as examples from Proto-Germanic verb paradigms illustrate (2):

(2) Verner within Proto-Germanic verbs

'I become'	'we became'	participle
*werþō	*wurðum	*wurðan(a)z
'I freeze'	'we froze'	participle
*freus	*fruzum	*gafruzan(a)s

In one of the most brilliant observations in historical phonology and presented in a paper that is a model of clear and compelling argumentation, Karl Verner (1875, partial translation in Lehmann 1967) showed that these differences corresponded to the position of the accent in some of the early Indo-European languages that maintained the original 'mobile' accent. As I'll exemplify in a moment, Indo-European accent could fall on different syllables in the word. For now, consider examples from Spanish (3), where you can contrast three different positions marking different word forms (I've added an accent mark not found in Spanish orthography to show where stress is):

(3) Spanish stress

término	'[the] end'
termíno	'I finish'
terminó	'he/she/it finished'

In languages like Russian or Japanese, the position of stress/accent not only varies by grammatical category but also by word, so that it must be learned for each word.

Verner observed that the unexpected voiced fricatives appeared where there was not an accent before the fricative (adapted from Salmons 2018: 53):

Verner's Law

1. When IE *p, *t, *k, *s follow an **un**stressed vowel (and come before another vowel or sonorant consonant or at the end of a word), they become Germanic *β, *ð, *ɣ, *z.
2. A little more abstractly: when a **Germanic** voiceless fricative directly follows an **un**stressed vowel, it becomes voiced in Germanic.

Verner eliminated the major set of 'exceptions' to Grimm, a reminder to follow Bloomfield (1933: 354, quoted above) 'in seeking a complete analysis of the residues.'

Second, segmental changes interact with prosodic changes, like in 'compensatory lengthening,' where some segment is lost and another segment is lengthened, so that the overall word (or other prosodic unit) keeps its original duration. A comparison comes from West Germanic, where languages like English, Low German and Dutch lost nasals before fricatives and lengthened the preceding vowel, while languages like German and Yiddish have kept the earlier forms, shown in (4), using 'pre-English' for the forms ancestral to languages with the change (see Salmons 2018).

(4)   West Germanic nasal loss with compensatory lengthening

Germanic	German	Pre-English	English
*munθa	Mund	*mu:θ	mouth
*fimf < *femfe	fünf	*fi:f	five
*gans	Gans	*go:s	goose

Similar changes are pervasive cross-linguistically, reviewed by Kavitskaya (2002) and others. In (5), some examples give you an idea of how widespread and diverse these patterns are, starting from Kavitskaya's appendices (2002: 191–9) and assembling data from throughout the book (see the book for details and data sources).

(5)   Cross-linguistic examples of compensatory lengthening

Language	Family	Element lost	Example		
Onandaga	Iroquian	r	*katórje?s	kató:je?s	'I am breathing'
Farsi	Indo-European	h, ?	ro?b	ro:b	'terror'
Turkish	Turkic	j, w, h, g	dyjme	dy:me	'button'
Komi Ižma	Uralic	l	kil-ni	ki:ni	'to hear'
Ngagan	Australian	j, l, r	marbu	ma:bu	'louse'
Ket	Isolate	?	i?	ie ~ i:	'day'

Kavitskaya accounts for compensatory lengthening starting from phonetics, in the duration of the vowels involved and drawing on an Ohala-type view of listener-driven sound change. Her broader argument is that synchronically compensatory lengthening isn't necessarily phonetically motivated, depending on whether synchronic alternations remain transparent or not. This is consistent with arguments later in this book – after sound change springs from phonetic motivations, it can 'move into' phonology and can be reinterpreted in various ways.

4.2   Change of prosodic systems

Prosody conditions segmental change, but prosody itself also changes. As just mentioned, Indo-European accent (probably mostly marked by pitch) fell on different syllables within the word, a tradition that some daughter languages like Sanskrit continue, as in (6), with some forms of the noun 'foot':

(6)   Accent in forms of 'foot,' Indo-European and Sanskrit

Case/number	IE	Sanskrit
nom.sg.	*pēs	pád
acc.sg.	*pédṃ	pádam
gen.sg.	*pedós	padás
loc.sg.	*pedí	padí
nom.pl.	*pédes	pádas

In many other daughters, though, accent has become fixed on a particular syllable within the word. In early Germanic, prominence came to fall consistently on the initial syllable and we have good reason to believe that, in traditional terms, 'accent' – marked by pitch – became 'stress' – marked mostly by loudness and duration. These two changes happened in neighboring languages as well, such as Celtic and early on in Italic, and eventually in some Slavic languages like Czech. Much farther east, a set of IE languages show final stress, like Armenian and various Iranian languages.

Halle (1997) provides a straightforward analysis of IE accent where some words were marked as accented and others weren't. From there, he uses a metrical theory of prosody to get patterns of IE and daughter languages that most closely resemble their parent tongue. Losing the basic distinction between accented and unaccented word classes almost automatically yields initial stress. And it's not hard to get final stress. There are excellent 'internal' or structural reasons for these changes in many daughters.

At the same time, the fixed-stress languages show clear geographical group-ings and the initial-stress languages have neighbors that have long had initial stress (like Finno-Ugric languages, such as Finnish). At the same time, the final-stress languages are found in an area with lots of languages with final stress (like Turkic languages). I have argued (Salmons 1992, but see the much better treatment by Ratliff 2015) that language contact correlates clearly with changes in stress or accent systems, especially from mobile to fixed. Learning a mobile accent system poses a challenge for especially adult learners, and fixed stress at the beginning or end of words is not only easier to learn but has the advantage of clearly indicating where words begin or end (see 'edge-marking' above). While the change would make sense, then, among bilinguals, Halle's analysis makes it the kind of change that could easily spread through a population. There are excellent 'external' reasons – here, language contact and bilingualism – for this change, alongside 'internal' motivations. This underscores why I reject efforts to see change in terms of 'internal' versus 'external' motivations, expecting social and structural factors to push in the same direction in common sound changes.

4.3 Tonogenesis

A large number of the world's languages are tonal. Ratliff (2015: 245) defines a tone language as one …

> in which individual words in the lexicon must include a specification for tone, such tones being drawn from a paradigmatic set of two or more contrastive level or contour pitches. Unlike accent (realized primarily by pitch) or stress (realized by a complex set of features, of which pitch is only one), tone is not limited to prominent syllables, but is realized on most 'tone-bearing units' in a way that does not privilege one or two syllables over the others in a word.

Thanks to decades of careful work – going back to Haudricourt (1954) on Vietnamese and Hombert et al. (1979) – we have a rich understanding of how tone arises, 'tonogenesis.' Classic cases involve what is called 'transphonologiza-tion,' the transfer of a contrast from one feature or set of features to another, to which we will return several times.

In White Hmong, a language of Southeast Asia also spoken in the United States since the arrival of refugees after the Vietnam War, this happened with the loss of coda consonants. We've seen that coda loss is common but, in these languages, effects of the codas remain as tonal distinctions, illustrated below in (7), from Ratliff (2015: 249). The numbers for White Hmong indicate how high the pitch is, 5 highest and 1 lowest; the modern spelling system uses final consonants to represent those orthographically.

(7)   White Hmong tonogenesis (Ratliff 2015)

1. Atonal stage	CV		CV?		CVH		CVC_{vl}	
2. Tonogenesis	CV(level)		CV(rising)		CV(falling)		CVC_{vl}(atonal)	
3. Tone split	*t- upper	*d- lower	*t- upper	*d- lower	*t- upper	*d- lower	*t- upper	*d- lower
4. White Hmong	[tɔ⁵⁵] 'deep'	[tɔ⁵³] 'hill'	[tɔ²⁴] 'mix'	[tɔ²²] 'wait'	[tɔ³³] 'pierced'	[tɔ³¹] 'sink'	—	[tɔ²¹ʔ] 'there'

The top row illustrates a pre-tonal stage, where the language had, in order, open syllables, syllables ending in glottal stop, syllables ending in /h/ and syllables ending in another consonant. In the second row, the two laryngeal consonants, glottal stop and /h/, are lost after creating tones that the language hadn't had before. The widespread view is that the constricting gesture of closing of the glottis for /ʔ/ creates a rising tone, while the opening gesture of /h/ creates a falling one, though these mechanisms have not been rigorously demonstrated yet. Later, we see another layer of change, where the distinction in onsets between voiced and voiceless consonants is lost, corresponding to higher and lower tones involving phonation type (known as a 'register' distinction). Modern patterns are in row 4, together with the modern spelling. These sets are further supplemented with reconstructed forms from Martha Ratliff (p.c.):

TABLE 4.1. Tonogenesis in White Hmong

Gloss	Reconstructed Hmong-Mien		White Hmong
To answer	*tau	Tone 1	55 tone: *teb*
Elder brother	*da	Tone 2	52 tone: *tij*
Body louse	*tɛmʔ	Tone 3	24 tone: *tuv*
Fire	*douʔ	Tone 4	22 tone: *taws*
To kill	*təjH	Tone 5	33 tone: *tua*
To die	*dəjH	Tone 6	breathy falling tone: *tuag*
Wing	*N-tat	Tone 7	22 tone: *tis*[a]
To bite	*dəp	Tone 8	21 tone: *tom*

Note: [a]Tone 7 merged with tone 4 in White Hmong.

Contrastive tone can arise from a wide array of sources, including one found in Tibetan, described by Caplow (2016a, 2016b). The Tibetan family includes tonal and non-tonal languages. Caplow examines data from non-tonal dialects at the extreme eastern and western ends of the area, Balti and Rebkong Amdo. From those, she is able to reconstruct shared stress, notably second syllable stress on disyllabic nouns, adjectives and numerals versus initial stress on disyllabic verbs. These correlate with the position of high tone in tonal varieties: second syllable stress 'has been phonologically re-analyzed as obligatory high tone on the second syllable of disyllabic words' (2016a: 215). Prosodic prominence has remained in place, but has changed from 'stress' to 'tone.'

The Algonquian family is spoken across a broad swath of North America, historically from northeastern Canada to the American Southeast, through the Great Lakes and Great Plains on to western Canada. Proto-Algonquian was almost certainly an iambic language – one where feet have a basic weak + strong pattern, versus trochaic languages such as English that typically have strong + weak pattern. It was not tonal, but tone has arisen in a set of geographically distant languages from different sources (see Mithun 1999: 24–6 for references, and also Biedny et al. 2019, manuscript). In some languages, like Montagnais, long vowels came to carry high tone. In that language, H develops on vowels with following glottal stops as well. Far across the continent, Cheyenne also developed high tone from vowel length. In Kickapoo, old coda /h/ led to a low tone, which apparently generalized to all spirant codas.

Algonquian also illustrates that tone tends to show areal distributions (Ratliff 2015: 245–6; Salmons 1992, among others; see Kirby and Brunelle (2017) for a more skeptical take). A set of Algonquian languages from the Great Plains have all developed tone, as shown in Figure 4.1 (Biedny et al. 2019, manuscript), in a broad area characterized by tone. This tonal area was first noted, to our knowledge, by Stacy (2004) and includes more languages than she notes and more than shown in the map, actually. Ratliff identifies a set of tonal areas around the world – East and Southeast Asia, sub-Saharan Africa, Meso-America – and Biedny et al. add the Great Plains to that list. Most striking – and I will say more about this below – is that tone across such areas is not being straightforwardly borrowed, for instance by borrowing words with tonal patterns intact and spreading tone to the rest of the lexicon, but rather often shows different sources and paths of development in individual languages. In Figure 4.1, languages without shading are non-tonal and those with light shading are Algonquian languages that have developed tone, while the more numerous languages shown in darker shading are unrelated tonal languages.

Afrikaans is developing tonal contrasts, replacing an old voicing distinction in syllable onsets. Coetzee et al. (2018: 205) trace this to low-level cues present in most [voice] contrasts (where 'f0' means 'pitch'):

Small consonantally induced f0 perturbations are most likely present in all languages that have a phonological voicing contrast … Why then do these f0 effects become exaggerated and even develop into independent phonemic contrasts in a small number of languages (as may be happening in Afrikaans), while they remain small and stable in most languages? An intriguing possibility for the Afrikaans development is language contact. What differentiates the Afrikaans situation from that of many other languages (including Dutch as Afrikaans's primary linguistic ancestor) is that Afrikaans was in close contact with tonal Khoisan languages during the early years of its formation, and has been in prolonged contact with tonal Bantu languages since. It is possible that this contact situation could have contributed to greater perceptual sensitivity to f0 differences in the Afrikaans speech community, and that this awareness

FIGURE 4.1. The Great Plains tonal area (by Gabrielle Mistretta, based on Mithun 1999: 609)

could have contributed to exaggeration of the f0 differences in Afrikaans over successive generations.

They ultimately doubt this scenario for sociolinguistic reasons, but we would need to know a lot more about the early history of the language: It's clear that many people acquired the language who were speakers of tonal languages or who came from families of people who were. That is, they would have brought this perceptual sensitivity with them in building an Afrikaans grammar.

4.4 Templates

In many languages, certain types of words or even virtually all words have particular structures, in terms of consonants and vowels or syllables and feet. This is famous in Semitic, with its triconsonantal roots, like the example of Arabic *ktb* for 'to write' that takes different vowels to form different word forms, like *kataba* 'to write' versus the verbal noun *katb* 'writing,' among many other forms. From the perspective of just segmental phonology, templatic patterns often look like conspiracies, sets of different changes that seem to produce a single outcome, something shown for syllable structure as a way to capture a set of diverse Germanic sound changes by Murray and Vennemann (1983). Work on how templates arise and change is recent. The example of Mixtec above was one of the earliest examples arguing that prosodic templates can shape sound changes in a language. Smith and Ussishkin (2015) represent the best general statement.

One example shows how strong these templates are, how modern Hebrew integrates English loans (Smith and Ussishkin 2015: 279, data from Bat-El 1994), in (8):

(8) Integration of English borrowings into Hebrew (Bat-El 1994; Smith and Ussishkin 2015: 279)

English noun	*Hebrew noun*
nostalgia	nostalgia
transfer	transfer

Hebrew verb	*Gloss*
nistelg	'he was nostalgic'
trinsfer	'he transferred'

The borrowed nouns just reflect English word structures, without adaptation to a template. For verbs, templatic requirements are stricter than on nouns and the verb for 'was nostalgic' has been adjusted to fit templatic requirements, for a particular 'shape' in terms of consonants and vowels.

The basic templatic word shape of a language can change over time as well. In the history of Chinese, Salmons and Zhuang (2018) argue, we can trace changes from typically disyllabic word forms in Proto-Chinese to monosyllabic in Middle Chinese and now back to disyllabic today, as in (9).

(9) Chinese prosodic templates (Baxter and Sagart 2014: 53; Salmons and Zhuang 2018)

Disyllabic Proto-Chinese	**Monosyllabic** Middle Chinese	**Disyllabic** Modern Chinese (with pinyin in brackets)	**Translation**
*kə·rˤak	落 *lak*	落下 (*luòxià*) *luɑ·ɕia*	'fall (v.)'
*mə·lat	舌 *zyet*	舌头 (*shétou*) *ʃə·təu*	'tongue'
*Cə·daŋ	尝 *dzyang*	品尝 (*pǐncháng*) *pʰɪn·tɕʰaŋ*	'taste (v.)'

We argue that this reflects a cycle of change with parallels throughout East and Southeast Asia. In the recent trend to disyllabic forms, a whole set of distinct and independent patterns converge, another 'conspiracy.' They include the following, using examples from Thai (Mixdorff et al. 2006; Yang and He 2012: 135–6):

1. Compounding with a synonym or semantically closely related word: $rai^{41}naa^{33}$ 'farmland' $< rai^{41}$ 'dry land' $+ naa^{33}$ 'paddy fields'
2. Reduplication: $tshoon^{24}tshen^{24}$ 'noisy'

Other words add apparent nonsense syllables or have been lexicalized from phrases into single words. Our interpretation is that those changes all serve the higher-level purpose of fitting a prosodic template.

In sum, sound change is hardly just particular individual sounds changing, but rather any sound structure changing. While some types of research into prosodic and tonal change are still new and developing (like with prosodic templates), we can see that prosodic and tonal changes are just as structured and systematic as segmental ones, and even intertwined with them.

4.5   Irregular and sporadic change

Let's shift gears to 'types of sound change' along another parameter, starting with changes prone, so it is claimed, to irregularity. The Neogrammarians clearly recognized that some kinds of sound change often appear as irregular or sporadic change. The Neogrammarians themselves did not see these as damaging the Regularity Principle, and called them 'types of sound changes for which consistent implementation is not a theoretical necessity' (Paul, in Auer et al. 2015: 82). These are typically illustrated with metathesis and dissimilation. Paul (Auer et al. 2015: 71) argues for the former, metathesis, that 'we are not dealing with a change – through displacement – of the elements of which the speech is composed. Rather there is only a transposition of these elements in certain individual cases.' Dissimilations, where identical or similar segments become less alike, are often but not always irregular. (Distance dissimilations were long regarded as rare, but recent work by Hualde (2018) on Basque and Jatteau and Hejná (2018) on Mongolian suggests that they may be more common than has been appreciated.)

Consider one example of each of these processes. First, Dahl's Law in Bantu (Teil-Dautrey 2008) describes how, when two adjacent syllables begin with voiceless stops, the first becomes voiced, as in the reflexes shown in this Kikuyu pair involving the diminutive prefix *ka-*:

(10) Dahl's Law reflexes in Kikuyu
      /ka-βori/   →   [ka-βori]   'small goat'
      /ka-ko/   →   [ɣa-ko]   'small piece of wood for burning'

Second, Spanish has undergone various metatheses, many irregular but some regular. One example is the inversion of /Cj/ sequences to modern /eC/ (Penny 1991: 56, 96, and elsewhere), where the metathesized glide becomes a vowel:

(11) Spanish glide metathesis

FERRĀRIU   >   *ferrero* > Spanish *herrero* 'blacksmith'
CAPIAM   >   *quepa* 3.SG.SUBJ. of *caber* 'to fit'
BĀSIU   >   *beso* 'kiss'

As we've already discussed, Ohala (1981, 2003) accounts for most sound changes as perceptual 'hypocorrection' or 'hypercorrection.' Listeners usually correctly perceive utterances, in part by normalizing or correcting the signal by factoring in contextual effects. Hypocorrection happens when a listener mishears a signal and interprets it without those 'corrective strategies' (as with assimilation), as we've seen. Hypercorrection occurs when the listener hears the signal correctly to begin with but incorrectly applies those strategies. Ohala sees dissimilation and metathesis as the latter. For instance, dissimilation often appears with segments that spread acoustically over a longer stretch of sound, like aspiration. That creates ambiguity for the listener as to where the feature was located in the signal, so that they may 'move' it to another segment perceptually. Indeed, Dahl's Law is traced to a time when the 'voiceless' stops of Bantu were aspirated, making it in effect deaspiration of the initial stop. Blevins and Garrett (1998, 2004) build similar arguments about metathesis, and provide a valuable cross-linguistic survey. A perceptual hypercorrection analysis of such changes is attractive, but is not the only factor at play: Teil-Dautrey (2008) shows that Dahl's Law helps to fill phonotactic gaps in Proto-Bantu root structure.

These cases take us back to a basic question about sound change. For Ohala (2003: 683), sound change …

> does not serve any purpose. It does not improve anything. It does not make speech easier to pronounce, easier to hear, or easier to process or store in the speaker's brain. It is simply the result of an inadvertent error on the part of the listener.

This kind of perceptual perspective has been developed into a theory of sound change and more recently of phonology by Blevins (2004: 33–4), which we will discuss in more depth later. It rests on three elements:[1]

- **Misperception**, where listeners mistake a sound for a similar-sounding one.
- **Reinterpretation**, where listeners associate an intrinsically ambiguous signal with a different phonological form than the speaker.
- **Selection from phonetic variants**, where listeners build a representation on an occurring variant that differs from the speaker's representation.

Blevins (2004: 23) proposes to explain sound change and most synchronic phonology:

> Principled diachronic explanations for sound patterns have priority over competing synchronic explanations unless independent evidence demonstrates, beyond reasonable doubt, that a synchronic account is warranted.

---

1   These are terms used by Smith and Salmons (2008) for and characterizations of what Blevins calls CHANGE, CHANCE and CHOICE, respectively.

Similar claims have a long history, views that give a prominent role to history in shaping the synchronic form of language, including Saussure (1986: 105), who wrote that 'Un état de langue donné est toujours le produit de facteurs historiques' (Any given language state is always the product of historical factors). Throughout, I argue for a robust role for history in synchronic explanation and a substantive role for abstract structure in understanding sound change (see Bermúdez-Otero 2006; Good 2008; and Chapter 9).

4.6   Cross-linguistically common and 'persistent' changes

If you read broadly about sound change, you'll encounter claims about what is 'common' versus 'uncommon' or 'unknown' and even 'impossible' in sound change (and language change). Establishing these trends is maddeningly difficult. I've already mentioned the issue in passing and we'll touch on it again several times in the coming chapters (e.g. in §5.6), so it warrants a brief introduction.

Consider an example seen as a particularly odd sound change: In Hawai'ian and various other Austronesian languages, *t has become /k/. It's odd in the sense that it leaves the language without /t/, an extremely common sound in the world's languages and one of only a small set of oral stops. But, as noted by Blevins (2004: 123), Foulkes and Vihman (2015) and others, this only seems to happen in languages that have lost a /k/ through other means, such as a change of k > ʔ. While Blevins in particular is concerned with phonetic motivations, the gap in the system at the velar place of articulation does get filled, though it creates a new one. What's rare versus common is a serious matter, for instance in deciding between competing analyses and especially in reconstruction: If we are confident that X > Y is vastly more common than Y > X, in a dataset where X and Y go back to a common ancestor, we posit X.

A common sound change is palatalization, prototypically a process where /t, k/ sounds become affricates or fricatives, like in the examples below. (See Bateman 2011 for a good overview drawing on data from dozens of languages.)

(12) English palatalization
    (a) what you doing?   [watʃju] ~ [watju] ~ [waʔju]
       Tuesday   [tʃuzdi] < /tju .../ ~ [tuzdi] < /tu .../
       truck   [tʃɹʊk] ~ [tɹʊk]
    (b) Latin   cāseus   cheese
       Old English   ceosan   choose

What you see is two different processes. In (12a), we have active, contemporary processes where speakers and dialects vary, while (12b) shows a historical process of palatalization. The targets differ as well, /t/ versus /k/, and the triggers too, /j, ɹ/ versus /i/, and so on.

In Algonquian, similar processes are also common, presumably developed independently numerous times in different languages, involving front vowels, especially high, and the glide /j/. Examples from various parts of the family illustrate (Pentland 1979):[2]

(13) Algonquian palatalization, Pentland (1979), following his orthography

Proto-Algonquian	t > c (= [tʃ]) ('Palatalization III')
Menominee	t > c (= [tʃ])
Narragansett	k > c (= [tʃ]) or tʸ
Montagnais	k > t, c (= [tʃ])
Blackfoot	k > ks

It's not always obvious what rules are phonologically active in a particular language at a particular time, and Menominee palatalization provides a nice example. The rule in Menominee (adapted from Macaulay forthcoming) is this:

(14) Algonquian palatalization, Macaulay (forthcoming)

t > tʃ / __ e(ː) or j

The mid front vowel triggers palatalization along with the palatal glide, but the high front vowel does not. It's not just that it's 'rare' to have palatalization of /t/ in this context (and you need to keep really clear that it's /t/, since /k/ is another major target of similar processes) but it is often claimed to be impossible. Bateman (2011) specifically claims that the situation described above is impossible. She posits an implicational universal: 'If lower front vowels trigger palatalization, so do higher front vowels.'

This is a real problem, but solvable: These palatalizations reflect the situation before an old Menominee vowel shift. In that shift, old *i lowers (what Oxford 2015 calls 'front-vowel lowering') and a new *i arises (from Oxford's 'glide-vowel coalescence'). In other words, this is a historical process – palatalization was active before the vowel shift and the contemporary distributions of /t/ and /tʃ/ have remained stable. We have to evaluate what is active versus what is an echo of a historical process no longer active. Menominee palatalization then falls easily into line with cross-linguistic patterns. Indeed, the English examples in (10) show a similar pattern: early *ceosan* 'to choose' had a front vowel triggering palatalization but the palatal /tʃ/ remains before a back vowel today, and the process is clearly not active, since words like *keep* and *keys* are common. As with the example of umlaut in Chapter 1, we again have a process where a conditioned change established and maintained itself after loss or change of the trigger. And as with umlaut, we have a change that didn't revert with conditioning changed.

Other patterns appear to persist over time. Iverson and Salmons (2008) puzzled over the repeated rise of aspiration in the history of Germanic, for instance, and in §6.3 we'll see that some scholars have declared that vocalic chain shifting is an enduring feature of Germanic languages as well.

This opens a chance to highlight a couple of points that aren't made often or clearly enough in terms of how sound changes do or don't make their way through a community. I sometimes sense an assumption that once a change gets going, it will inevitably reach completion. This is a kind of teleological thinking

---

2   These examples leave aside other processes that Algonquianists call palatalization. The analysis parallels that in Cudworth (2019), and grew from discussions about this issue.

(as we'll discuss later) and there seem to be clear counterexamples to at least the naïve version of that view:

- **Stalled changes.** Just because a change starts doesn't mean that it eventually reaches conclusion. The Northern Cities Shift (NCS, see the next three chapters) is an example of this, where the shift is 'falling apart' in Chicago and other places (McCarthy 2011), that is, the patterns used by many speakers no longer follow the NCS. Only parts of it seem to have reached beyond the southeast corner of Wisconsin. Similarly, the Second or High German Consonant Shift (§9.1) did not generalize fully anywhere and shows steadily narrower changes from south to north. While the loss of Proto-Algonquian *k is complete in Arapaho and Atsina, it remains partial in Cheyenne.
- **Ebb and flow.** Other changes don't just stop, but stop and start and even stop again. Hickey (2002) treats a particular kind of stall, where variation remains present in the community for long periods of time without resolution, with a whole set of examples from English and Irish English, including light versus dark /l/. Pitts (1986) argues for 'flip flop prestige' in the presence of glides before vowel in words like *tune*, *news*, *duke*.

Contrast this with the **Constant Rate Hypothesis** (also called the Constant Rate Effect), developed by Kroch (1989) for syntactic change but extended to sound change by Fruehwald et al. (2013). They define it this way:

> when a new syntactic variant begins to enter the grammar, its use may be more or less favored in different contexts, but it increases in frequency in every context at the same rate over time (the 'Constant Rate Effect'). This shows that the different contexts express the same underlying change, a single incoming rule which is unspecified for context. The differing frequencies in each context, then, are orthogonal, additive, and extragrammatical, or at least grammatically inert.

Fruehwald et al. support this from the history of German final fortition and in §7.4, I give a chart by Labov showing vowel changes that look like something closely related to these patterns. How to integrate this important generalization with stalled changes and ebb and flow changes has not, to my knowledge, been undertaken. These are areas that badly need systematic exploration, with a broader set of languages and changes.

4.7   Conclusion

We've moved in this chapter from segmental changes to changes 'above the segment,' an area of rapid and exciting progress these days, including on matters such as prosodic templates which were barely discussed in the field not that long ago.

I've stretched the notion of 'types of change' to talk about changes thought to be irregular or 'sporadic' as well as those that appear to be common or even persistent. For both topics, there is tremendous need for new and better work.

One way that I expect future progress in this area is by better integration into a modular view of sound systems, something I'll talk about in Chapters 9 and 10.

Let's move on now to our last bit of introduction to the field, the kinds of evidence that we can draw on to demonstrate that sound change has happened. Here, too, we'll find that using all the data and all our tools is extremely valuable.

Beyond this book

1.   Digging deeper: Data

Change in stress and metrical systems has been unevenly investigated across the languages of the world, especially in terms of using modern views of metrical and stress theory. Hayes (1995) gives an excellent starting point for understanding the synchronic systems – with some attention to history. Compare his synchronic analysis to what you find in language histories. There are lots of contributions to be made in understanding particular languages and language families.

2.   Digging deeper: Theory

The idea of language change organized around prosodic templates – their emergence, changes in templates or loss of templates – has hardly begun. A careful reading of Smith and Ussishkin (2015) can give you a springboard into finding such patterns and using templates to understand them in many languages.

3.   Moving beyond what we know

- To what extent do your language histories deal with factors 'above the segment' in treating sound change? Is there explicit discussion of prosody and/or metrical structure?
- Many languages have undergone restructuring of stress systems, changes in syllable and foot structure, loss or development of distinctive tones or changes in the tone system, and so on. After reading this chapter, do you see any new angles for thinking about these?
- It seems clear that 'ebb and flow' changes and 'stalled' changes are under-discussed for many or most languages. Can you find further examples? Are there good ways to account for them?
- A good account of *k loss in Algonquian would be a serious contribution.

5

Evidence for Sound Change

Materials of concern in historical linguistics are available primarily through written records called **texts**.

Lehmann (1973: 59)

5.1 Introduction

This chapter introduces the empirical bases for the study of sound change. When I was a graduate student, data came overwhelmingly from written texts, as in the quote from Lehmann above (also Hoenigswald 1960: 4). Changes were presented as before-and-after scenarios: Proto-Indo-European versus Germanic consonants, Latin vowels versus their reflexes in Italian, or Middle English versus Modern English long vowels. This naturally limits us to languages with long written traditions, where we can, for instance, clearly compare Middle English and contemporary English or Latin and French. And it often means that examples come mostly from European languages – Hoenigswald barely mentions non-Indo-European languages that I can see, for example.

These are exciting times for linguistics and for historical linguistics in particular, with rapid progress on myriad fronts. In few areas has the progress been as dramatic as in our empirical foundations: Yes, we still draw data from written records, but we do it in new ways and it's now one source among many, and how we use written records is now very different. The discovery of previously unknown ancient manuscripts and inscriptions is commonplace. In 2006, someone looking at a book in the University of Leipzig noticed that the book's binding material was in Old Saxon. He had a closer look and this led to us having two more pages of the earliest manuscript in that language. In 2009, scholars found a palimpsest, two pages of which had been used for writing earlier and where the earlier writing had been removed to reuse the writing surface (see (1)). New technology allowed people to read the earlier text, and you can see the Gothic word *atdraga* 'pull down' in lighter shading below. These pages probably date to the sixth century, see Finazzi and Tornaghi (2013).

(1)   Gothic palimpsest (Finazzi and Tornaghi 2013)

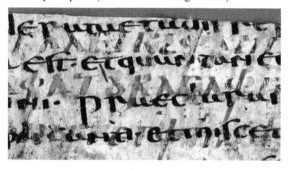

The goals of this chapter are to: (1) outline the main types of evidence for sound change, written and otherwise; (2) balance the advantages and disadvantages of various kinds of evidence; and (3) argue that these complicated kinds of evidence actually fit together well and yield much more information than one might first think. We'll talk through old and new ways in which we use those records, and then turn our attention to the newer kinds of datasets we draw on, including spoken data (from new or historical recordings). Thanks to digital technology, we have new ways of dealing with all that data, from free software for acoustic analysis to ready access to large electronic corpora and corpus analysis tools. I'll first talk about alphabetic systems and some obvious and not-so-obvious problems with their interpretation (§5.2), then 'diffuse' writing systems, based on Chinese and how scholars can glean information from ancient writing (§5.3). While sound recording is a recent innovation, we have recordings of speakers born two centuries ago, long enough to allow deeper data on sound change (§5.4). Indirect but still valuable evidence for sound change comes from experimental work and computer simulations (§5.5) and from comparative work (including reconstruction) and cross-linguistic typology (§5.6).

5.2   Written evidence: Alphabetic

Many people are surprised to learn that writing systems have seldom been invented in the course of human history. Most written languages are written in systems that have been adapted from another language. The process of converting a spoken language into a written form is called 'scripting' (Seiler 2014: 31, using a term coined by Ursula Schaefer). Let's begin with the kind of writing I'm using now – alphabetic – where symbols correspond to particular sounds. In the case of English, those correspondences are very abstract, basically for historical reasons, as we will discuss.

Historical phonologists have learned to extract amazing data from even limited written texts. Evidence includes occasional spellings (hardly 'misspellings' where there is no established system!) and hypercorrections, alliteration, meter, word division across lines, puns, orthoepic works – works giving advice on how to pronounce a language – and other explicit descriptions of speech sounds and pronunciations. In Gothic, it has long been noted that word breaks across lines correspond, generally, with syllable structure. Rhymes and puns reveal patterns of pronunciation, and explicit comments about pronunciation tell us much, though see Minkova (2014: chapter 8) on difficulties. In the short Gothic *Skereins* text, for instance, CVCCV are broken over lines as *aflif-nandeins* 'of remaining' and *at-ta* 'father' (Miller 2019). These, along with comparative evidence, allow us to confirm that the language had long versus short vowels and heavy syllables. At the end of this chapter, I'll say a little more about occasional spellings and hypercorrections. But let's start with basic issues of alphabetic writing and its interpretation.

Committing a language to writing involves, among other things, adapting or creating symbols for sounds that the language from which the alphabet was borrowed did not have. Latin, for example, lacked the sounds /ð, θ/, found in the early Middle Ages across Germanic. The indigenous Germanic writing tradition, the runic alphabet, was probably built on Southern European models, and had symbols for these sounds. One, <þ> or 'thorn', made its way into early writing across many Germanic languages; it was well established in Old Norse and is still used in Icelandic. From early on, though, other spellings were common across West Germanic languages, including <th>, which we use today for both /ð, θ/, as in *th*is and *th*ing. Seiler (2014: chapter III) reviews a set of possible sources of that spelling convention: Irish, Greek, Latin and indigenous sources. Our /w/ also showed complexities, spelled with <u> or multiples (leading to our usual name for the letter, 'double u') or the rune *wynn* <ƿ>.

Even more complex than adapting a writing system to a language that had those sounds already may be the case of figuring out ways to represent new sounds that emerge after a writing system is established, like in the case of German umlaut. Scribes and writers didn't consistently mark it even in the Early Modern period, 800 years after the vowels arose. The high front rounded vowel /y/ was represented early on with <iu>, and a dizzying array of variants over time, including a following <e> (<ue>), an <e> above another vowel (<ů>), and the modern two raised dots (ü).[1]

In the nineteenth-century European tradition of historical linguistics, the linguists doing historical analysis were often the same people doing philological groundwork: editing and publishing ancient texts. Hermann Paul, already mentioned as one of the heavyweights of theory in the day, not only wrote the classic statement of the Neogrammarian position, called *Principles of Language History* (first published 1880, see Auer et al. 2015), but also wrote the standard handbook of Middle High German grammar (first published 1881, updated to the present day). He not only carried out linguistic analysis, but also literary work, and he co-edited what is still the major journal for German historical linguistics and philology, *Beiträge zur Geschichte der deutschen Sprache und Literatur*. He clearly had something close to total mastery of what was known in those days about those languages and about language change. Paul was hardly alone in

---

1   A rich story of scripting is Smalley et al.'s 1990 account of the development of an alphabetic script for Hmong. In other cases, writing systems weren't adapted directly, but just seeing written language inspired people to develop new ones, as with Sequoyah's early nineteenth-century invention of the Cherokee syllabary (Bender 2002).

this breadth: Eduard Sievers was a master of phonetics and poetry, for instance. These people understood the complex variation and vagaries of transmission from working directly with original manuscripts. In their grammars, though, they wrestled mightily with the presentation of variation. The classic pattern, still found in the current editions of those handbooks, is to present descriptions and developments in the body of the text, with regional and chronological variation consigned largely to footnotes. (An old joke among Germanic historical linguists is that changing a footnote in one of these books is a worthy goal for a dissertation.) But, as we'll see, this work may have biased some of these scholars toward major literary texts and away from certain readily available data, such as glosses scratched onto manuscripts. While variation was recognized as a fact about the datasets at hand, variation was not deeply woven into the analysis of change in many cases.

In the second half of the twentieth century, the situation changes. As argued in §2.5, Weinreich et al. (1968) provide a profound turning point in the study of language change with their explicit focus on the role of variation. They write about 'Hermann Paul, who apparently was the first to isolate the language of the individual as the most legitimate object of linguistic study' and then 'trace the hardening of the paradox in the Saussurian period, when homogeneity of language – assumed to be found in the idiolect – was drawn upon as a prerequisite for analysis' (1968: 98–9). This mindset is present in work on sound change until late in the century, but with complexities. Lehmann, in the book quoted at the beginning of this chapter, pays attention to Labov, an indication that he sees an opportunity or maybe a need for change.

At the same time, most researchers over time came to align themselves more with the linguistic side of historical work or more with the philological side, and, at worst, with a lack of respect for what others were doing, down to crass stereotypes of theory-mad linguists who didn't understand or value the actual data at hand versus plodders poring over manuscripts without any thought to making generalizations. These ghosts still occasionally pop up and there have been and are a few scholars who perform both roles. Happily, the pendulum seems to have swung back: Today, people are working hard to integrate rich empirical understanding with generalizations situated in linguistic theory. This is captured in the mission statement of the journal *Diachronica*, which I edited for almost two decades: 'Contributions which combine theoretical interest and philological acumen are especially welcome.'

We can illustrate this reintegration with work by Schiegg (2015, discussed in Salmons 2016 and 2018, on which this section draws). Schiegg examines early medieval glosses in German manuscripts, from the stage of the language called 'Old High German' (basically texts written up to about 1050, abbreviated OHG), the home turf of legendary scholars such as Hermann Paul. Glosses are words or phrases written often between the lines of Latin texts. Those earlier scholars didn't always ignore glosses entirely, but they mostly banished their discussion to footnotes (with the exception of Sievers, who edited a collection of glosses). Looking through older, traditional histories of German, glosses are usually mentioned, but are seldom discussed in any detail. If you recall the Lauersdorf Principle from Chapter 1, this is a problem, since some estimates have it that two-thirds of our attested OHG words are in glosses. (For more information, see http://glossenwiki.phil.uni-augsburg.de/wiki/index. php?title=Hauptseite)

Old High German was frequently written into Latin manuscripts, once talked about, certainly among non-specialists, as simple explanations or translations of words or phrases – crib notes for people without strong enough Latin skills. (This is not far from what Wikipedia has today under 'gloss (annotation).') If you've ever looked at foreign language books in a college-town used bookstore, you probably know this function. Close analysis of these glosses shows a wide range of functions, from editorial comments and instructions (such as 'learn this part by heart') to giving information on pronunciation or grammar.

Of particular interest to Schiegg are 'drypoint glosses' (*Griffelglossen*), pressed or etched into the writing surface without ink. These, he argues, were not intended to be widely read. Scribes were carefully trained in spelling and writing conventions – OHG is widely regarded as orthographic chaos, but Seiler (2014) reveals great systematicity – and it is easy to imagine that these more or less hidden written forms reflected informal usage. You might be more likely to write 'gonna' in a text message but 'going to' in formal writing, using the more inno-vative form in less formal contexts. Schiegg sifts out evidence for when certain sound changes took place with gloss data. Like other specialists before him, he sees progressive forms, like the reduction of final syllables (recall umlaut in Chapter 1), and the reduction of other unstressed syllables. For example, verbal prefixes *ar-* or *fir-* become *er-* or *fer-*; where they once had /a/ or /i/, they come to be spelled with <e>, like Modern German *er-* and *ver-*. But we also have evidence of very archaic forms, such as spellings suggesting continuation of an earlier /iu/ form where handbooks suggest that it had already changed to /y:/ (2015: 280–5). While both were spelled <iu>, the older form is marked by a special sign pointing to its diphthongal status. These conflicting pieces of evidence may reflect glosses entered at different times or by different readers/writers. When we start to track all the data, we make progress and see new challenges.

Let's first put a dagger through the heart of one common myth about written records. Newcomers to the field often seem to take spellings at face value in ways that I don't expect from English speakers – our orthography is catastrophi-cally inconsistent: Think about <g> in *go*, *germ*, *garage*, *sing*, to give a minor example. To establish the phonetic and phonological value of historical writings, we continue to use methods developed in philology. Minkova provides nice over-views of these (2014, 2015) and I'll say a little more about this below.

For one set of vowels and diphthongs, the mismatch goes back centuries, and we can talk about that while asking a bigger question about interpreting this kind of written evidence: How can we identify changes in progress in such texts? The 'gonna' example points to the conservative character of writing. As a newer form, *gonna* is not what we learn to write, and we're told not to write it. (As I'm typing, the spellchecker flags it.) But spelling can be more profoundly conservative. In English, we write long vowels with symbols that differ sys-tematically from what they mean in most European languages. This reflects the 'Great Vowel Shift' (taking this image from Salmons 2018: 251), mentioned already in Chapter 1:

(2)   The Great Vowel Shift, Early Modern English

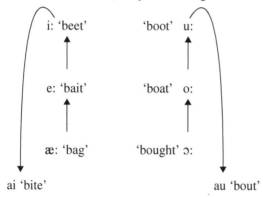

The symbol <i> in many languages reflects /i/ or something closely related, and <ee> would be /e:/, for instance. We spelled these sounds in a traditional way for centuries after these sound changes. In fact, the vowel in *boot* has fronted in many kinds of English – North American and British – so that the spelling is increasingly two major steps away. (See Lass 2015 and Minkova 2015 for discussion of related issues in the history of English.)

The question is how we identify changes in such a system. If we have poetic texts, rhymes can play a crucial role ... before the unrounding of front rounded vowels discussed in Chapter 1, *king* and *ring* did not rhyme: The former was *kyng* in West Saxon. With unrounding, they rhyme. People have figured out more ingenious strategies. For example, when you learn to write you don't learn to spell everything in the language, and when you have to write something new, like a name of a previously unknown place or person, you may fall back on what you hear or say. The earliest evidence for some early German umlaut comes precisely from such names. The front rounded vowels that are now spelled *ü* and *ö* in German were not spelled regularly even in the Early Modern period (1350–1650). By about the year 1000 some spellings suggest these pronunciations, but they had to have existed even much earlier than that. Gütter (2011) examines manuscripts well back into the ninth century and reveals that place names show distinct spellings exactly where we have umlaut today. The Swiss town name *Büren*, for example, is spelled *Puirron* as early as 827. It is exceptional spellings that tell us something, the places where writers don't have a model to follow.

These examples show that identifying and tracking sound change in alphabetic texts is far from obvious and simple, but with effort we can squeeze out a lot of information. For excellent overviews of the topic using historical English data, see Lass (2015) and Minkova (2015).

Let's turn now to some challenges in interpreting old scripts and texts that may be less familiar to most readers. We will not even talk about sound change directly, but about how we create a basis for talking about sound change: How do we establish phonetics and phonology in such materials?

(3)   The Rosetta Stone

British Museum [GFDL (http://www.gnu.org/copyleft/fdl.html) or CC
BY-SA 4.0 (https://creativecommons.org/licenses/by-sa/4.0)], via Wikimedia
Commons

The Rosetta Stone is a beautiful fragment of black stone with three versions of
a long inscription, one in Greek and one in hieroglyphic Egyptian. Because the
texts are closely parallel, the latter could be deciphered by comparison to the
Greek. More difficult was the decipherment of 'Epi-Olmec' hieroglyphic writing,
laid out in Justeson and Kaufman (1993). A set of inscriptions in southern Mexico
date back in part to before the Common Era. With the discovery of one relatively
long inscription, found in Veracruz and pictured below, Justeson and Kaufman
were able to gain a foothold into the interpretation of these inscriptions.

(4)   Epi-Olmec writing

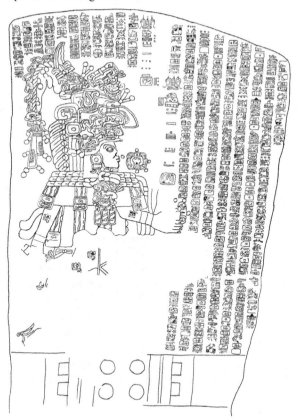

Paulo Calvo [CC BY-SA 4.0 (https://creativecommons.org/licenses/by-sa/4.0)],
from Wikimedia Commons

First, they assumed the language would be part of the Mixe-Zoquean family
spoken today in the region. Considerable reconstruction has been done for these
languages, so that they had some idea of what the relevant form of the language
would look like. Second, they assumed that the writing system was 'logosyl-
labic,' i.e. had symbols representing morphemes. Given that, they anticipated that
certain grammatical patterns would occur, such as particular verbal suffixes. They
were helped along by our understanding of other scripts and types of inscriptions
in the region, especially calendars which use distinctive ways of writing dates,
allowing comparison to Mayan hieroglyphs. This complicated triangulation
led them to identify particular symbols with particular words and morphemes,
including their phonological shapes, identifying grammatical markers like the
plural *-taʔm* and lexical items like *kuy* 'wood, tree' and *mak* 'ten'. As Patrick
Honeybone neatly summed it up: 'once we've cracked the writing system, we
can use it as further evidence for phonological forms.'

While much remains to be done, studies like these present us with examples
of using all the data and how they give clarity about what was recently murky
linguistic prehistory.

5.3 'Diffuse' writing systems

Above, we looked at issues of scripting and sound change in texts using the Latin alphabet. That writing system has been adapted for many languages and often expanded, e.g. with diacritics for additional consonants (ś, š, ç, ć), vowels (ü, ö, ä), length (ū, ō) or features like nasalization or tone. Still, the total number of symbols needed to write in Latin, Cyrillic, Greek, Runic or other alphabets is small, a couple of dozen. The same holds for syllabaries, like those used for Cherokee and other languages. Unger (2015) calls these 'compact' systems, which he contrasts with the 'diffuse' writing system of Chinese, which was adopted for other languages across much of East Asia.

The challenge for interpreting Chinese writing without a key to the system is real. In 谢谢 'thank you', usually transliterated as *xièxiè*, though there is a phonetic element, the characters don't directly tell us the sound values. Instead of a tiny set of symbols, we find a relatively open-ended one. Yet thanks to a long tradition of research, we know a lot about the phonetics and phonology of Chinese from a millennium and a half ago. There are some Chinese words written in Tibetan alphabetic script and some Sanskrit words are found in Chinese texts (Unger 2015: 88). Far more important are 'rhyme tables' and the technique of *fanqie* (Baxter and Sagart 2014; Norman 1988; Unger 2015): The former, notably the *Qie yun* from the year 601 CE (but known from later manuscripts), arrange words by the four relevant tones and then by the rhyme. This all interacts with *fanqie*, a system that puts together words with the same initial consonant and then the full rhyme (nucleus and coda). This image from Baxter and Sagart (2014: 10) gives a pair of homonyms (the two larger characters):

(5) Rhyme table

In this pair, the first element indicates, as noted, the initial consonant of the word and the second gives us the rest of the word, the rhyme, using Baxter and Sagart's spelling system:

(6) Interpretation of (5)
    tok   huwng

That is, the word in question would be read as *t(ok)* + *(h)uwng* = *tuwng*. Still, these comparisons are algebraic comparisons of ancient forms. They become usable only when they can be matched with modern forms from various Chinese languages or dialects, or with known loanwords from Chinese. Here is Baxter and Sagart's supporting modern evidence for this item:

(7)   Comparison across languages

	德	多	特
Middle Chinese	*tok*	*ta*	*tok*
Mandarin	[tɤ³⁵]	[tuo⁵⁵]	[tɤ³⁵]
Cantonese	[tɐk⁵]	[tɔ⁵⁵]	[tɐk⁵]
Sūzhōu	[tɤʔ⁴]	[tɒ⁴⁴]	[tɤʔ⁴]
Sino-Korean	*tŏk* [tʌk]	*ta* [ta]	*tŭk* [tɯk]
Sino-Japanese	*toku*	*ta*	*toku*
Sino-Vietnamese	*đúc* [ɗuk D1]	*đa* [ɗɑ A1]	*đắc* [ɗak D1]

This complicated network of associations provides forms that are connected to modern forms where we do know the sounds and you can see changes even here.

The reconstruction of virtually every aspect of this stage of the language is controversial (see Schuessler 2015 for one good overview). Indeed, even the periodization is disputed (not everybody calls the relevant stage 'Middle Chinese'), but you can see how much can be learned from this work. Unger (2015: 98) concludes that 'The long history and richness of the Chinese writing system are by no means insurmountable obstacles to phonological reconstruction.'

These last two sections – on alphabetic and other writing systems – contrast types of evidence: You might think that you can trust alphabetic systems to some degree in studying sound change and you might imagine that you can't squeeze much out of non-alphabetic ones. Neither would be close to the mark. In working with written materials, we constantly confront the pitfalls of alphabetic systems and find ways of mining non-alphabetic systems.

We're not always lucky with ancient scripts. The decipherment of early inscriptions from Greece in scripts known as Mycenean Linear A and Linear B has been a long slow process (see https://www.hf.uio.no/ifikk/english/research/projects/damos/ for a database of Linear B). Many documents and scripts remain undeciphered, like the Voynich Manuscript, where an internet search will lead many people down a serious rabbit hole. But let's turn to a happier time, an era where we don't have to rely on writing at all but have audio recordings that we can listen to and do acoustic analysis of.

5.4   Audio evidence, in apparent and real time

With Thomas Edison's phonograph or grammaphone (patented in 1857), it became possible to record and play back sound (Hickey 2017c). English dialect recordings began in the early twentieth century with Wilhelm Albert Doegen's recordings for the Berlin Sound Archive. It wasn't until the 1930s and 1940s that recordings for linguistic research became common. This includes work at the University of Wisconsin–Madison by Miles Hanley in New England (Purnell 2012) and then widespread recording by Frederic Cassidy in the early 1950s, leading to the *Dictionary of American Regional English* project in the late 1960s and early 1970s (Cassidy and Hall 1985–2017), on which more in a moment. Wisconsin faculty were recording immigrant languages early as well: Einar Haugen and Lester W. J. Seifert recorded Norwegian and German/Low German respectively in the 1940s.

There is already a good overview of this area (Maguire 2015) and a solid volume on the topic (Hickey 2017a). How historical recordings can inform linguistic research is neatly summarized by Hickey (2017b: 3, with examples, details and references throughout that volume):

TABLE 5.1. Classification of insights from early recordings, adapted from Hickey (2017b: 3)[2]

Level 1: Early recordings reveal previously unattested features. This is not common, but an example would be the use of a rolled [r] attested in the recordings of Baroness Asquith and Virginia Woolf for earlier RP.

Level 2: Early recordings display combinations of features not previously attested. For instance, in early twentieth-century Irish English non-rhoticity and a monophthong in the GOAT lexical set is found, a combination which does not occur anymore.

Level 3: Early recordings have combinations of features not continued in a variety. In early twentieth-century Australian English, a retracted START vowel and a fronted STRUT vowel co-occurred whereas these vowels converged later in the twentieth century in Australia.

Level 4: Early recordings display features which help one to decide between alternatives for the development of features in a variety. For instance, in early South African English the retracted START vowel is nothing like as prominent as it is today, suggesting that this was an internal development in South Africa after initial anglophone settlement.

Level 5: Early recordings confirm features known from later recordings and observations of present-day speakers. For instance, the early recordings of English from Tristan da Cunha document clearly the presence of non-etymological initial /h-/ which is known from studies of Modern English on the island.

Level 6: Early recordings confirm general patterns assumed for the development of varieties. For example, the speech of some older speakers from Ghana shows that for four key variables, Ghanaian English moved away from RP and more toward endonormative realisations of the variables in question.

Levels 1 and 2 and to a lesser extent levels 3 and 4 are valuable for providing new and often unexpected insights into language history but even levels 5 and 6 are important: We work hard to increase the certainty of our analyses and raise the probability that our analyses are right.

Maguire surveys methodological challenges of real-time data on change, pointing to the problem of apples-to-apples comparisons, surely one of the most serious challenges. We are of course dependent on the kinds of data we have, and to establish in a rigorous way that change has happened we need the most closely parallel data across points in time.

An outstanding solution to this problem is found in a set of papers by Harrington and colleagues (Harrington 2006, 2007; Harrington et al. 2000a, 2000b). In England, Queen Elizabeth has broadcast an annual Christmas message every year since 1952. Aside from being delivered by the same person to essentially the same audience, these messages are generally similar in form, content and tone. (I'll explore other changes over the lifespan in the next chapter.) British English pronunciation has been changing rapidly over this period and these papers consider relevant social changes, in particular the weakening of older social class lines and how this might have impact on 'Received Pronunciation.'

The figure below (see p. 78) plots a set of the Queen's vowels (measuring vowels in Bark rather than F1 and F2). In each image, '5' represents the values of the Queen's vowel in the 1950s, '8' in the 1980s and 'S' provides a comparison to Standard Southern British in the 1980s. As you can see, in every case except the HEAD vowel, her pronunciation has changed in the direction of ordinary people. That is, in those figures, the 8 is closer to the S than the 5. Harrington et al. find that 'there has been a drift in the Queen's accent towards one that is characteristic of speakers who are younger and/or lower in the social hierarchy' (2000a: 927).

---

2   Words in all caps indicates Wells's vowel classes – https://www.phon.ucl.ac.uk/home/ wells/stanlexsets.htm – reflecting various patterns of contemporary English vowels with historical context in terms of phonological conditioning.

(8)   The Queen's vowels over time

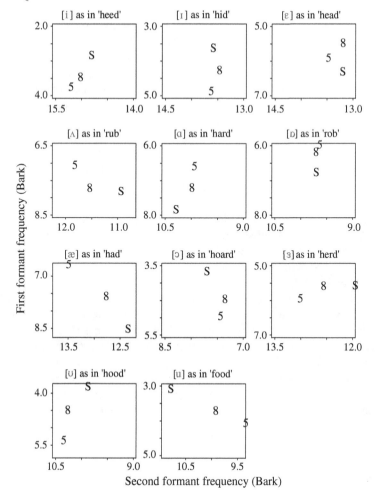

Note: The three symbols '5', '8' and 'S' represent the average positions of different vowel types in the Christmas broadcasts of the 1950s and 1980s, and in standard southern British of the 1980s, respectively. The axes are the first two formant frequencies in Bark, a scale used to model the way listeners perceive vowels. Positions towards the top of each square correspond to less mouth opening; the left corresponds to sounds made by constricting the vocal tract nearer the lips rather than further back.

Harrington et al. (2000a) title their paper in *Nature* 'Does the Queen speak the Queen's English?' and reach this closing statement (2000a: 927):

We conclude that the Queen no longer speaks the Queen's English of the 1950s, although the vowels of the 1980s Christmas message are still clearly set apart from those of an S[tandard] S[outhern] B[ritish] accent. The extent of such community influences is probably more marked for most adult speakers, who are not in the position of having to defend a particular form of English (the Queen's English in this case).

They note that this seems surprising in terms of issues of class and prestige, on the assumption that people of higher social status would not imitate the speech of those of lower social status. As we'll discuss in Chapter 7, 'prestige' is a problematic notion and people do accommodate how they speak to others around them, regardless of status.

Another kind of data comes from traditional dialect fieldwork. In the American Upper Midwest, focusing on Minnesota and Wisconsin, fieldwork for linguistic atlases was done in the 1940s and on into the 1950s, involving very 'close' (phonetically detailed) transcription. (One atlas was eventually published and the fieldnotes exist for the other.) Beginning in 1951, Frederic Cassidy made recordings for the Wisconsin English Language Survey, which set the stage for the *Dictionary* mentioned above, with recordings in Wisconsin and Minnesota from 1964–9. 'Wisconsin Languages' – a project of faculty and students at the University of Wisconsin–Madison – has carried out more recent fieldwork. The earliest speakers involved, seventy-four in total, were born between 1850 and 1879. Many of these interviews included similar or even the same material, such as having consultants read the short passage 'Arthur the Rat.' (It exists in a couple of variants and a web search will get you all of them.) The University of Edinburgh Phonetics Recording Archive has another large set of recordings, including many of Arthur: https://datashare.is.ed.ac.uk/handle/10283/345

Purnell et al. (2017) use the US sources to extend the history of Upper Midwestern English, looking at three vowel changes which have been taken to have different histories in the region:

1. the monophthongal pronunciation of the long /oː/ vowel in words like GOAT, long assumed to reflect Scandinavian influence on English;
2. the merger of /a/ and /ɔ/ in words like LOT and THOUGHT, often assumed to reflect the eastward spread of a merger over time (often known as low back merger); and
3. the raising of the /æ/ vowel in words like TRAP (often known as ash-raising or æ-raising), reported in the southeastern part of this area and mostly among speakers born since about 1950.

In each case, examination of historical data, audio and transcribed, changes our understanding. Monophthongal /oː/, that is /oː/ without the typical offglide we find in American English (and other varieties), is marked on Figure 5.2 by circles, while speakers who had offglides are shown with triangles. Scandinavian settlement was heaviest in northwest and western Wisconsin and eastern and northeastern Minnesota, and the distribution of monophthongal forms does not correlate with that. This monophthongal realization of the vowel is instead scattered across the region and it appears to have consolidated itself in the region and as a stereotype of speech in the region.

We found /a/ ~ /ɔ/ merger early on as well, also scattered across the region, and before most sources would have expected it. The raising of /æ/ begins earlier and has a wider geographical distribution than previously reported. The conditioning is also unexpected: Through the Great Lakes area associated with the Northern Cities Shift, following apicals favor the raising, while in Wisconsin (and areas beyond) following velars, especially /g/, trigger raising (recall Purnell's work noted in §3.2). We'll discuss the Northern Cities Shift in the next chapter, but, for now, just note that it involves, among many other changes, a raising of /æ/ especially before alveolar obstruents like /d/. We found that the earliest speakers show pre-apical raising, which then shifted to prevelar. Figure 5.1 illustrates the kinds of distributions we found, here for the GOAT vowel.

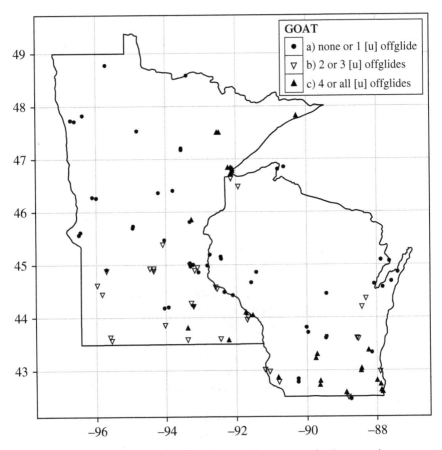

FIGURE 5.1. Monophthongal /oː/ in Wisconsin and Minnesota in early recordings

Together, these patterns yield a different history of regional English, redefining the geographical distribution and history of spread of a set of defining features.

5.5 Experimental and simulation evidence

We have already talked about experimental work that helps us understand sound change, like Ohala's research into the listener's role in sound change in Chapters 1 and 3, with more to come in Chapter 8. The laboratory can be helpful in other ways and this section is a brief reminder that experimental and simulation evidence are indeed evidence for sound change. I'll just mention one example of each.

First, in Ohala's work on 'hypocorrection' – a failure to compensate for contextual effects in perception as a source of sound change – a major question is how and why we do this. In a series of articles, Yu (2010, 2015; Yu et al. 2011) has presented evidence that 'the magnitude of perceptual compensation varies as a function of cognitive processing style' (2010: 5) interacting with the sex of listener. He measured cognitive processing style by the Autism Spectrum Quotient (AQ), where everyone, including neurotypical people, shows a range of different behaviors. His experiment asked listeners to identify syllables as /su/, /sa/, /ʃu/ or /ʃa/. He synthesized these into continua, varying from clear /s/ to clear /ʃ/. This is a familiar technique and it allows us to find out at what point on a continuum listeners shift from hearing one sound to another. When /s/ is produced before a rounded vowel like /u/, it becomes more like /ʃ/, because the lip rounding and lip protrusion of /u/ change the /s/ toward /ʃ/. Nonetheless, people are more likely to hear an /s/ in this context, presumably because they are compensating perceptually for the following vowel.

Yu relies on two particular measures within the AQ, namely AQAS, which measures attention switching abilities, and AQCM, which measures communication skills. The results show that women with low AQ scores normalize less, i.e. engage in less perceptual compensation, than others (see (9) below). This suggests that sound changes involving hypocorrection may tend to originate in this particular part of the population. This speaks to one of the most consistent patterns in sound change, the tendency for women to lead in change. That is, as sound changes move through a community, women are often about a generation or so ahead of men in adopting the new forms (see Labov 1994, 2001, and much other work). This association would have been, at best, extremely difficult to establish through observations of change in progress or otherwise.

(9)   Correlation between AQ scores and vowel perception (Yu)

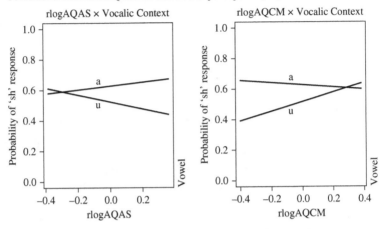

Second, Wedel (2015 and elsewhere) has produced computer simulations of language change, where agents and sets of agents are programmed to communicate, that is exchange some symbol – producing it for other agents and interpreting the output of other agents. An error rate is built in, so that the sound or form in question isn't always accurately conveyed. By building in biases in the communication, pressure is created toward or away from some variant. Those biases can be positive or negative, favoring or disfavoring some variant over another. Wedel argues that speakers and listeners strive to maintain contrast, generally and specifically when pairs of words compete in some sense. In the figure below (10), Wedel (2015: 161) illustrates four 'words' in the lexicon of one agent, with an initial stage given in (a). After 4,000 exchanges (b) shows the result for the lexicon when there is no bias for keeping words distinct – they are similar enough that they all merge. In (c), the same number of simulations has been run but with a bias against word-level ambiguity, so that the forms remain distinct. These simulations lack the real-world complexity of sound change, but allow us to do what Wedel calls 'impossible experiments.' In particular, the effects of some real-world bias (toward vowel-to-vowel assimilation, or loss of final laryngeal distinctions) may take many, many generations to come to represent sound change. Here, running the simulation for thousands of generations is not a problem. Moreover, this approach allows for precise manipulation of variables. If you think that one particularly powerful speaker exerts great influence on a community's speech, you can program one agent to be that influential. If one form is harder to learn than another, you can bias the program that way. In (10), you see the effects of maintaining contrast (distinct clumps of dots) with and without a bias for distinction.

(10) Simulations showing the effect of a selection against word-level ambiguity (Wedel)

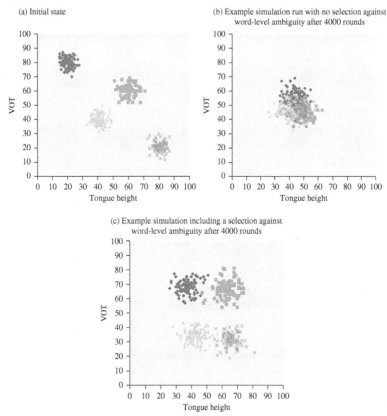

(a) Initial state

(b) Example simulation run with no selection against word-level ambiguity after 4000 rounds

(c) Example simulation including a selection against word-level ambiguity after 4000 rounds

This approach begins to capture long-term trends that we simply cannot observe directly. It provides new ways of testing hypotheses, and will likely become more valuable as such.

5.6 Comparative and typological evidence

As linguists, a lot of what we do in practice is look for patterns in complex data. The literature on sound change is filled with claims of the sort – already alluded to earlier in 3.4 and 4.6 – that some particular change is common and the reverse change uncommon, like p > f versus f > p, that is, spirantization of stops (discussed earlier) appears more common than stopping of a fricative (though interdental /θ, ð/ may be exceptions). Still, we have numerous examples where historical /f/ is realized as /p/, such as a historical hardening process in Icelandic (Árnason 2011). Icelandic is prone to fortition processes so that this example is not shocking. Here are a few asymmetries in direction of changes that come up (drawing in part on Honeybone 2016):

(11) Asymmetries in frequency of particular sound changes (Honeybone 2016)

Common	Uncommon
p > f	f > p
k > s	s > k
k > tʃ	tʃ > k
θ, ð > f, v	f, v > θ, ð – unattested?
y > i	y > u

If we can establish such typologies, even as tendencies, they can help us understand changes across related languages and reconstruct proto-languages. Historical phonologists take typological evidence of what changes are more likely to inform their decisions about the direction of change in interpreting systematic differences, basically what we have seen with Grimm's Law and other sound changes.

That said, the use of typology in historical and comparative linguistics has been met with surprising hostility at times. The system of Indo-European obstruents presented in our discussions of Grimm has, in fact, proven problematic. Scholars since Jakobson have noted that the basic system – involving voiceless, voiced and 'voiced aspirate' or murmured stops – is unusual if not unattested in modern languages. (Many languages of South Asia have a four-way system, with voiceless ≠ voiced ≠ voiceless aspirates ≠ 'voiced aspirates,' but this three-way contrast is at best very rare.) In addition, the system more or less lacks *b and voiced stops are generally rare – and not found at all in inflectional affixes– and CVC roots cannot contain two voiced stops.

To account for these unusual patterns, the 'Glottalic Theory' was proposed, independently but almost simultaneously, by Hopper 1973 and Gamkrelidze and Ivanov 1973 (reviewed in Kümmel 2015; Salmons 1993). An important observation was that the patterns just noted for the voiced series would be unremarkable in a series of implosive or ejective stops. These utilize a manner of articulation involving glottal constriction along with a supralaryngeal place of articulation. That is, the proposal was that we should posit ejectives/implosives in place of the traditional voiced stops (with additional, follow-on changes). This suggests revising our reconstruction based on a range of cross-linguistic evidence to fit what we know about sound systems. While reconstructions have long involved some level of typological evidence, this proposal challenged the phonological core of the traditional reconstruction of Indo-European. The reactions to this idea were often vociferous, if not always informative. For example, Dunkel (1981) demeans typology as 'anti-factual' and 'circular,' and characterizes typological generalizations as 'opinions.' The matter has not been resolved, but it can be mitigated by adopting the posture that reconstructions are always tentative projections, subject to revision based on new data. Recall from Chapter 1 that while data in this book is italicized, for reconstructed forms flagged by*, I don't use italics. Take that as a reminder that I don't think of reconstructed forms as real, positive data.

5.7 Corpus evidence

A particular kind of written evidence comes from corpora, written data compiled to allow quantitative analysis. Thanks to the rapid development of electronic linguistic resources, a whole field of corpus linguistics has grown up quickly, including all the hallmarks of a new field, like handbooks and journals.

Corpora are nothing more than collections of linguistic data, typically offering data in some way(s) consistent across texts. In the many historical corpora now available, these may be the same text types (such as legal documents, personal letters), from the same or similar locations, and so on. People today think of corpus-based work as something from the computer era, but there's a long tradition of corpora. J. R. R. Tolkien famously assembled massive amounts of data from historical texts to greatly advance our understanding of language variation in English, leading eventually to the creation of the *Linguistic Atlas of Late Medieval English*. Many dissertations on German built remarkable datasets. A modern example in English is Vaught (1977), giving data on the neutralization of final laryngeal distinctions in early German texts, parallel to the modern process of final fortition in German (see §§3.4 and 4.6). Vaught was able to show that some texts present more evidence of this process than others (like the early Old High German *Isidor*) and some consonants were more prone to neutralize than others (such as /g, k/, but less with /d, t/).

Studying sound change with corpus data is less straightforward than many issues in syntax and morphology – it's just easier to track whether adjectives precede or follow nouns or what past tense verb form is being used than it is to suss out whether vowel neutralization has taken place; look at English spelling for how orthography can fail to match phonology. And this subfield bias is reflected in the handbooks and journals: some handbooks on corpus linguistics lack chapters on sound change, and phonetics and phonology are broadly underrepresented outside of audio corpora (on which see Maguire 2015). Still, there are excellent examples of corpus-based studies of sound change. Two examples illustrate this, both largely without great computational horsepower, in part to underscore that we don't always need huge state-of-the-art databases. These examples should not, however, obscure the rapidly increasing sophistication in computational work, including machine learning, such as Baumann (2018, with further references).

First, Egurtzegi (2017) examines the rise of a new vowel in Zuberoan (Souletin) Basque. Most varieties of Basque have the familiar five-vowel system (a, e, i, o, u) but a small set of dialects have developed an /y/ that comes from fronting of an older /u/, as a secondary split (defined in §3.2). Following French orthographic conventions, /u/ was written traditionally as <ou> and /y/ as <u>. Using this and building a corpus of early Zuberoan texts and examining these vowel spellings, Egurtzegi is able to show that the fronting is conditioned, specifically being blocked by a set of following consonants or clusters, /r, rtʰ, rt, rd, s̺, ts̺/. While numerous texts do not mark the distinction orthographically, enough do that he can find clear patterns. One early seventeenth-century source clearly distinguishes fronted and non-fronted varieties in these contexts, <goure> 'our' and <ourthe> 'year' with blocking, but <uda> 'summer' and <guciac> 'all' with fronting. The relevant varieties of Basque have long been in intense contact with Romance languages (Occitan, Gascon and French), which likewise developed /y/ from old /u/, to which we'll return in §6.6. This shows that the gradual diffusion of an innovation across closely related Romance languages eventually appears to have spread into a genetically unrelated language, under intense bilingualism.

That this example comes from Basque dialects points to something else worth noting: Corpus building is slow and labor intensive and large tagged corpora and relational databases to date have skewed toward languages with more speakers and/or with more historical texts. This is changing, including for historical corpora, though it will take time.

Turning to our second example, historical corpora are allowing us to gain much greater understanding of how colonial Spanishes arose and when. A widespread view has been that early settlement, in the 1500s, led to the quick development of a koine – that is, a new regional variety developed from contact among related dialects, in part by leveling – based on the various dialects brought from Iberia, including, for instance, by many southerners from Andalusia and elsewhere.

Medieval Spanish had a complex set of fricatives and glides, which have merged in various ways in modern varieties. One example is called *yeísmo*, the merger of old /ʎ/ and /j/ into the latter.[3] The distinction is still spelled in Spanish today:

(12) /ʎ/ and /j/ in Spanish
    El   caballo   cayó
    /el   kaˈbaʎo kaˈjo/
    The   horse   fell

This merger has happened in most western hemisphere varieties of Spanish, including the US state of New Mexico, where Spanish has been spoken since the late 1500s. This included a resettlement of the community after 1693, following their temporary displacement when indigenous peoples revolted and took back the area. The population was demographically rich, including people born in Europe and what is now Mexico as well as indigenous people. Given the history, the community was quite isolated for a long stretch of its early history. Sanz-Sánchez (2013) assembled data from the *Spanish Archives of New Mexico II*, covering the years 1683–1795. The archives contain a lot of bureaucratic writing but also documents by 'semiliterate individuals who were clearly not versed in the conventions of written interaction' (2013: 74). He assumes that (2013: 75):

> confusion of well-established spelling conventions with a phonemic value are indicative of merger. Thus, consistency in the use of etymological spellings by one given scribe cannot be taken as evidence of non-merger, but the use of non-etymological spellings (for example *mallor* 'mayor' or *cabayo* 'horse' for standard *mayor* and *caballo*) indicates at least some degree of merger.

Writers less accustomed to spelling norms offer especially good opportunities for seeing evidence of merger. Sanz-Sánchez shows that New Mexico-born writers

---

3 /ʎ/ and /j/ are similar, both voiced palatal sounds, the former a lateral approximant and the latter a fricative.

maintained the distinction far later than one would expect, changing the chronology of this merger. This has big implications for the history of Spanish in the western hemisphere: The tendency has been to assume that koine or new dialect formation takes place quickly after new communities are formed, but in Latin American contexts there was ongoing migration of Iberian Spanish speakers to the western hemisphere for generations, and late formation of new varieties suggests that this had linguistic consequences in terms of when the varieties became 'focused,' that is, variation narrows and the variety starts to stabilize.

This is methodologically similar to what Litty (2017) does, and in a setting where things were likewise unsettled by ongoing demographic changes for several generations. She examines sound change in both English and German as spoken in Wisconsin, from the Civil War to the present. Earlier work (Purnell et al. 2005) found that young Wisconsin speakers are neutralizing the laryngeal distinction in final position (recall §3.5), pronouncing pairs like *buzz* and *bus* or *bid* and *bit* (almost) the same, in ways that sound like the second word of each pair. We attribute this pattern to the influence of immigrant languages that lack such a distinction, especially German but also Polish and Dutch and others. Analyses in Laryngeal Realism treat German as a case of final fortition – insertion of a [spread] feature – while English appears to have a neutralization by loss of the [spread] feature in sounds like /t, s/. The surprising finding was that this feature appears to have receded among mid-twentieth-century speakers and to be now re-emerging, a so-called 'boomerang' effect.

Litty examined personal letters from the nineteenth century for clues to attestation of this among German Americans. She finds spellings that reflect neutralization in straightforward ways, like *baks* 'bugs' and *frose* 'froze', but also spellings that suggest hypercorrection, like *babtist* 'Baptist'. And she finds these spellings in both English and German letters. She then compares those patterns to acoustic analysis of historical recordings (in both languages) and her own recordings of contemporary speakers. Neutralization of some pairs does disappear in her data (like /p, b/ and /s, z/) but /t, d/ remained present in the community. The boomerang actually produces a new and different pattern.

While good corpus work is happening without massive data or particularly sophisticated quantitative approaches, that is a burgeoning area as well. Sanstedt (2018) uses a corpus analysis of spellings to investigate Old Norwegian vowel harmony. Surely corpora are, for many linguists, our best shot at playing the game of 'big data.' In a *New York Times* article cautioning us about what we can and cannot do with big data, Marcus and Davis (2014) conclude that 'Big data is here to stay, as it should be. But let's be realistic: It's an important resource for anyone analyzing data, not a silver bullet.' Large corpora in no way free us from the responsibility of building theories and testing them. They just offer us new tools for doing that.

5.8 Conclusion

Until recently, historical linguists drew our evidence overwhelmingly from one source, written texts, and not even all that are accessible to us. We are now drawing on vastly more data and richer kinds of data, often far more reliable than old written texts. Data that we knew but didn't use – like glosses – have proven their value. Sound recordings open a new world on sound change, if one that still has limits (and we'll explore some of those later), while experimental work and simulations allow us to model patterns that are difficult, at best, to observe in the real world.

In some ways, the current challenge is to start assembling a whole picture from the disparate types of data, as we saw with Litty's and other work in this chapter. This kind of work not only uses 'all the data' but assembles detailed pictures of community and individual language use and sociolinguistic variation, creating a far fuller picture than one might expect to be possible given the 'bad data' at hand. It points to a bright future for progress on difficult past problems.

Beyond this book

1. Digging deeper: Data

Minkova (2015, but also in many passages of 2014) gives an exemplary discussion of how to interpret orthography for understanding historical change in English. You might explore applying her approaches and principles to earlier spelling of other languages.

2. Digging deeper: Theory

In the chapter, I mentioned the controversies around using typology in the reconstruction of the Indo-European obstruent system. Kümmel's work (as cited and in other work) is a particularly valuable entry into that discussion. After reading it, do you have a sense of how typology should (not) be used in reconstruction? In your language histories, is typology being used for reconstruction? If so, how? Can that be improved on?

3. Moving beyond what we know

How can you use the tools described in this chapter to advance understanding of some particular problem in languages that you're working with or looking at? For example (and these are only examples):

- Are there corpora you can use to track some sound change(s)? Carry out some brief searches to look at changes that might be trackable.
- What real-time resources exist, written and audio? If you can access audio material, listen to some of the earliest for features that don't sound like what you hear in the same area today.

Part 3

Where sound changes

6

The Learner

The general condition for linguistic change can ... be stated in a very simple way: *children must learn to talk differently from their mothers.*

Labov (2001: 415)

6.1 Introduction

Think about how your parents talk and how you talk, or just listen to older and younger generations in any family from wherever you live. There will be differences, certainly small ones and probably large ones, discussed since the Preface.

A widespread change in English is the fronting of back vowels, where Feagin (2003) shows the progress of changes in /u:, o:/ with real-time data from Alabama, though the same basic pattern holds across the south and the east, with parallels in England. This has continued, with young southern speakers now showing very fronted /o:/ vowels. The second formant (F2) is a rough measure of how back or front a vowel is, with higher values indicating farther front. These are illustrated in (1).

(1) Back vowel fronting: F2 values by birth year (after Feagin 2003)

/u:/	1880s	1950s–
	ca. 1400–1600 Hz	ca. 2250–2350 Hz
	some fronting	very front
/o:/	ca. 1100 Hz	ca. 1600 Hz
	little fronting	clear fronting

For an American southerner like me this means that my great-grandfathers, grandfathers, father and I have each presumably taken a step down this road, gradual steps and surely not always perceptible ones.[1] In both low back merger

---

1   And we'll see in the next chapter that the progress of such changes is heavily correlated with gender, thus the limit to male lineage.

and back vowel fronting young people have learned to talk differently from their elders. How and why?

We have focused mostly to this point on how speakers and listeners might shape and reshape sounds and sound patterns, but we've seen that language acquisition plays a critical role. That said, if you browse a shelf of textbooks and handbooks of historical linguistics, you may be surprised at how unevenly the topic is covered. Searching indexes for 'acquisition,' 'learning' and 'child language' will show how some authors barely mention the topic, while relatively few give it coherent coverage.

With that generalization, though, agreement shatters. Child or first language acquisition offers rich opportunities for language change generally, based on the inherent **discontinuity** in transgenerational transmission: Each and every human being has to assemble a language from the input they receive filtered through the powerful resources human cognition provides us, in terms of storage and processing.

We'll deal with a range of learners and settings in which learning happens, but the role of child language acquisition in language change has been a focus of attention since the nineteenth century. A widely quoted passage is from the phonetician Henry Sweet (1900: 75):

> If languages were learnt perfectly by the children of each generation, then languages would not change: English children would still speak a language as old at least as 'Anglo-Saxon,' and there would be no such languages as French and Italian. The changes in languages are simply slight mistakes, which in the course of generations completely alter the character of the language.

This comes in a discussion of the 'natural method,' how we acquire our native tongues. While 'we begin young, and we give our whole time to it,' he concludes with something not often quoted:

> the results are always imperfect. Indeed, so imperfect is this natural method, that even with the help of school-training and the incessant practice of everyday life, very few ever attain a really thorough mastery of their own language.

From the perspective of a linguist today, speakers are speakers and their command of their languages is hardly imperfect. (That rhetoric still lingers in even some scholarly circles when it comes to heritage speakers and other bilinguals and even creoles, see DeGraff 2003.) So, Sweet's notion of perfect learning is somewhat different to how we would talk about things today.

Still, the point is incorrect and necessarily so, based simply on Weinreich et al. (1968) discussed in Chapter 2: For languages to remain stable through 'perfect learning,' each generation would have to be exposed to the same input. The ubiquity of variation means no child gets exposed to the same speech that their parents did. Even modest exposure to other dialects or to new social varieties should lead a child to build a different grammar. If the distinction between [a] and [ɔ] is less clear perceptually than the distinctions between most other English vowel pairs, and if particular words vary between the two pronunciations, the learner has a harder time learning this distinction than others. Labov (2010: 99ff.)

points out that there are relatively few minimal pairs of the *cot* versus *caught* type and almost none of those are likely to be confused in practice … the first names *Don* and *Dawn* are an exception. Labov also sketches the complex history of how vowels came into the /ɔ/ class. Low back merger is motivated on several different fronts; the distinction poses more challenges to learners than most other distinctions. Ultimately, variable input challenges our notion of 'perfect'; at the least, acquiring a different grammar from an older generation or peers hardly represents 'imperfection.'

Here, some nuance gives us 'natural' reasons for change across generations in ways that do not involve imperfect learning. We get different input for a set of reasons, including moving in different social contexts and coming into contact, from an early age usually, with speakers who don't speak exactly like us or our caregivers. It's easy to change the frequencies with which we use variables and if those change systematically, that can be enough, it appears, to trigger different learning in children. I'll also argue that different input to children can lead to what we call 'skewing': Children are given specifically different pronunciations – child-directed speech – and that may motivate some subtle, chronic types of shifts.

There are several famous storylines about how this works and we'll review some of the narratives:

- What is innate, i.e. built into our cognitive hardware?
- Is there a critical period for language acquisition, a period after which we are less able or unable to learn at least certain new linguistic patterns?
- Does imperfect acquisition play a role?

After discussing cross-generational transmission and discontinuity (§6.2), the rest of the chapter is about who's doing the learning and changing – children, (pre-)adolescents, adults and those acquiring a second language or dialect. I'll cover what factors appear to shape acquisition and change. To the first point, who is learning, traditional discussion has focused on the child acquiring its first language(s) (§6.3), but more recent work has given important attention to the role of (pre-)adolescents (§6.4) and also adults (§6.5). In language and dialect contact, people learn new varieties – making L2 and second dialect acquisition important in much sound change. To the second, I'll say a little about innateness, simplification during acquisition, types of input and social factors. Our commitment to using all the data and using all the tools available to us naturally leads us to what Stanford (2015: 470, and elsewhere) calls an 'all-of-the-above' approach to the subject.

6.2 Cross-generational transmission

A simple representation of how sound change can come during language acquisition comes from Hale (2003, 2007), who sees 'noise' (I'd use another word here) from the source grammar to the Primary Linguistic Data (PLD) that leads the learner to build their own grammar.

(2) Sources for 'noise' in the PLD

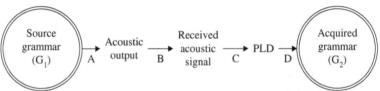

This process is iterative, taking place every generation. Moreover, to some degree, learners are almost never exposed to a single source grammar. A representation of transmission highlighting variability in input is given below, developed by Howell (2012), building on van Gelderen (2006: 283), this image from Litty (2017: 5). UG provides the basis from which a learner starts and they get input from speakers with various grammars (Lg^x) from which they build their own grammar (Gr^x). This is what they use to produce their own language and what provides input to the next generation.

(3) Transmission of language from generation to generation with heterogeneous input (Howell 2012)

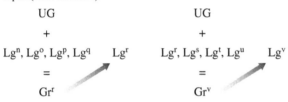

UG		UG	
+		+	
Lg^n, Lg^o, Lg^p, Lg^q	Lg^r	Lg^r, Lg^s, Lg^t, Lg^u	Lg^v
=		=	
Gr^r		Gr^v	

This begins to give us a sense of the complexity of the basic process of transgenerational transmission of language to new learners. While building of an initial grammar is pivotal, that's hardly the end of learning, or change.

6.3 The child

Hermann Paul provides a clear early statement about the role of children in sound change (originally published 1880, here from Auer et al. 2015: 63):

> Early childhood is a stage of experimentation in which an individual gradually learns through a variety of efforts to repeat what is spoken in the environment. Once this is achieved as successfully as possible, a period of relative stasis begins. The earlier substantial fluctuations cease and from then on there is great uniformity in pronunciation, as long as no disturbances arise through a strong influence of other dialects or a formal written language.

But there is always variability in performance, and he notes:

> This variability in pronunciation, which remains unnoticed due to its limited range, holds the key to understanding how a phonetic change in prevailing usage can gradually occur without those involved having the slightest idea of it.

In shifting focus to what is innate, Chomsky (1964: 112) writes:

> the structure of the grammar internalized by the learner may be, to a presently quite unexpected degree, a reflection of the general character of his learning capacity rather than the particular course of his experience.

This was applied to sound change by Kiparsky (1965: 1–4, emphasis added), beginning with a critique of Paul:

> As more important than the inadequacies and inconsistencies of Paul's theory I would regard his fundamental insight that the phonology of a language can change in two ways: by *Lautwandel* and by *abweichende Neuerzeugung*. I will translate them as *sound change* and *imperfect learning*, respectively, subsuming both under the general term *phonological change*. Sound change is brought about by the joint operation of *innovation* and subsequent *restructuring*. Innovation in phonology is change in the way phonological representations are executed by speakers of a language; restructuring is the resulting revision in the phonological representations. As the latter were considered to be phonetic by Paul, and restructuring immediately followed on innovation, the distinction between innovation and restructuring was to him purely theoretical and devoid of any practical consequences. *But with richer conceptions of phonological structure it takes on a cardinal importance for diachronic phonology.*

Those higher-level, phonological representations and how they shape sound change are the focus of Chapter 9, but Kiparsky gives hypothetical examples of how acquisition could drive sound change, such as 'fortuitous ignorance' (1965: 2–13), where children's input happens to lack examples of some particular phenomenon; he gives the example of a child exposed to some kinds of Old High German umlaut but not others – so that they build a grammar without the latter.

Beyond the idea of missing input, one common way to imagine sound change through acquisition is by simplification. That is, young children in the process of learning cannot produce the adult-like structures they hear, so they change them. In fact, we find all three possible correlations between child language and sound change are attested (Bybee 2001: 202–3, adapting her ideas somewhat):

- **Patterns in child language are rare or non-existent in sound change.** Consonant harmony is common in child language, but not in adult speech or sound change. That is, children often change the place of articulation of consonants to match those of other consonants in a word, so that *bug* becomes [gʌg]. And we have already talked about the process of spirantization, where stops become fricatives, while the reverse appears to be much less common. In child language, we do see fricatives becoming stops, like *shoe* pronounced as [du].
- **Patterns in sound change are rare or non-existent in child language.** We have discussed assimilation and reductions as remarkably common and predictable kinds of change for various reasons. Yet these are not reported in child language beyond patterns the language already has, according to Bybee.

- **Patterns in child language parallel those in sound change.** Unrounding of front rounded vowels (as we've discussed with the development of umlaut) and loss of nasalization on nasal vowels are found in both child language and sound change. As Bybee puts it: 'Substitutions that persist into late stages of acquisition would be the ones that are most likely to have a permanent effect on the language,' as these examples illustrate.

Stepping back to the role of child 'errors' in general, Foulkes and Vihman (2015: 312) review sets of studies of child speech and sound change and conclude that 'early errors are highly unlikely to lead to change.' That is, Bybee's third scenario seems to them to be a rare one.

This hardly exhausts the ways that children might build different grammars from those of an older generation. As argued in various places in this book, a lot of sound change comes from re-analysis of data rather than the sort of mechanical replication in the three scenarios above. We might need to look at more abstract patterns (like re-analysis) and principles in acquisition and change. A body of work by Archibald (1996, 1997) shows that second language acquisition of prosody depends heavily on the speaker's native system. Speakers of Polish and Hungarian, basically fixed-stress systems, acquire English stress with notable success, including patterns sensitive to lexical category, noun versus verb, and syllable weight, those where stress falls on CV: or CVC syllables. So, for instance, they can master generalizations such as that nouns have penultimate stress due to heavy penult (*aroma, agenda*) and verbs 'final stress due to heavy final syllable' (*maintain, achieve*).

Native speakers of tone languages who learn stress languages as adults, according to Archibald, have difficulty perceiving, let alone producing, English stress. He connects this with the absence of a metrical grid in the tone language he investigated, Chinese. That is, speakers of (some) tone languages appear to organize language in ways independent of a metrical system, making perception and production of stress extremely hard to learn. Even relatively advanced learners do not seem to acquire sensitivity to lexical category differences in accent. Archibald (1997: 175) accounts for this by arguing that speakers of tone languages store English stress lexically rather than by rule:

> The picture that is emerging from all of these results is that the subjects in this study did not seem to be acquiring the principles of English stress assignment with regard to such things as the influence of syllable structure or grammatical category on stress assignment. They seem to be treating stress as a purely lexical phenomenon; something that has to be memorized as part of the phonological representation of a word.

A crucial test case is the evidence from Japanese, which has what is traditionally called a 'pitch accent,' a system with a prosodically prominent syllable in the word including a metrical grid. Given an L1 with this metrical priming, the speaker can perceive stress well enough, unlike the Chinese speakers studied, but still fails to acquire stress, including generalizations based on lexical category. For these Chinese and Japanese subjects alike, all advanced learners, there was no significant progress over time. The conclusion is that while most other parameters can be changed, tone language speakers, never having acquired a metrical grid natively, eventually lose the ability to reorganize their prosody in such basic ways. These patterns seem to hold equally well the other way around, i.e. for speakers of stress languages trying to acquire tone languages later in life.

These are fundamental structural features, which are or are not relevant to a child's first language. If a feature isn't relevant and isn't activated early on, an older learner has to reach for other kinds of solutions to acquire and store those patterns – a kind of acquisitional kludge.

I started this chapter arguing that changing and even variable input to children can motivate change without any 'imperfect learning' at all. Two different examples show how this can be, both focused on how adults talk to young children (child-directed speech, or CDS), drawing on two completely different kinds of data.

First, Foulkes et al. (2005) gathered data from northeastern England (Tyneside), where the pronunciation of /t/ is sociolinguistically variable, produced in vernacular speech in some environments as glottalized (most often realized with creaky phonation) as opposed to standard-like [t]. The glottalized variants are not only more dialectal or vernacular but also, like many vernacular features, they are used more commonly by men than women, including in formal settings such as the reading of word lists.

Foulkes et al. looked at the speech of the caretakers of small children. They first found big differences between how the mothers spoke to other adults versus children. With children, they used far more [t] forms and fewer glottalized forms. Second, they found that men and women talked differently to small children, as shown here (Foulkes et al. 2005: 187), with men being more vernacular with word-medial /t/, as in *water*.

(4)   Gender differences in (t) glottalization in Child Directed Speech (Foulkes et al.)

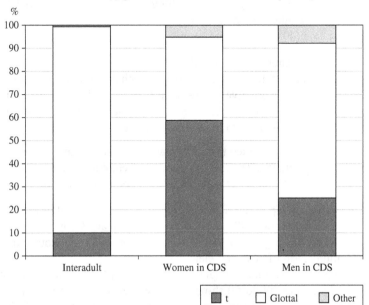

Speakers varied, including by who they were talking to. Mothers varied their pronunciation depending on whether they were speaking to boys versus girls, again giving girls considerably more standard-like speech. Not only that, as the figure below in (5) (Foulkes et al. 2005: 191) makes clear, pronunciation changes as the children age.

(5)   Changes as children age (Foulkes et al.). Use of [t] in CDS, word-medial context, by child age and gender (34 informants with $n \geq 5$ tokens)

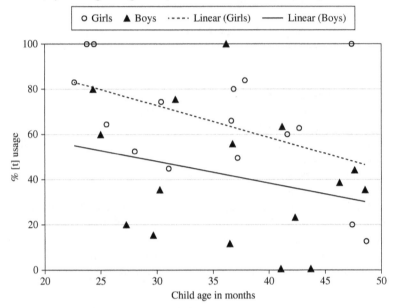

From early on, boys and girls were getting different input for a sociolinguistic variable and learning that adult speakers likewise varied by gender in this regard. They conclude (2005: 198) that:

> Speech from parents to boys differs from that to girls because parents have different expectations about appropriate speech patterns for boys and for girls, respectively. Girls are given more chances to learn phonological variants that are positively evaluated, because there is a heightened expectation that girls will – or should – grow up to use those variants.

> Indeed, it could be argued that CDS may contribute to the creation of gender-based differentiation. The fact that gender differentiation in our CDS data was more apparent for younger children would support such a claim.

Getting different input can shape different grammars and this kind of sociolinguistic variation looks like a good example of that. But it also touches on a major issue in the progress of sound change, where girls and women are usually a generation ahead of boys and men.

Turning to our second example, Salmons et al. (2012) look at speech across generations to identify vowel shifts in progress. Just as in the back vowel fronting example at the beginning of this chapter, various other shifts in sets of vowels – 'chain shifts' like the Northern Cities Shift – unfold by slow and steady change in the same direction over generations. That shift, reaching from upstate New York to southeastern Wisconsin, involves changes to a set of vowels as illustrated here from Labov (1994: 191, but see also Gordon 2001):

(6)   Northern Cities Shift

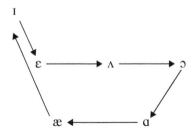

This accent is stereotypical of Chicago speech and involves things like *block* sounding more or less like *black*, and *bad* sounding like *bed*. This kind of shifting, which in some sense goes back to the Great Vowel Shift (introduced in §5.2) and on to early Germanic, seems chronic. Stockwell (1978: 337, emphasis added) tackles the chronology of the Great Vowel Shift this way:

> The vowel shift occurred no more at the usually cited dates than at any other date in the documented history of English. That is, it did occur then, and also (equally, I believe) over the past 200 years, or over the 200 years between the birth of Alfred and the death of Aelfric, or any other period of that length. *This kind of vowel shifting is a pervasive and persevering characteristic of vowel systems of a certain type.*

CDS is often characterized by emphasis and over-articulation of particular sounds and patterns (aka clear speech, and hyper- versus hypo-articulation). When we place particular syllables under prosodic prominence, it changes the pronunciation of the vowels in many kinds of English. That is, the word *beds* in the first pair of sentences will have a different vowel in this context of contrastive stress than that of either *beds* in the second, where another word is being emphasized.

Rob said the tall CHAIRS are warm.
No! Rob said the tall BEDS are warm.

Rob said the tall beds are COLD.
No! Rob said the tall beds are WARM.

Salmons et al. (2012) hypothesized that in cultures where people engage in CDS and where CDS has this prosodic character, the child's input is systematically skewed toward emphatic realizations. In dialects undergoing change in these vowels, Salmons et al. predicted that the change would be toward the more emphatic pronunciation. These need not be large differences to trigger changes. As Foulkes and Docherty conclude (2006: 422), 'Subtle differences in input may yield subtle differences in children's own productions.'

A younger generation's typical vowels (neither stressed nor unstressed) would be moved systematically in the direction of the earlier generation's stressed vowels. Schematically, this is the prediction across generations:

(7) Skewing

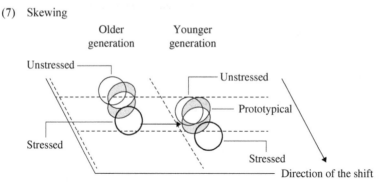

This was largely borne out in Salmons et al.'s 2012 data. In western North Carolina, as part of the 'Southern Vowel Shift,' the vowel in words like *bit* and *hid* is becoming more peripheral, moving to the edge of the vowel space, and sometimes 'breaking' into two syllables. In (8) below, you can see the realization of /ɪ/ for three generations – A2 is the oldest, A1 is in the middle and A0 is the youngest. Typical realizations versus stressed realizations are marked by open circles and filled circles respectively. This captures the basic dynamic of movement to the edge of the vowel space, though Salmons et al. also expected some upward movement, based on descriptions of the Southern Shift.

(8) Skewing of /ɪ/ across generations

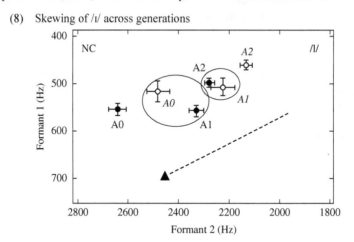

We concluded (Salmons et al. 2012: 182) that:

in some cases children may not be misperceiving or making different generalizations from those of earlier generations. Instead, in certain cases, they may simply be getting different input which leads to sound change, a type of sound change that advances incrementally over multiple generations and even millennia. Such change would be initiated via skewing, and subject to later adjustment during vernacular reorganization. Ultimately, directly structural factors in how vowels are pronounced and the input presented to learners should be accorded a position in change across cross-generational transmission of language alongside social factors. Putting our recent findings in the context of Labovian and other views on sound change strongly suggests a new kind of tight and complex interaction between the social and the structural.

If these kinds of changes were directly driven by social factors, it would be hard to explain how and why they move in the same direction over multiple generations. Social factors in language change have often, and usually unfortunately, been compared to fashion, like the length of hair or skirts. It's hard to imagine fashion moving consistently farther along a single dimension over time, practical limits aside (and see 'persistent' changes, §4.6).

This work has potential implications for women leading in sound change, including with regard to early input. Foulkes et al. (2005) point to different input for boys and girls. With the kinds of 'skewing' just discussed, girls could be getting more skewed data, that is, data with more advanced forms of a change. This is extremely speculative but also testable.

6.4   The (pre-)adolescent

While children early on acquire language and come to understand patterns of social variation, this hardly means that their speech is set. The next step comes with the emergence of social identities and formation of intense peer groups. Labov (2001: 447) asserts that girls as the leaders in sound change …

> increase their use of the linguistic change in progress by re-organizing the vernacular they first acquired. The simplest assumption is that this increment is a continuous one from the period when children first emerge from the linguistic domination of their parents (4–5) to the time when their linguistic system stabilizes (17–20).

This then involves ordinary acquisition of language by children, but allows for ongoing change. In the Labovian tradition, this is treated as an interplay between two patterns, which D'Arcy (2015: 584) defines this way:

- **transmission**: the unbroken sequence of native language acquisition
- **incrementation**: the unidirectional progression of a change over time.

The seminal work on this topic is by Eckert, famously with her 1989 book. Doing ethnographic work in Detroit area high schools, especially one that she calls 'Belten High,' she identified two distinct groups, which she labels 'Jocks' and 'Burnouts,' aligned with middle-class and working-class culture respectively. Using data from the Northern Cities Shift, she shows how it is not simply a young person's socio-economic background that correlates with their vowels, but rather which of the groups they identify with. Focusing on the /ʌ/ vowel, she finds (1988) that the Burnouts had far more Northern Cities-like patterns than the Jocks: the Burnouts used more back and lowered variants. In this study, and others following in Eckert's footsteps, we see direct evidence of young people learning to talk differently from their mothers.

While much work on adolescent speech focuses on well-known patterns like the Northern Cities Shift, Chambers (1992) looks at broader dialect change. He investigates the speech of six children of Canadian families who moved to England; so, a case of young people coming into a different dialect setting. Integrating this evidence with other studies of dialect acquisition when young people move, he proposes eight principles for what is and is not acquired in these settings (from Chambers 1992: 677–701):

1. Lexical replacements are acquired faster than pronunciation and phonological variants.
2. Lexical replacements occur rapidly in the first stage of dialect acquisition and then slow down.
3. Simple phonological rules progress faster than complex ones.
4. Acquisition of complex rules and new phonemes splits the population into early acquirers and later acquirers.
5. In the earliest stages of acquisition, both categorical rules and variable rules of the new dialect result in variability in the acquirers.
6. Phonological innovations are actuated as pronunciation variants.
7. Eliminating old rules occurs more rapidly than acquiring new ones.
8. Orthographically distinct variants are acquired faster than orthographically obscure ones.

Briefly, words are surely learned faster than pronunciations and also certain kinds of sound patterns are better acquired by early learners and others later. It may be easier to lose an old rule than acquire a new one. An example is what Chambers calls 'T-voicing' or flapping, where *putting* and *pudding* are both pronounced the same. This is the norm in Canada but not in England and his data show that the speakers lost the Canadian pattern.

The patterns that only early acquirers master are the most challenging and/ or complex structurally. The most amazing example comes from an earlier study by Payne (1980) looking at the pronunciation of children in King of Prussia, near Philadelphia. Children of families who moved to King of Prussia mostly acquired the local variety. However, the patterning of /æ/ in this dialect is incredibly complex, with a raising and tensing rule (/æ/ pronounced closer to [eːə]) that applies variably in some contexts (such as before *l*), but does not appear in a set of usually unstressed words (*and*) and shows three specific lexical exceptions – *mad, bad, glad* – a set of words widely discussed by Labov and others. For this particular rule, Payne finds that simply being born in King of Prussia is not enough: Children whose parents were from King of Prussia learned the rule, while children of parents who had themselves moved to King of Prussia did not. This suggests that extremely robust and consistent early input may be necessary in acquiring particularly difficult patterns. This has implications for settings involving rich dialect and language contact generally: Some kinds of patterns, phonological and otherwise, require particularly rich early input and sufficient amounts of contact to master; heterogenous input in the community and even in the family can hinder the learner from gaining full command of certain phenomena.

This is highly consistent with the effects of prosodic skewing sketched above: While vernacular reorganization does indeed reorganize sound patterns, it is reorganizing what has been acquired or not acquired early on. This all supports the basic argument of this chapter that we keep learning over the lifespan, but what we do and don't acquire becomes more constrained with time. Reorganization will alter effects of early input, such as what learners acquire from child-directed speech produced by parents, as described by Foulkes et al. 2005 or Salmons et al. 2012.

6.5 The adult

We have growing evidence for change later in life. The question, as we have now seen, is exactly what changes and how. While the range of views on this issue cannot be fully reconciled, it is safe to say that they are not as far apart as many see them being. In part, there is an issue of what counts as 'grammar change.' The way I read the available evidence, a lot changes in adulthood, but these changes are of particular types, not fundamental structural changes.

A compelling case for change beyond the critical period comes from Montreal French by Sankoff and Blondeau (2007). French spoken in Montreal has shifted in recent decades in how /r/ is pronounced, from widespread use of an apical (tongue trilled) [r] to a uvular variant [R]. Sankoff and Blondeau analyzed recordings made in 1971 and 1984 with similar groups of speakers (a 'trend' study) but also had access to a set of people who were recorded in both 1971 and 1984, that is, the same people over a decade later (a 'panel' study) (2007: 566):

(9)   Panel versus trend study (Sankoff and Blondeau)

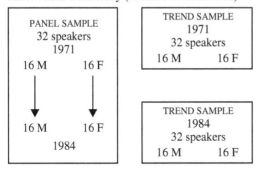

In (10) you can see the changes in the pronunciation by speaker. The vertical axis shows percentage of the innovative uvular variant and the horizontal axis shows age. The filled diamonds show how many uvular variants each speaker produced in the earlier recordings while the open squares show the same for the later recordings. The arrows indicate how much each individual speaker has changed over real time.

(10) Changes by speaker (Sankoff and Blondeau). Individual percentages of [R]/([R] + [r]) for the 32 panel speakers for 1971 and 1984. Trajectories plotted for all speakers who showed a significant difference between the two years

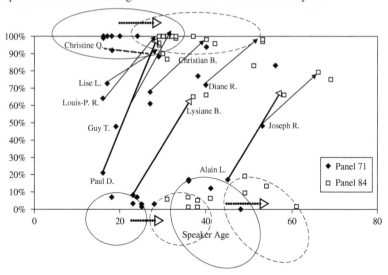

Many of these speakers shift, often dramatically, from [r] to [R] over this time, while some were already using the innovative [R] in 1971. Most notable for our purposes is that those who do not shift toward [R] were speakers who basically did not use [R] at all in 1971. What has changed is the frequency of variants where speakers had learned both early on.

An important aspect of this paper ties back to our discussion of input to early learners: A child starting to learn French among adults like those studied here in 1971 was getting quite different input than one starting among the same speakers in 1984. To speculate for a moment, while both would have been exposed to two kinds of /r/, the frequencies and social patterns would have been large enough to allow for different generalizations about how to build their own grammars. It would not be surprising to find that the earlier child was developing a strong sense of and maybe command of highly variable rhotics, while the later one might have seen apical [r] as something a few people, especially older ones, used. Perfect learning among exactly the same people not much more than a decade apart could yield a different sound pattern and social understanding of sound patterns.

Taken together with results like Chambers's, we see clear kinds of change at any stage of life, including adulthood. While the shift from [r] to [R] is striking, changing frequency of a variable is different from a speaker of a stress language learning a tone language in a native-like way later in life. (See §9.3 for more on rhotics and change.)

6.6 Conclusion

We have seen once again the pressing need to consider all the factors at hand, to take an 'all-of-the-above' approach (Stanford 2015). Yes, language changes beyond child acquisition, in limited and constrained ways under specific circumstances and then on through the lifespan.

Think back to the effort to represent graphically how transgenerational transmission works from the beginning of the chapter. If we restrict ourselves just to the kinds of input we get over our whole lives, we now see a vastly more complex picture, one that cannot be readily displayed graphically. The picture in (11) below gives a schematic reminder of a hypothetical pattern of how input can change and what we (can) do with it over the lifespan. This makes the simplest possible assumptions in the kind of social settings we often find in contemporary western settings:

- The child is exposed in its early years mostly to a small group of people, especially immediate family. At this stage, the child uses whatever innate machinery we have to acquire a basic grammar – including a sound system. The learner is typically exposed to some social variation at that point, e.g. gender/sex- and age-based variation, and Foulkes et al. (2005) show that the child is getting variable input from caretakers.
- Before and through adolescence, the learner has command of what we can think of as a full grammar and is mastering parameters of social variation. As the young person does that, they form peer groups and adjust their speech to those groups: 'vernacular reorganization.' This can significantly change speech patterns in terms of the variants and frequencies of variants, but the fundamental structures are likely to remain those already acquired.
- In adulthood, we may be mobile and active across a wider range of social settings, and so are exposed to greater variation. We may learn to identify and understand a broader range of speech than earlier. At this stage, successful acquisition of some new features and kinds of features becomes difficult, like mastering native-like tonal patterns if you grew up only with a stress language. Still, our language is far from fixed: We acquire some new things – words, derivational morphology and so on – and clearly change our use of variable patterns, like with Montreal /r/. But these aren't really at the heart of grammar, core phonology or syntax.

(11) Differential patterns of change over the lifespan

This takes the simplest case, assuming a monolingual environment, atypical for the world's population as a whole. Stanford (2015) and other research is beginning to sketch how such more complex bilingual and multilingual circumstances work.

If this seems complicated, well, it is. But it is also clearly structured and constrained. When we consider all the data, a lot of the apparent contradictions and conundrums disappear. Under the right circumstances – such as the rules with /æ/ in King of Prussia and supported by Chambers's findings as well – children may not acquire some patterns found in the broader community, when their input is not sufficiently consistent and the patterns are sufficiently complex. Beyond the early years, young people certainly change their speech, in ways that underscore the notion of 'reorganization' – these people are finding a place in society and adjusting their speech to fit that, not acquiring new phonologies. And even adults change their speech, if often in terms of changing frequencies or variants or probably some advance or retreat of some speech patterns.

The social setting of sound change has been present throughout the book up to this point and has begun to come into focus in this chapter and most clearly in the figure in (11) just above. Let us now turn directly to society and its role in the transmission and diffusion of sound change.

Beyond this book

1. Digging deeper: Data

The summary overview of changes by age given in (11), just above, makes pretty strong claims about what changes how and when over the lifespan. It suggests two kinds of follow-on data projects: First, looking at literature that rejects all or most claims about a critical period and/or that argues for change later in life, can you reconcile such work with this graphic? Second, can you find phenomena that challenge the scenario itself?

2. Digging deeper: Theory

Read a couple of the works cited in this chapter about the relationship between first (or second) language acquisition and sound change. How could we improve on testing this relationship? For instance, should we really expect acquisition to closely parallel the ultimate outcomes of sound change? Or should we be looking at how re-analyses made by children look like sound changes?

3. Moving beyond what we know

- Labov (1994: chapter 5) and others have noted sets of languages that show vocalic chain shifts, mostly in Germanic but also other languages, almost all in Europe (1994: 122). We need to build our set of examples in other languages and language families of the world. Find and describe a novel example.

- One test of the 'skewing' claims is whether communities without patterns of child-directed speech like those in much of American English show persistent changes like English vowel shifts. Survey work on child-directed speech in different languages and cultures in search of possible correlations to persistent shifting of the type found in Germanic.

7

Society[1]

7.1 Introduction

This chapter is dedicated to a single question: How does a sound change take hold across a group of people, spread through social and geographical space?

People seem to imagine sound change starting somehow with one person and spreading to a broader community. (I would argue that if a single person adopts a new pronunciation and nobody else adopts it, it may be a sound change but it's not a very linguistically interesting one.) Richard Dawson coined the word *meme* and was the first to use it, meaning 'a unit of cultural transmission, or a unit of *imitation*' (Zimmer and Carson 2011: 474). If that happens with sound change, how and why would others adopt that innovative form? A new word can be directly useful in ways that a new pronunciation may not be. Unlike the coining of a new word, sound change is not necessarily abrupt in this way. Instead, speakers, listeners and learners are inundated with variability. If you think back to any of the examples of sound change that we've developed so far, changes start from a pool of variation, where groups of speakers have different pronunciations. You've seen this with the geography of Upper Midwestern US vowel changes. And we already have evidence that people with particular cognitive processing patterns are prone to pick up innovations faster than others (Yu), and how young people adapt to peers (Eckert), and so on. In this chapter, I contextualize these issues in the bigger picture of how changes work their way through a whole community and over space.

I'll survey a set of issues, beginning with the relationship between social and structural factors in change, where you can already anticipate that I'll argue for examining both and integrating them into a coherent single account (§7.2). In §7.3 we'll return to sound change in progress, with an eye to how we can identify spread through a community, while §7.4 turns to two different ways that sound change spreads through communities: 'transmission' versus 'diffusion.' Whether people are aware of a sound change matters in how changes do or don't spread through a community and we'll sketch several examples of that in §7.5.

---

1   For more detail on some of these issues, see Salmons (forthcoming b).

Section 7.6 lays out some basic issues of sound change in dialect and language contact.

7.2   The social and the structural

Many researchers are interested mostly in structural aspects of change – what's happening with vowel formants or phonological alternations – and others mostly in social aspects of change; issues like those we'll deal with in terms of how a change spreads through a community. That's all well and good, but it connects to the worst example of one-toolism in the field: People constantly – from long ago down to the present day – have spent great time and energy arguing that some particular change is 'internally motivated' or 'externally motivated,' as I mentioned in the Preface. Dorian dedicates a 1993 essay to challenging 'the weakness of simplistic dichotomous thinking' (Dorian 1993: 152) and concludes that:

> Precisely because there will seldom be the ideal breadth and depth of material on which to base an assessment of change in terms of external or internal motivation, it is useful to consider the hazards of casually invoking that tempting but overly simple dichotomy.

I argue that in that ideal case what we will find is an interaction of internal and external motivations. The most phonetically and phonologically 'natural' assimilations or reductions still have to make their way into community speech. And the socially best motivated sound change has to be interpreted and implemented structurally by speakers, heard by listeners, learned by children. In other words, thinking in terms of multiple causation is the only way to go. Malkiel (1983: 251) wrote:

> Depending on each researcher's range of experience, catholicity of taste, and doctrinaire position regarding certain controversial matters such as the principle of teleology in evolution, he will incline to favor either external or internal factors, either the hypothesis of gradual improvement (under adverse circumstances, deterioration) of structure or the alternative hypothesis of mere regrouping of the structure's constituents, either an explanation allowing for the intervention of speakers, at varying levels of consciousness, in the events affecting their speech or the rival explanation operating with unguided clashes of blind forces.

He concludes (1983: 268):

> By starting out with the expectation of overwhelmingly plausible pluricausality we stand a chance of reaping two major benefits: In terms of improved cognition, we shall do fuller justice to the complexities of reality, and in terms of academic tone and scholarly climate, we shall eschew that stridency of debate which, in the case of strict alternatives, the stern demand for a partisan choice has invariably carried with it, to the detriment of a serene and balanced appraisal.

We'll focus on particular social and/or structural aspects in our work, but we should keep in mind the need for this kind of breadth.

7.3   Spread in progress

You now understand that variation is central to change and even a prerequisite for it. As Weinreich et al. (1968: 188, quoted in §2.5) put it: 'Not all variability and heterogeneity in language structure involves change; but all change involves variability and heterogeneity.'

The relationships between variation and change raise issues for tracking change in individuals and communities. If we look at variation in a community and among individuals who are part of that community, we see a set of distinct patterns. Bowie and Yaeger-Dror (2015: 604) present the following taxonomy (adapted from earlier versions by Labov 1994: 83; Sankoff 2006: 1004).

(1)   Patterns of linguistic change (adapted from Bowie and Yaeger-Dror 2015: 604)

	Synchronic pattern	Individual	Community	Interpretation
1.	Flat	Stable	Stable	No change
2.	Monotonic slope with age	Unstable	Stable	Age grading
3.	Monotonic slope with age	Stable	Unstable	Generational change/'apparent time'
4.	Flat	Unstable	Unstable	Communal change

Much modern work on language variation and change has focused on type 3, where people differ by age – younger people and older people talk differently in a community, and individuals are stable over time in their behavior. This change in 'apparent time' gives a picture of people learning and keeping speech patterns as they age, identifiable in samples taken at one time in the community. This contrasts with age grading, in type 2, where speech patterns are associated with certain age groups. I've long wondered whether 'uptalk', the use of question-like intonation in statements among many young American English speakers, may be abandoned as they age. While we all change our use of slang and other vocabulary over the years, age grading is not widely attested with sound change (Chambers 2009: 201; Cukor-Avila and Bailey 2013: 253–4).

Determining which type we have in a given situation is not always easy, but we now often have enough real time data to go beyond apparent time data.

7.4   Spread through the community

In the last chapter, I introduced the Labovian notion of 'transmission,' what many people see as the normal way that a language is handed on from one generation to the next, with ongoing but relatively minor changes ('incrementation'). Labov (2007) argues that this process leads to the kinds of splits among languages that we see represented in historical-comparative linguistics with trees. He contrasts with this what he calls 'diffusion,' a kind of spread 'across communities [that] shows weakening of the original pattern and a loss of structural features' (2007:

344). Labov associates this with 'waves.' He argues that the difference is how these changes are adopted: transmission – by children up through adolescence through the kind of incrementation discussed in the last chapter – and diffusion – where adults learn new sounds and sound patterns to the best of our limited abilities *qua* adults. Transmission is a primary pattern in the learning of languages over generations while diffusion is really a secondary process, just as many linguists assume that the fundamental relationship among languages are tree-like while waves reflect some kind of contact.

Labov illustrates these with data from the Northern Cities Shift, discussed since Chapter 5. The map in (2) shows the core Northern Cities area (the black line) and an offshoot going from Chicago down to St. Louis (broken line).

(2)   The Northern Cities Shift on the St. Louis Corridor (Labov 2007)

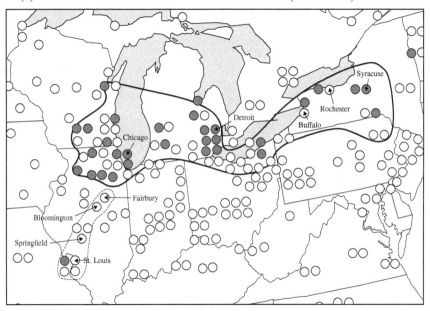

In (3), Labov's analysis shows a set of speakers according to whether they show some feature of the NCS. Without detailing all the measures, the first, 'AE1,' is his label for æ-raising, the first stage of the shift. 'EQ' reflects a reversal of /æ/ and /ɛ/, a later element of the shift.

His northern Illinois speakers show clear and consistent NCS shifting, but as you move toward St. Louis you see the pattern break up and, in the corridor itself, we find mostly broken pieces.

(3)   Individual patterns along the corridor: stages of NCS in speakers from Northern
      Illinois and the St. Louis corridor, with ages, rank ordering and correlation of
      age and rank

NORTHERN ILLINOIS	AE1	O2	EQ	ED	UD	AGE	RANK
Sterling IL	✓	✓	✓	✓	✓	34	1
Elgin IL (1)	✓	✓	✓	✓	✓	19	1
Elgin IL (2)	✓	✓	✓	✓	✓	42	1
Joliet IL	✓	✓	✓	✓	✓	30	1
Rockford IL (1)		✓	✓	✓	✓	37	2
Belvidere IL	✓		✓	✓	✓	33	2
Hammond IN	✓	✓	✓			45	3
Rockford IL (2)	✓				✓	65	4
Lena IL	✓					47	5
r-correlation							.74
age coefficient							.08*
ST.LOUIS CORRIDOR							
St. Louis MO (1)	✓	✓	✓	✓	✓	48	1
St. Louis MO (2)	✓	✓		✓	✓	57	2
Springfield IL	✓			✓	✓	60	3
Fairbury IL	✓			✓		25	4
Bloomington IL	✓			✓		27	4
Springfield IL (1)				✓		32	5
Springfield IL (2)					✓	67	5
St. Louis MO (3)					✓	53	5
St. Louis MO (4)				✓		38	5
r-correlation							−.21
age coefficient							n.s.

How these changes have spread is dramatically different in the two areas and
supports a view of transmission within the NCS area but diffusion along the
St. Louis corridor. Chapter 6 suggests that patterns of input change over the lifespan. Children in Springfield may, for example, have considerable contact with
NCS speakers from early on. Children exposed early on to more or less full NCS
systems from adults or even peers early in life have better chances of acquiring
the complete system, while those with less and/or later exposure might acquire
pieces but not the full system. In short, it would be valuable to have studies of
what children are being exposed to in these areas.

   This kind of large-scale study of spread is valuable, but we also want to understand how things work on a more local level. The classic work has used social
networks – widely used in social anthropology, sociology and history – pioneered
in linguistics by James and Lesley Milroy (L. Milroy 1980; Milroy and Milroy
1985, and elsewhere) but since adopted by many others. These networks are
connected to the larger society. For example, in a society with high mobility –
like most western societies today – our social networks are susceptible to almost
complete replacement with a move across the country or from a rural community
to an urban one.

Social networks are simply the set of relationships any individual has with others, and they provide 'a means of capturing the dynamics underlying speakers' interactional behaviors' (Milroy and Llamas 2013: 409). This contrasts with earlier work correlating linguistic features with fixed social categories, that 'working-class' people or older rural men speak some particular way. Fundamentally, we can think about a person's networks as strong or weak. Strong ties are dense – people in a person's network are more tied not just to that person but also to one another, the classic 'tight-knit' group. They are also multiplex – a person knows other people in more than one role, like the neighbor who is also a relative and who works in the same place you do and so on. Dense and multiplex networks connect with relatively stable language use. Weak or loose networks correlate with more change, and specifically people at the edges of networks are prone to innovate, captured in Granovetter's 1973 title: 'The strength of weak ties.' Milroy and Llamas (2013: 419) summarize:

First, persons central to a close-knit, norm-enforcing group are likely to find innovation of any kind to be socially risky but the adoption of an innovation already on the fringes of the group less so. Second, weak ties are generally more numerous than strong ties, providing links to many more individuals. Conversely, information relayed through strong ties tends not to be innovatory, since strong tie networks are more likely to be shared (that is to belong to overlapping networks). Thus, mobile individuals who have contracted many weak ties but occupy a position marginal to any given cohesive group are in a favorable position to diffuse innovation.

Take an example from a village in westernmost Austria. In Grossdorf, Lippi-Green (1989) found that the vowel [ɔ] was becoming [a], with the change favored when the vowel occurred before a nasal plus another consonant (like *Mantel* 'coat') and less favored before l + consonant (like *kalt* 'cold'). As is typical in network studies, she built scores for speakers to measure how integrated they were into various local networks, by kinship, work and cultural institutions. Men who were less integrated into those networks used the [a] form considerably more as shown in the tables below (4). The first column shows how often men used the new form and the next three are measures of how integrated they are into three kinds of social networks, kinship and workplace and voluntary associations. As you can see, those with lower overall integration use the innovative form more.

(4)   Social networks and innovation in an Alpine vowel change (Lippi-Green)
      a) Old generation males; network innovation

Informant code	% innovation	Kinship	Workplace	Voluntary association	Total
Average all males	14.2	3.8	5.1	1.8	10.7
95% Range *Males* *born 1906–1934*		3/5	4/7	1/2	9/13
Kaspar	0	4	7	3	14
Jokel	0	5	7	2	14
Mìchel	0	2	7	2	11
Sefftone	12.2	1	5	2	8
Melchior	16.6	5	0	1	6
Kolumbian	26.6	3	4	2	9

b) Young adult males; network innovation

Informant code	% innovation	Kinship	Workplace	Voluntary association	Total
Average all males	14.2	3.8	5.1	1.8	10.7
95% Range *Males* *born 1955–1962*		3/5	4/7	1/2	9/13
Jodok	5.0	5	7	3	15
Ignaz	20.4	5	7	1	13
Klemens	20.8	4	4	1	9
Leo	21.2	2	1	1	4

Much work on social networks has been done in urban areas – Howell (2007) on Dutch in early modern Amsterdam – but Lippi-Green shows clear network patterns in a rural setting.

Another angle is how fast change spreads through a community. As Labov (1994: 65) puts it, there is a 'general observation that sound changes begin at a slow rate, progress rapidly in midcourse, and slow down in the last stages.' This yields the S-curve widely discussed in language change. The figure below in (5) (Labov 1994: 67) gives us a snapshot of where a whole set of vowel changes in Philadelphia were at one point in time, using apparent time – age of speakers at that time. These range from changes just beginning, such as the lowering of the vowels in words like *bit* and *bet* (marked with 'i' and 'e' in the figure) on to one nearing or at completion, like the raising and fronting of /æ/ in certain environments, such as before nasals (a process we discussed for King of Prussia earlier) and the raising and backing of /a/ before /r/, in words like *bar*.

(5) Places along the S-curve of Philadelphia vowel changes in progress

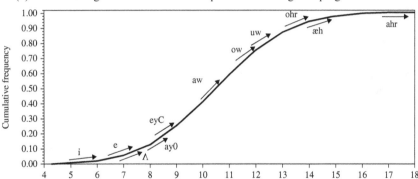

This one figure captures a whole complex set of changes at once, placing each vowel change at its place on the curve at one point in time. (To see how complex efforts to capture variation and change have gotten at times, see the remarkable presentation in Cedergren and Sankoff (1974), a paper that builds variability into classic generative phonological rules while keeping an eye on social differences.)

Most work in the field focuses on changes that go to completion. Even working historical linguists might reasonably have the impression that once the sound change train leaves the station, there's no stopping until you reach the destination, a complete change. This is, as discussed in §4.6 with 'stalled' and 'ebb and flow' changes, hardly the case.

7.5 Awareness and its consequences

Labov (1966) introduced a distinction between change from above and below. Change from above is 'introduced by the dominant social class, often with full public awareness' (Labov 1994: 78) and change from below is systematic and appears first in the vernacular. People remain unaware of such changes until they are well developed (see Eckert and Labov 2017). Examples include most of the vowel changes Labov has dedicated his career to. In this section, I lay out a few issues of how awareness does or does not seem to play in the spread (or retreat) of sound change.

We adjust our speech to that of those around us, converge toward their way of speaking, often unconsciously and in subtle ways, usually referred to as 'accommodation,' see Auer and Hinskens (2005) for an excellent illustration. (Of course if you want to distance yourself from interlocutors, you can also distance yourself from them.) Trudgill (2010: 189) argues that accommodation 'is inevitable because [it] is not only a subconscious but also a deeply automatic process.' He (like others before him) connects this to a basic human 'drive to behave as one's peers do.' These behaviors have long-term consequences for speech varieties: Purnell and Yaeger-Dror (2010) provide a set of case studies from North America where especially in inter-ethnic communication, people accommodate, often selectively, to the speech of other groups, so that African Americans may adopt some but not all features of the Northern Cities Shift in that region of the

US. While we have lots of evidence for accommodation, this is yet another area where we need more work to connect it clearly to longer-term change.

'Prestige' has been long and widely appealed to as a or even *the* motivation for why speakers adopt or don't adopt particular features.[2] This remains true today – alas, often even among dear friends and colleagues – and it's worth laying out some historical precedents to indicate how deeply rooted this tradition is. Sturtevant (1917: 26) talks about the issue in terms of fashion (partially quoted also in Milroy 1989, and §6.3):

> Just as fashions in dress are binding upon all members of a given class and are imitated by all who look up to that class, so fashions in language are binding upon all people of culture and are followed by other members of the community to the best of their ability. This is irksome for those who rise from a lower to a higher class in the community, or who go from a provincial neighborhood to a college or university. It is not easy, and it often seems quite useless or even disloyal to one's origin, to alter one's speech at the behest of fashion; but in many cases the thing must be done.

Bloomfield (1933: 403) uses the term often in his book and includes this stark statement (keeping in mind that he writes [ɛ] for our [æ]):

> The most powerful force of all in fluctuation works quite outside the linguist's reach: the speaker favors the forms which he has heard from certain other speakers who, for some reason of prestige, influence his habits of speech. This is what decides, in countless instances, whether one says *it's me* or *it's I, rather* with [ɛ] or with [a], *either* and *neither* with [ij] or with [aj], *roofs* or *rooves, you ought to* or *you'd better*, and so on, through an endless list of variants and nearly synonymous forms. Dialect geography and the history of standard languages show us how the speech of important communities is constantly imitated, now in one feature and now in another, by groups and persons of less prestige.

Bonfante (1947: 357) likewise says it with particular clarity:

> The main factor in the triumph of a language or of a linguistic innovation (which is the same thing) is its prestige. This is not only military, political, or commercial; it is also, and much more, literary, artistic, religious, philosophical.

Weinreich et al. (1968: 123–4) react to these views: 'The direction of imitation, Bloomfield believes, is determined entirely by the "prestige" of the model ... this is now known to be factually incorrect ... .' Labov (1972: 308) pushes onward to argue that prestige 'must be defined in terms of the people using [the term] and the situations in which it is used.' (Labov and others distinguish 'covert' from 'overt' prestige, the former for forms that carry value within a group.)

Milroy (1989: 225, 1992a, 1992b; Salmons 1990) argues that 'the notion of prestige has been too readily appealed to in explanations of language variation and change, and that such appeals result in apparent contradictions and conceptual

---

2   The following paragraphs closely parallel some of chapter 3 of Salmons (forthcoming b).

confusions.' Milroy proposes, much like I did above, that we think about these settings in terms of how speakers understand their identities and 'acts of identity' (Le Page and Tabouret-Keller 1985). That is, people adopt forms based on a sense of solidarity and group membership, and so on, rather than based on 'influence or reputation derived from achievements, associations, or character, or (esp.) from past success; a person's standing in the estimation of others' (to take the *OED* definition of 'prestige'). Milroy develops various examples of language change that are difficult or impossible to capture if prestige is a major motivation. Many (or most?) of the examples in this book are instances of change moving away from 'prestige' norms in the relevant sense. The best solution in many cases is, I suggest, to drop the word 'prestige' and replace it with the more specific factors that make up 'prestige.'

Kloeke (1927) built a detailed theory of how the Holland dialects of Dutch exercised great influence on other Dutch dialects in the Early Modern period. His title is: *De Hollandsche expansie in de zestiende en zeventiende eeuw en haar weerspiegeling in de hedendaagsche Nederlandsche dialecten* (The Hollandic expansion in the 16th and 17th century and its reflection in contemporary Dutch dialects). A piece of this story, made known in English by Bloomfield (1933), is development in the old Germanic /uː/ vowel, which fronted during this period, so that *muːs 'mouse' and *huːs 'house' became /myːs/ and /hyːs/, eventually diphthongizing to /mœys/ and /fɩœys/ over most of the Dutch-speaking area (using IPA, while the map below has Kloeke's /øy/). In fact, this is the form found in the modern standard language, spelled *muis* and *huis*. Assuming regular sound change, both words should show these changes over the same territory. But they don't. Bloomfield's version of the map (1933: 328) is reproduced below (Figure 7.1) and you can see a set of areas in the east marked with broken diagonal lines (and the second item in the key), over one long north-south stretch and two small areas to the north of it, where the *house* word has a front vowel, /yː/, but the *mouse* word retains the old /uː/.

Kloeke dedicates much of his book to the distribution of these two words, and proposes a sociolinguistic story, starting from two competing spheres of influence, one Hollandic and the other connected to Hanseatic trading cities farther to the east. Consider Bloomfield's summary (1933: 33):

> Whoever was impressed by the Hollandish official or merchant, learned to speak [yː]; whoever saw his superiors in the Hanseatic upper class, retained the old [uː]. The part of the population which made no pretensions to elegance, must also have long retained the [uː], but in the course of time the [yː] filtered down even to this class.
>
> ...
>
> The word *house* will occur much oftener than the word *mouse* in official speech and in conversation with persons who represent the cultural center; *mouse* is more confined to homely and familiar situations. Accordingly, we find that the word *house* in the upper-class and central form with [yː] spread into districts where the word *mouse* has persisted in the old-fashioned form with [uː].

FIGURE 7.1. 'Mouse' and 'house' in Dutch dialects

That is, the proposal is that people's pronunciation reflected whose sphere of political and social influence they were in. For those in the Hollandic sphere, people with 'no pretensions to elegance' eventually adopted the [y:] in words used in the town square, but kept their old vowel in words from the private realm.

Setting aside the issue of prestige, the argument is that innovation or retention here was driven by two competing political powers and by the mismatch in the social situations in which each word was more likely to be used. It's a beautiful story, but, like many tales, the historical record is more complicated. Stroop (1981) shows a fuller set of data for diphthongization as a broader phenomenon – that is, he looks at how this change developed not just in two words, but across a set – and we see that there are some inconsistencies and irregularities in the distributions in general, patterns that can have nothing to do with the meaning or use of these two particular words. Instead, these rough edges probably reflect the influences of multiple social and linguistic factors.

Where we really do become conscious of sound change, we can react to it. You already know about hypercorrection (defined and discussed in Chapters 1 and 5), where speakers recognize that their speech differs from social expectations of some kind (such as being non-standard) and they go too far in 'fixing' it, like adding an /r/ to *wash*. Related phenomena abound; my favorite is 'hyperforeignism' (Janda et al. 1994). In English, the sound /ʒ/ is pretty much restricted to words borrowed from other languages. While it's the usual pronunciation of words like *measure* and *pleasure*, many people adjust words like *garage* to sound more usual for English, pronouncing it with [dʒ]. The association of /ʒ/ with non-English words comes to bear when we encounter foreign words that actually would have /dʒ/ in the source language, like *Beijing* or *Tajikistan*. Making the association to where /ʒ/ occurs, namely in foreign words, some people produce *Bei*[ʒ]*ing* and *Ta*[ʒ]*ikistan*. People who know French are prone to laugh when they hear Americans pronounce *coup de grâce* without the final /s/. We not unreasonably associate French with having orthographic final consonants that are not pronounced (like *ballet, cachet*) but in this case it would be (signaled by the final -*e* if you know French); losing that consonant turns *grâce* into *gras*, and a 'blow of mercy' into a 'blow of grease.'

Another example is in some sense related to this. English historically had a sound pattern and then a sound change that were unrelated – as far as I can tell – but that interact in an important way. The language had a restriction on the amount of material that could be contained in a syllable rhyme, so that coda clusters like -*sp*, -*st*, -*sk* were limited to syllables with a preceding short vowel. That is, ɪsk, ʊsk, and ɛsk were legitimate ways to fill out a syllable but *i:sk, *u:sk and *e:sk weren't. We had words like *fisk* 'fish' and *englisc* 'English', but nothing like /fi:sk/ or /li:sk/. Later, the cluster *sk* changed into a single segment, [ʃ], at some point creating a new phoneme. By accident, then, a small gap emerged: English phonotactics licensed long vowel plus a single consonant but there happened to be no examples of this with the particular consonant [ʃ]. Over time, borrowings and new creations trickled in to provide a few items with this structure, coming from a lot of different languages (from Iverson and Salmons 2005):

(6) Borrowed words with tense vowel plus [ʃ]
  i:
  capiche   < Italian 'understand'
  hashish   < Arabic 'dried hemp'
  baksheesh   < Arabic 'tip, gratuity'
  maxixe   < Portuguese 'Brazilian dance'
  fiche   < French 'slip of paper'
  u:
  tarboosh   < Arabic 'brimless cap'
  farouche   < French 'wild, savage, fierce'
  o:
  gauche   < French 'left, maladroit'
  skosh   < Japanese *sukoshi* 'a little bit'

English sound patterns had changed, in a concrete sense, but was there sound change? I would argue no. Many speakers integrate some of these words into English – *niche* can be pronounced with a tense or lax vowel and/or with /ʃ/ or /tʃ/ – but nobody integrates all of these. I would argue that a synchronic theory of sound patterns has essentially nothing to say about this gap or its filling. Words like *gauche* [go:ʃ] and *skosh* [sko:ʃ] were never ungrammatical in English per se, once we had the shibilant; the long-vowel words simply happened not to be present. We can easily describe these, but trying to account for them by rules or constraints or templates in the grammar would be an overreach of the sort I argued against with regard to final fortition in §3.4. No sound change has taken place, only lexical changes (coinages and borrowings). Instead, the grammar of the language has remained in this regard constant and the explanation of a minor synchronic pattern has to be sought in history. Speakers today tacitly recognize their oddity, we argued, because of where we find new words with this structure – in affective, onomatopoeic words, many pretty recent and generally etymologically obscure. These examples are all from the late 1800s or later:

(7)   New words with tense vowel + /ʃ/ in contemporary English
      swoosh
      whoosh
      squoosh
      sheesh
      smoosh
      moosh
      koosh

This pattern, by no means prohibited by contemporary English phonology, represents an 'accidental gap' that still echoes today.

The examples just discussed show how awareness – or lack thereof – of sound patterns and their social interpretation interacts with sound change. The most extreme intervention would be for a community to deliberately and consciously alter their speech. Clear evidence of such patterns in sound change would be important to the field, and I'll return to the topic in §8.4.

7.6   Language and dialect contact

The social side of sound change could be claimed to be all about contact – given how we've been talking about variation, sound change spreads in contexts where people don't speak exactly the same way. I'll introduce two models of language contact in a broader sense as it bears on sound change: Van Coetsem's view of borrowing and imposition and Matras's approach.

To the first, Van Coetsem (1988, 2000; Howell 1993; Winford 2005) distinguishes borrowing from imposition in contact. Borrowing is the adoption of material into one's dominant language. Words are readily borrowed and while real 'phonological borrowing' was long thought to be rare, it is easy to find examples – we've already talked about segments like /ʒ/ and phonotactics like long vowel plus /ʃ/ in English. Both are part of English phonology today, having spread beyond foreign vocabulary (if, in the former case, often by hypercorrection). German's nasalized vowels and /ʒ/ clearly come from French as well, though they remain restricted to borrowed items, like *Bonbon* and *Journalist*, and haven't spread into the native vocabulary. (Indeed, not all speakers have these sounds.) Imposition is the result of speakers bringing L1 features into their L2 repertoire, basically where we are unable to overcome L1 features in a new language. Much structural interference can be characterized as 'imposition' from L2 acquisition.

These are basically complementary processes, seen from the perspective of the speaker and their language dominance. Howell (1993: 189, see now Natvig 2017 and work since) captures the connection between borrowing and imposition in this stability gradient:

(8)   Stability: Borrowing versus imposition
      More open to borrowing   →   Less open to borrowing
      Less affected by imposition   ←   More affected by imposition

Less stable domains: *More stable domains:*
lexical items, derivational morphology   phonology, inflectional morphology,
                                             semantic system, syntax

To the second approach, Matras (2009) discusses contact in terms of whether it is 'matter' or 'pattern' that is being transferred; that is, whether we are dealing with 'concrete word-forms and morphs' versus 'the arrangement, meaning and combination of units of matter' (2009: 8, with those terms coming from Sakel 2007). This provides a different perspective on phonological contact effects, shown below. This characterizes contact settings more broadly – at the community rather than individual level – and is a useful typology, especially in historical situations.

(9)   Matras on phonological convergence

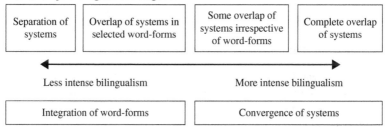

Not all sound change under contact is so simple. The loss of tone under contact is intuitively plausible to you, probably: Having compromised input to acquire tones and having available a system that is easier to learn, like fixed stress, could motivate this. But that tone spreads areally (recall §§4.3–4) without direct borrowing probably strikes you as more puzzling, though we may have ways of accounting for it. In other cases, sounds appear to have been introduced by language contact but play different roles within the new system. We discussed Zuberoan Basque /y/ in §5.7 (Egurtzegi 2017). That surely has its origin in the /u/ fronting of neighboring Romance languages, yet in Basque the fronting is inhibited by a set of consonants while it is unconditioned in Romance.

7.7   Conclusion

I have surveyed a range of ways that social aspects interact with structural aspects and the ways that sound change can and does spread. Integrating the social and the structural underscores the need to build variation into our understanding of sound change at the most basic level. I've argued that the relationship between the social and the structural depends in part on awareness of changes, and ultimately that means different types and levels of awareness – our subconscious reaction to a subtle vowel variant is different from our reaction to something that is fully enregistered with a social value.

In this chapter, again, we see great complexity, something we have to expect given that we're dealing with not just human cognition but human cognition as it works in the context of human society. But as in other cases, this is complexity that yields to nuanced analysis. The tremendous opportunities for understanding by putting those pieces together in the right way are vast.

I close by asking you, please, to never invoke 'prestige' as a motivation for sound change. With that, let's move on to phonetics and sound change.

Beyond this book

1. Digging deeper: Data

A huge issue in the study of change in progress is gender, with, most notably, young women typically leading in sound change. In languages and communities you know, how strong is that pattern? Most of that work has been done assuming gender as a binary, which researchers generally no longer do. (There's still relatively limited work on this with regard to sound change, but Podesva and Van Hofwegen 2014 provide a good overview.) Do you see ways that the increasingly complex interpretation of gender identity can change this picture?

2. Digging deeper: Theory

People like Van Coetsem, Winford and Matras – all cited in this chapter – have really advanced our understanding of language change in contact settings, though often not with a particular focus on sound change. Read some of that work and look at where accounts of sound change could be sharpened.

3. Moving beyond what we know

- For years I have tried to convince colleagues and students that 'prestige' is a counter-productive notion for motivating language change, probably a nonsensical one at its core. People don't necessarily roll their eyes, but a lot of them do continue appealing to the notion. Prove me wrong! Take a couple of language histories and search for the term 'prestige.' Are there better – more direct and explicit – ways of accounting for whatever change is motivated that way in the text? Or is 'prestige' really the best story?
- In the language histories you're working with, how many sound changes run counter to standards and norms and prescriptions? You may need to look at relatively recent changes, since we often lack good information about language ideologies and attitudes farther back in the past.
- I've mentioned twice the borrowing of /ʒ/ into English from French. If you read the specialist literature, like Minkova (2014: 141–3), you'll find that there's some more texture to the story. For example, the French word for *pleasure* today has a [z]. Similarly, we have a set of French

loans in English that have [ʃ] where French has [s], like our words *sugar* and *sure*. Track down the histories of such words and those two sounds. How does contact interact with structural and other social factors in such cases?

Part 4

Sound change in grammar

8

Phonetics and Sound Change

8.1 Introduction

We've talked repeatedly about the roles that phonetics can play in sound change, and how articulation, acoustics and perception can drive sound change.

The image in Figure 8.1 from Denes and Pinson (1963: 5) first made me consider the whole speech chain. Sound change involves every link of this chain. Work on the phonetics of sound change is often centered around perception, but phonology and other modules ('the linguistic level') are involved, along with articulation ('the physiological level') and sound waves ('the acoustic level'). This is all happening in the brains, ears and mouths of speakers and listeners. You might expect transmission to be seamless here – that a particular articulation leads to particular acoustic patterns that lead to particular percepts, but Purnell (2008) (§3.2) illustrates one mismatch, where speakers used unexpected articulations to achieve the acoustic effect associated with prevelar raising.

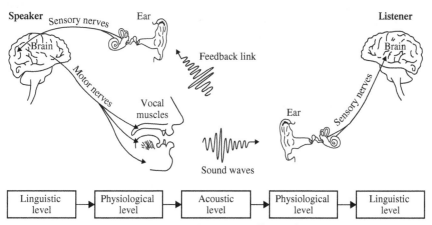

FIGURE 8.1. The Speech Chain: the different forms in which
a spoken message exists in its progress from the mind of the speaker
to the mind of the listener

We've already applied Ohala's listener-driven perspective to umlaut data in Chapter 1. Below I repeat the graphic on how this would model the beginnings of umlaut.

(1) Listener-driven umlaut (after Ohala)

   (a) Successful reconstruction

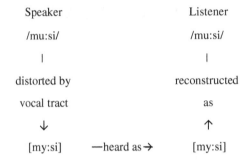

           Speaker   Listener

           /mu:si/   /mu:si/

              | |

        distorted by   reconstructed

        vocal tract   as

           ↓   ↑

         [my:si]   —heard as →   [my:si]

   (b) Hypocorrection

         Speaker   Listener   Listener-turned-speaker

         /mu:si/   /my:s(ə)/   ↴

           | |

      distorted by   interpreted   produced

      vocal tract   as   as

         ↓   ↑   ↓

   [my:sə] —heard as → [my:s(ə)/]   [my:s(ə)/]

One goal now is to explore this influential model more fully, including recent developments (§8.2). In §8.3, I revisit another issue from Chapter 1, the role of articulation in sound change. Some work on phonetics involves strong arguments against abstraction and phonology and I'll touch on those in §8.4, before briefly addressing the question of whether all sound change is phonetically motivated in §8.5.

8.2 Perception and acoustics in sound change

The figure above reminds you of how Ohala sees hypocorrection as central to much sound change. For something like umlaut the pattern should make sense intuitively, since the assimilation is actually making the target vowel articulatorily and acoustically much more like the product of the change … the /u:/ is moved considerably toward /y:/ for coarticulatory reasons.

    A less obvious example of his kind of hypercorrection is 'spontaneous nasalization,' the introduction of vowel nasalization or a nasal consonant where there was no trace of a nasal before. Matisoff (1975) shows that this kind of rhinoglottophilia can be found across the world's languages, including in 'certain upper class dialects of British English' where *heart* can be pronounced, in his transcription, [hããt]. Ohala has given, in various publications including 1993, this set of examples from South Asia:

(2) Examples of spontaneous nasalization (Ohala 1993)

Sanskrit	Prakrit	Old Hindi	Modern Hindi	Bengali	Translation
pakṣ	pakkha	pãkh	paŋkhã		a side
akṣi	akkhi-		ãkh		eye
uččaka-	uččaa-		ũčã	uɲča	high
satya-	sačča-	sãč			truth
sarpa-	sappa-		sãp		snake

He finds the reason for the insertion of nasality or nasals in the presence of high air-flow segments, often [h] but also voiceless fricatives generally, aspirated stops and affricates. He has supported this cross-linguistic tendency by perceptual experiments where listeners do rate such forms as sounding more nasal. That is, the relatively open glottis in these segments 'is partially assimilated by adjacent vowels which, in turn, creates an acoustic effect which mimics nasalization' (1993: 241). There's more going on, though, since it is not only in those environments where such forms arise, as in Matisoff's example I just gave of British English *art* pronounced as [ããt]. Whether this is analogy to words like *heart* or a phonological generalization is not clear to me, but it would be an interesting question to pursue.

Ohala has, over the years, presented many instances of sound changes that may seem counter-intuitive in terms of articulation but which make sense in terms of acoustics, how listeners interpret sounds in context. This is one of them. But there's a bigger program in terms of the typology of sound change. Specifically, Ohala (1993: 259) establishes guidelines for distinguishing between hypo- and hypercorrection. For instance, 'Sound changes attributed to hypocorrection, then, would involve listeners copying at face value those details of speech that originally owe their existence to the influence of physical phonetic properties of the speech production system' (1993: 260). Sound changes due to hypercorrection, he argues, 'do not conform to known constraints on speech production.' Further differences include these:

Criterion	Hypocorrection	Hypercorrection
Loss of conditioning environment?	Possible	No
Results in new segments?	Possible	No
Change from robust to less robust segment?	Possible	Usually no

This distinction has been discussed often, and the examples I know align with this table, but further testing of it would no doubt lead to deeper understanding and refinement of the model.

Ohala also argues that various theoretical claims follow from his approach (1993: 261–8), including these.

1. **Sound change is non-teleological.** Ohala objects to the long tradition of
   arguments that sound change reflects ease of articulation or perception
   or any kind of simplification. Instead, 'there is no intention by either
   the speaker or the listener to change pronunciation. Indeed, the whole
   purpose of the listener's interpretive activity is to attempt to deduce the
   pronunciation intended by the speaker, i.e. to preserve, not to change, the
   pronunciation norm' (1993: 262).
2. **Sound change is phonetic.** Here, Ohala's focus is on variation, and we've
   already seen from other perspectives that the turn toward giving variation
   its place in sound change is revolutionary. Distinct in his approach is
   parsing or failing to parse variation accurately. He does not quite dismiss
   any role for the sound system, but finds 'structuralist' efforts weak and
   lacking in rigor. (See the the next chapter for a less pessimistic view.)
3. **Sound change in the laboratory.** While studying sound change in lab
   settings is an old art, Ohala worried a quarter of a century ago that this was
   not a 'mainstream' concern. There's no cause for worry on that count. The
   specialty known as Laboratory Phonology alone covers this, but experimental work is pervasive and surely mainstream.

Ohala describes his experimental results as involving 'mini-sound changes.' He
is simply far less interested in 'maxi-sound changes,' which 'arise due to some
of these mini-sound changes spreading selectively whereas others fail to spread;
cultural and psychological factors undoubtedly play a role in this' (1993: 268).
He has created a powerful focus on a part of the Denes and Pinson picture that
was not fully appreciated before. While understanding sound change clearly
requires a broader and more inclusive approach, his work leads directly to important research agendas, like Blevins's Evolutionary Phonology, which is far more
typological and less experimental, and newer experimental approaches, like those
of Yu (§5.5) and Kirby (see below).

8.3   Articulation and sound change

In §2.6, I mentioned one view about speech articulation and sound change: Blasi
et al.'s evidence that agriculture has led to changes in our dental structure that
make the production of f-sounds easier. Other work these days explores whether
small individual and group differences in anatomy might bias speakers toward
particular ways of articulating sounds. Dediu and Moisik, for instance, argue
that a preference for one or the other of the two main variants of English /r/,
'bunched' versus 'retroflex,' correlate with 'hard palate width and height, the
overall size of the mouth, and the size (i.e., prominence) of the alveolar ridge'
(2019: 21).

Such presumably unusual situations aside, the real focus on articulation and
sound change has been on general motivations in speech production, today
usually integrated with perceptual and other factors. As its name suggests,
Natural Phonology (Stampe 1969 and work since) seeks to account for sound
change in terms of what those working in the framework regard as 'natural'
processes, anchored in physiology. Articulatory challenges or 'problems' in

producing certain sounds or patterns have their own 'solutions,' called 'processes' (Donegan and Nathan 2015: 432). This follows the 'ease of articulation' views noted in Chapter 1, but Natural Phonology is broadly concerned with the inhibition of such processes. Donegan and Nathan (2015: 432) write:

> Processes may emerge as the infant learns to associate articulatory gestures or configurations with their audible results, but unlike the rules of generative phonology, they are not learned by observation and comparison of forms. What is learned, in learning to pronounce a language, is to inhibit processes, or to inhibit them under certain circumstances, and thus to pronounce their potential inputs. In sound change, inhibitions on processes may be relaxed, so that additional processes apply, or processes apply more generally.

This view, then, is anchored in acquisition, though the focus on inhibition differs from many other related perspectives.

A more recent model is Degree of Articulatory Constraint (DAC), laid out with comparative Romance data by Recasens (2014). It focuses on coarticulation, especially involving the tongue, and the 'basic tenet' is that (2014: 3):

> the degree to which phonetic segments are more or less permeable to the coarticulatory effects exerted by other segments and influence them at the phonetic level can be accounted for by their own production requirements.

This allows specific predictions about coarticulation and its direction (anticipatory versus carryover) and Recasens tests these with processes like assimilation, dissimilation, elision and insertion. Widespread across Romance are cases of regressive assimilation of velar stops (k, g) before front vowels or glides becoming dental stops (not unlike our discussions of palatalization in §4.6), for example French *ceuillir* 'gather', [kʲør] is realized as [tʲør] in Besançon Francoprovençal. To account for these, Recasens proposes first an articulatory change and then a perceptual one (2014: 131–2):

1. 'An increase in front dorsal or laminodorsal contact causes the front velar stop to shift to an (alveolo)palatal stop', and then
2. 'the categorization of the outcoming realizations [c, ɟ] as /t, d/ by listeners.'

That is, a first step in production, driven by coarticulation, triggers a second step in perception. Together, they yield a sound change. An intermediate step is attested in various places as well, so that Italian *chiave* 'wrench' appears in the Pisa variety of Tuscan as *tiave*. This can continue beyond dentals to 'velar softening,' as Latin [kɛnto] 'hundred' becoming Italian [tʃɛnto] and Catalan [sɛn].

Recasens's work is part of a broader move today explicitly connecting perception and production. Beddor et al. (2018) make this connection at a more abstract level: They hypothesize that people who use more coarticulation and do it more consistently will pay more attention to coarticulation as listeners. They tested this experimentally by tracking nasality and find that 'a speaker's coarticulatory patterns predicted, to some degree, that individual's perception, thereby supporting the hypothesis: participants who produced earlier onset of coarticulatory nasalization were, as listeners, more efficient users of nasality as that information unfolded over time' (2018: 931). This is part of a broader body of work that moves us away from the listener error view of perception and toward a focus on variation and how people make different analyses of what they hear.

At the same time, it is important to keep in mind that sound change can involve whole sets of cues rather than a single one. Kirby (2014a, 2014b) tackles the rise of tone in Khmer spoken in Phnom Penh, Cambodia. The standard variety is not tonal, and distinguishes sets like /ku:/ 'pair' ≠ /kʰu:/ 'old' ≠ /kru:/ 'teacher'. But this dialect is developing patterns with the loss of trilled /r/ in onset clusters, so that /kru:/ 'teacher' can be realized as [kù:] (low (rising) tone) or [kʰǔ:] (aspiration and falling-rising pitch) or [kṳ:] (breathy voice). Even though the f0 differences are modest, Kirby shows that they are enough for listeners to distinguish the old r-ful forms without an /r/ present. While this might look like a new path of tonogenesis (/r/ > low tone), Kirby attributes this to acoustic effects of /r/, including breathiness.[1]

8.4 Does sound change have to be phonetically or even linguistically motivated?

A cornerstone of Ohala's view, carried on by younger scholars in this tradition, sees sound change as beginning in phonetics. This view has had deep roots in the field since the Neogrammarians, including Paul (1920 [1880]), and has run through the Natural Phonologists, as well as Blevins, whose working hypothesis for Evolutionary Phonology is that 'recurrent synchronic sound patterns have their origins in recurrent *phonetically motivated* sound change' (2004: 8, emphasis added).

Most changes I know seem to have roots in phonetic variation. But is this necessarily so? Depending on how narrow your definition of sound change is – and I'm working with a broad one – it definitely includes phonological motivations, where something about the phonological system itself motivates sound change, e.g. to create a more symmetrical system. (As noted, Ohala seems to concede a modest role for such.) We'll explore these ideas in the next chapter.

There are attempts to motivate sound change in other ways. In §7.5, I noted in passing the proposal that speakers might engage in deliberate efforts to change their language. A vigorous attack on phonetic or phonological motivations comes from Blust (2005, and elsewhere). He presents ten changes that he repeatedly deems 'bizarre' from Austronesian languages, given below in (3). These are all conditioned changes (except possibly 4) and none shows phonological alternations. By 'bizarre,' Blust means that such changes appear unusual cross-linguistically, though exactly how we determine that is unclear with the current state of knowledge of diachronic typology (Chapter 3 and §5.6). His bigger claim is that these changes cannot be structurally motivated, that is, they are not triggered by anything in phonetics or phonology.

---

1 Beddor et al. (2018) and Kirby (2014a) demonstrate how we can bring cutting-edge experimental work and simulations to concrete problems in the study of sound change.

(3) 'Some bizarre sound changes in Austronesian languages' (Blust 2005: 221)
  1. *w/y > -p in languages of western Manus
  2. *w/b > c, nc in Sundanese
  3. Intervocalic devoicing in Kiput, Berawan
  4. *dr > k^h in Drehet
  5. *b, *d, *g > -m, n, ŋ in Karo, Batak, Berawan
  6. C > C:/__V# in Berawan
  7. *b > -k- in Berawan
  8. *g > p-, -j-, -p in Sa'ban
  9. *an/aŋ > ay and *em/en/eŋ > -aw in Iban
  10. Postnasal devoicing in Murik

Blust reviews three motivations for sound change: (1) phonetic and (2) phonological motivations for actuation, how changes get started, and (3) sociolinguistic motivations for implementation, how changes spread (Chapter 7). For these changes, he argues or asserts that they are single-step changes, not reflections of chains of development, and that each lacks any 'articulatory, auditory, or structural motivation,' leaving only sociolinguistic factors as motivations (2005: 221). He eventually concludes (2005: 264):

> I have tried to consider explanations that would allow us to salvage the theory that all sound changes are linguistically motivated, but some changes appear to remain fundamentally intractable. No amount of speculation about possible intermediate steps is likely to provide a plausible phonetic motivation for more than a few of the changes considered here, and alternative structural explanations are also problematic. By default the only remaining explanation appears to be that speakers may sometimes engage in a conscious, arbitrary manipulation of linguistic symbols which produces systematic or semi-systematic results that resemble phonetically motivated sound change.

His view is that 'although many sound changes begin as a result of automatic phonetic processes working on the mechanics of speech, others not only are spread through linguistic communities, but arise through a conscious effort to distinguish the speech of one social subgroup from that of another' (2005: 264).

If you're following carefully, you will recall that his first change, where glides harden into oral stops, looks like glide fortition in several languages from around the world discussed in §3.3. There, both phonetic and phonological motivations have been proposed by Mortensen and Hall, respectively. (With Blevins 2008: 2 and others, I would assume that the two glides *y and *w merged to *w, making this a two-step change.) Blevins has motivated many of these changes phonetically (2004, 2008, and elsewhere). And the cases have sometimes been easy to make. For instance, for his fifth change, of voiced oral stops to nasals, Blevins has shown that related languages show prenasalization – /b/ realized as [ᵐb], and so on – and some languages have carried that on to loss of oral closure, yielding synchronic /m/. That's a straightforward sound change, just not a single-stage one.

Blust puts himself in the awkward position of making a sweeping negative claim – that these changes cannot be motivated linguistically – only to have others provide precisely such motivations. Often, a step forward is to acknowledge the possibility of complex changes, not the single-step analyses he expects. Yes, we prefer simpler analyses (Ockham's razor) but not at the cost of incomplete analysis. Modern research shows that complex unfolding is the norm.

I have yet to see convincing examples of non-linguistic motivation in sound change, beyond the kinds of social motivations like accommodation in §7.5 (or perhaps its opposite, distancing oneself linguistically from certain groups). For one thing, we have to know a lot about the social and cultural settings of change to know what is deliberate or conscious. The shift from looking at long past changes in terms of pre- and post-stages to looking at change in progress has borne tremendous fruit, as we've seen time and time again, but it would be necessary in order to establish motivations for change, stages of change and so on. I'm certainly not claiming that such social motivations don't exist, only that this is not how we could reliably establish them. We need positive evidence rather than assertions about what cannot happen.

8.5   The phonetics of sound change and attacks on abstract structure

If you read around in the strands of research discussed here – Ohala, Natural Phonology, Evolutionary Phonology and so on – you'll see a variety of interpretations of what is phonetic and what is phonological and what roles each plays in sound change. Some, like Ohala, stop shy of denying the existence of phonology in the usual sense and, as above, concede that structural considerations may play some role in sound change, but see it as marginal. Others, like Blevins, give an explicit but relatively minor role to phonology in synchrony – she sees it as limited to prosodic structures (like syllables and feet) and distinctive features, while almost all of phonology reflects diachrony and, overwhelmingly, phonetic rather than phonological patterning in the traditional sense. Natural Phonologists, as I understand them, basically do not differentiate phonetics from phonology, with the former doing all the work. Other approaches, like Bybee's Usage-based Phonology, follow similar lines.

Broadly speaking, Port and Leary (2005: 258) move dramatically away from any notion of abstract grammatical structure and machinery, rejecting that language is a 'formal symbolic system,' in favor of viewing language as emerging from use. They particularly attack the notion that sound systems are made up of segments (see also Bybee 2001: 36, among others) . This work has increased our understanding of variation as central to change, by attention to frequency effects (such as Todd et al. 2019, but now Labov 2020) and presenting evidence for phonetic detail in representations, among other issues. Debates about the role of abstract structure are substantive disagreements about the most basic questions of human language, if not as dramatic as earlier battles over linguistic theory, cf. Harris's 1993 *The Linguistics Wars*. While our world is today often more collegial in this regard (at least the one I'm living in now), it's worth reading something like the special issue of *The Linguistic Review* from 2007 discussing Jackendoff (2002) and including his response to the discussions (Jackendoff 2007).

Large parts of these disagreements boil down to long-standing debates about the existence and/or nature of Universal Grammar: What is our innate (and apparently unique) capacity as humans to acquire and use language? Earlier and some contemporary views posit truly massive capacity (recall the issue of grammar as a micro-manager in §3.4), but contemporary discussions in 'big t' linguistic theory have moved dramatically toward seeing much work done in general cognition, rather than being specific to language (see 'third factors' in §3.4). One place this has relevance for us is in the existence of a universal set of distinctive features. I haven't made such an assumption – most distinctive features are well established across languages and I have regularly used them, but without claiming that [high] and [low] or [spread glottis] and [voice] are innate. (If they aren't hard-wired, our vocal and perceptual apparatus at least makes them easy targets for developing contrasts and contrasts susceptible to sound change, but that's beyond our focus in this book.)

What troubles me, though, is that instead of looking at how these matters can be integrated into phonology (synchronic and diachronic), some scholars discard phonology in the sense developed in the next chapter. Port and Leary write that 'Today the premise that language must be completely formal is impeding progress in phonology' (2005: 958). There's a definitional issue, but acknowledging the roles of usage and phonetic detail hardly seem at odds with there being an abstract, formal system. Whatever its shortcomings, generative and other formal approaches to phonology have yielded tremendous insights into how sounds pattern and change, and I just do not see efforts in these counter-currents to account for those insights. Until I do, I work to understand both the phonetics and the phonology, the abstract and the concrete, the structural and the social, and to integrate those into a coherent whole.

8.6 Conclusion

In this chapter, I've argued for a large but still constrained role for phonetics in sound change. It's a critical piece of the big picture, and looms particularly large at certain points in the unfolding of change.

Ohala concludes the paper I discussed in this chapter this way: 'I have presented a general plan to explain the *initiation of sound changes* found in similar form in diverse languages,' adding then (1993: 268–9, emphasis added) 'I have attempted to show the relevance of phonetic research to an understanding of the *mechanism of sound change initiation*.' The relevance of phonetics for the study of sound change is widely accepted today, and that relevance is heavily focused on the origins of sound change, but it yields only an incomplete picture of sound change. Phonetics plays a role, but so does abstract structure – phonology – to which we now turn.

Beyond this book

1. Digging deeper: Data

I think most language histories talk about at least some sound changes basically in terms of phonology, changes in contrast or features. If you find such examples, what kinds of phonetic accounts could be used to advance the story?

2. Digging deeper: Theory

Many readers at this point have some ties to some bigger view of sound patterns, often ingested from lectures and course readings in linguistics classes from introductory courses on phonetics or phonology. Whatever your perspective may be, look at foundational works and start laying out what the relationship between phonetics and phonology (in the senses I've been using those terms) is.

3. Moving beyond what we know

Take a couple of examples of sound change from language histories and/or the technical literature. Look at the role of phonetics in the account of these changes:

- Are phonetics and phonology clearly distinguished or not?
- If not, can you sort out a distinction?
- Is the account balanced in including phonetics and phonology?
- What about other facets?

It's common for language histories to have somewhat outdated analyses and many of those have not been addressed in recent research. If you have some background in phonetics, look for older accounts of sound change where contemporary knowledge can help us sharpen and revise those accounts.

9

Phonology and Sound Change

9.1 Introduction

I closed the last chapter with a discussion of how phonetics helps us account especially and specifically for the INITIATION of sound change. While phonetics is critical and indispensable to the full picture of sound change, it is only one part. I noted in §8.5 various moves to limit or even reject the role of real abstract structure in the study of sound systems, including the rejection of what I would see as phonology itself. This is not the place for a defense of phonology – Dresher (2009), Hall (2011), Hyman (2018) and many others have done that cleanly in recent years for issues such as contrast and underlying representations. And important recent work has begun to pursue the role of phonology in phonetic change, notably Fruehwald (2017). I simply adopt a model of grammar that includes a robust phonological component. This chapter also in many ways sets up Chapter 10, where we go beyond sound systems, farther beyond what we could do with phonetics alone.

While phonetics is traditionally divided into concern with articulation, acoustics and perception, most definitions see the core of phonology as being its focus on CONTRAST and sound as SYSTEMS. Martinet (1952, 1955) and others have explored notions of balance and symmetry in systems, including how 'holes in patterns' (*cases vides*) in systems get filled, extending to chain shifting. We've talked about this with vocalic chain shifts and Grimm's Law, and we will see another example in just a moment. Still, Martinet is explicit that gap filling is not a simple, mechanical process, and writes about filling 'holes in patterns' that (1952: 19, similar language in 1955):

> This phrase is undoubtedly picturesque, but it is apt to deter linguists from a painstaking analysis of the successive processes involved. 'Paper phonetics' has been severely and justly criticized. Juggling with the symbols of phonemic charts would be equally dangerous and reprehensible. Isolated phonemes do not rush into structural gaps unless they are close enough to be attracted, and whether they are attracted depends on a variety of factors which always deserve careful investigation.

Martinet argues that we need to examine what sounds are distinctive in a language and how they are organized into groups, with reference to what features we need to characterize them. This also means looking at the processes that sounds and groups of sounds participate in, in terms of rules or constraints, as I'll discuss for 'phonological activity.' If we take these points as a basis for an abstract system of sounds, the study of sound change has been phonologically oriented since early discussions of Grimm's Law (Cser 2016). As I have stressed throughout, that sound change is beautifully systematic – covering places of articulation and manners of articulation – and shows powerful parallels to other changes in Germanic languages, including the High German Consonant Shift and modern Liverpool English (Honeybone 2001). We can motivate pieces of such shifts phonetically, for instance treating aspiration as a motivation for voiceless stops becoming fricatives. But phonetics alone can't account for the full patterns we have.

Consider likely phonetic motivations of part of Grimm's Law and related changes, the spirantization of stops, already introduced in §2.2 and §3.2. With /p, t, k/, the velar /k/ is normally aspirated far longer and has a far shorter closure than the labial /p/, so that the odds of missing complete closure in production or hearing incomplete closure in perception increase. And these stops have longer aspiration at the beginning of stressed syllables than unstressed syllables. Heavier aspiration has better chances of being heard as fricative or fricative-like.

Now let's look at the Second or High German Consonant Shift, a change, as just noted, that parallels Grimm's Law, the First Consonant Shift, to an extent (thus the name(s)).[1] While aspiration is often taken for granted as a, or the, motivation, the complex results show that there must be more than aspiration at play in its eventual distribution. This shift happened before our earliest written records of German. It was most robust in southern German, petering out farther north, leaving a systematic set of shifted and unshifted stops. These are illustrated in (1) and (2) below, first showing examples from Old Saxon, the ancestor of Low German, which lacks the shift (like English), compared to southern (or Upper) German forms with the shift. Example (2) lays out the complex areal distribution of the shift, starting with Old Saxon at the top and working southward from there, ending with very poorly attested Longbardic.

(1)   Unshifted (Old Saxon) and shifted (Upper German) cognates

West Gmc	Unshifted Old Saxon	Shifted Upper German	Gloss
*t-	tehan	zĕhan = [ts]	'ten'
*-tt-	lātan	laʒʒan = [ʃː]	'to let'
*-nt	lenten (MLG)	lenzo = [ts]	'spring(time)'
*-lt/rt	herta	herza = [ts]	'heart'

---

1   I have written much over the years about this and the tables and data are drawn from those works, though the substance of this discussion is very different.

West Gmc	Unshifted Old Saxon	Shifted Upper German	Gloss
*p-	plegan	p**f**legan	'to care for'
*-pp-	ap**p**ul	ap**f**ul	'apple'
*-mp	dam**p** (MLG)	dam**pf**	'steam'
*-lp	hel**p**an	hel**f**an	'to help'
		hel**ph**an = [pf]	
*-rp	wer**p**an	wer**f**an	'to throw'
		wer**ph**an = [pf]	
*k-	**k**orn	**ch**orna = [x]	'grain'
*-kk-	ac**k**ar	ac**ch**ar = [x:]	'field, acre'
*-nk	than**k**on	dan**ch**ōn = [x]	'to thank'
*-lk/rk	fol**k**	fol**ch**a = [x]	'people'

(2) The Second Sound Shift: Distribution of fortis stops in Old High German by place and context

	CORONAL					LABIAL						VELAR			
Pre-OHG	t-	-tt-	C+t	-t-	-t	p-	-pp-	-mp	-lp	-rp	-p(-)	k-	-kk-	C+k	-k(-)
OSaxon	t	tt	t	t	t	p	pp	mp	lp	rp	p	k	kk	k	k
MFranc	z	zz	z	ȝȝ	t/ȝ	p	pp	mp	lp	rp	f(f)	k	kk	k	ch
Rh-Franc	z	zz	z	ȝȝ	ȝ	p	pp	mp	lp/	rp/	f(f)	k	kk	k	ch
									lpf	rpf					
S Rh-Fr	z	zz	z	ȝȝ	ȝ	p	pf	mpf	lpf	rpf	f(f)	k	kk	k	ch
E Franc	z	z	z	ȝȝ	ȝ	pf	pf	mpf	lpf	rpf	f(f)	k	kk	k	ch
Bavarian	z	z	z	ȝȝ	ȝ	pf	pf	mf	lf	rf	f(f)	kχ	kχ	kχ	ch
Aleman	z	z	z	ȝȝ	ȝ	pf/f	pf/ff	mf	lf	rf	f(f)	ch	kχ	ch	ch
Langob	z	z	z	s(s)	s	p	p(p)	mpf	lpf	rpf	p/f(f)	k	kk	k/kχ	ch

Adapted from Salmons (2018: 121), ultimately from Sonderegger (2003: 263).

That aspiration played a role is widely accepted and I'll take it as uncontroversial. In both Grimm's Law and this shift, for example, /p, t, k/ did not shift when they follow *s-, so that words like *speien* 'spew' and *sprechen* 'speak' continue Indo-European forms in *sp-. Such s-clusters lack aspiration in the modern languages (*pit* versus *spit*, *Paß* versus *Spaß*) (Iverson and Salmons 1995, and elsewhere).

With those phonetic roots in mind, consider Voice Onset Time (VOT) values in modern English. VOT is how long it takes for the vocal folds to start vibrating (for voicing to begin) relative to the end of a consonant, like the release of a stop. These patterns are grounded in the physics of speech, where a closure farther back in the mouth, like with /k/, allows less expansion of the inside of the mouth than /p/. (You can hold /p/ longer because air pressure builds up, basically puffing your cheeks a little; with /k/, you lack that flexibility.) This yields longer aspiration with /k/ than /p/.

(3) Mean VOT, msec., isolated words (three speakers), Lisker and Abramson (1967: 17)

	Stressed	**Unstressed**
/p/	59	38
/t/	67	45
/k/	84	55

(4) Mean VOT values, msec. (Weismer 1979)

	/i/	/e/	/ɪ/	/ɛ/	/u/	/æ/
/p/	57.33	56.73	44.06	48.46	57.60	52.80
/t/	67.06	67.86	63.33	65.13	66.00	63.93
/k/	79.40	67.40	71.66	62.66	70.60	66.53

If aspiration triggers the shift, it should start with /k/, probably first before /i/, and only reach /p/ last. Yet the distribution of the shift is profoundly different: In initial position (as in the numbers in (3) and (4) just above), /k/ shifts the least, followed by /p/, while /t/ shifts the most. And /t/ shifts broadly across different environments, while /p/ and /k/ shift most only in post-vocalic position.

Where we find more shift does not correspond to where there was presumably more aspiration: /k/, the most aspirated, shows by far the least shift, while /t/, in the middle in aspiration, shows the most shift. This suggests that at some point the change moved beyond its phonetic motivations – probably involving both articulation and perception – and generalized, perhaps with cross-generational acquisition playing a role. That process of generalization is where phonology takes charge. A tradition of research shows that the abstract patterning of consonants varies systematically by place of articulation (Rice 1994, 1996, examples from the latter).

First, coronals – like /t, d, s, n/ – show strong tendencies to assimilate to adjacent consonants at other places of articulation. In English, the prefixes *in-* or *un-* change the nasal to the following consonant's place, as in *u*[m]*believable* or *i*[ŋ]*conceivable*. Many languages show similar patterns, such as Korean:

(5) Korean assimilation (Rice 1996: 494, with sources and further examples)
    kotpalo   ko[pp]alo   'straight'
    han-ben   ha[mb]en   'once'
    pat-ko   pa[kk]o   'to receive'
    han-kaŋ   h[aŋk]ag   'the Han river'

Second, many languages restrict the set of consonants that can appear at right edges of prosodic domains, like in codas or word-finally. Coronals are routinely allowed where other consonants are not. Rice gives the examples of Koyukon (an Athabaskan language) and Finnish, which have both /m/ and /n/, but allow only /n/ at the ends of syllables. Spanish and Greek and myriad other languages show related restrictions.

Third, coronals can be 'transparent' to certain processes that are blocked by consonants at other places of articulation. Old High German umlaut, in some southern dialects, failed when velars, especially clusters, intervened between trigger and target, creating south-north pairs like *Innsbruck* versus *Osnabrück*, from *brukki. This did not happen with coronals.

Rice understands these phenomena in terms of how and whether consonants are given place features. Drawing again on privativity (§3.4) she focuses on where structure is or isn't assigned to a sound:

(6) Place markedness (Rice 1994)

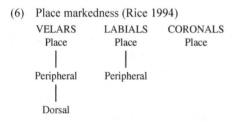

Without place features of its own, a coronal can take on features from adjoining consonants, appear in places where place structure is not allowed, or be transparent to distance assimilation. Iverson and Salmons (2006b) show that this correlates with the generalization of the Second Consonant Shift: Less structure corresponds to more shift. We need much more detail on the mechanisms and to explain how these generalizations take place.

Other parts of these shifts suggest phonetic origins and phonological generalizations. Grimm's Law involved a change of voiced stops to voiceless, and the Second Consonant Shift again provides a partial parallel. /d/ regularly becomes /t/ through much of the territory (German *tun* and *Taube* correspond to English *do* and *dove*), but /b/ and /g/ devoice only in the far southern areas. A purely phonetic story is ultimately a dead end. At noted, it is easier to voice /b/ than /g/ … maintaining vocal fold vibration in an oral stop requires keeping air moving across the glottis and the labial closure allows a far greater amount of air to build up (expanding the space of the whole mouth) than a velar (with little opportunity for expansion behind the velar closure). These phonetic patterns are well established (Gamkrelidze 1975), and suggest phonetic motivations for shifts like Grimm's Law and the High German shift, where place of articulation and stress should correlate with earlier shift. In both, shift appears to have taken place after the related shift of /p, t, k/. Many people interpret this as a kind of gap filling, where the partial or complete loss of a series of stops triggered a follow-on change. We see this with the High German shift, where /t/ has mostly shifted to become an affricate or fricative and /d/ then becomes /t/, especially in the south. Most Germanic languages have eliminated interdental fricatives, including Old High German: /θ/ becomes /d/, starting in the south and traceable through the written records of the period. This looks like a chain shift, specifically a 'pull chain' where /t/ > /ts, s/, then /d/ > /t/ and finally /θ/ > /d/.

Note how 'local' the beginnings of these changes look. The directly phonetic patterns don't automatically lead to or motivate the shift of a whole series, let alone extend to other series in a system. At the least, these have generalized from the most phonetically motivated contexts to the whole series of stops in Grimm's Law, all voiceless stops becoming fricatives and all voiced stops devoicing. And somehow the shifts of all three series (voiceless, voiced and 'voiced aspirated') are implicated. (In the High German Consonant Shift, we see somewhat more modest generalizations, but still generalizations.) If we adopt a view of speech sounds as organized in terms of distinctive features, we can readily capture these broad changes. Where we focused on local phonetic motivations in the previous chapter, it's this broader, more abstract perspective that we take now.

The chapter organization is simple: In §9.2, I sketch a simple model of grammar, a pretty traditional one (Hyman 2018) and familiar to most students of linguistics from classic generative linguistics, and sharing similarities with earlier structuralist models. I focus on the relationship between phonetics and phonology, especially how 'big' phonology is … just what parts of the realm of sounds and sound changes are attributable to this abstract system (or set of subsystems) versus other systems, including phonetics. Section 9.3 turns to a foundational issue for phonology, contrast, including issues of markedness and privativity. The discussion revolves around notions I've introduced: merger, split and chain shifts. In §9.4, I introduce a long-standing challenge for understanding the broader grammatical system, the relationship between what is actually 'active' synchronic phonology versus synchronic reflections of sound change. Section §9.5 introduces a sound change that is hard to understand without assuming that speakers have a robust abstract system of sounds. These are historical featural reversals and I argue that they deserve a place alongside chain shifts in thinking about phonological change. In §9.6, I tie these pieces together.

9.2   A model of grammar

Traditional models of grammar are modular, where elements are plucked from a lexicon and processed in assembly-line-like fashion through various stages, usually including phonology and syntax, and eventually phonetic implementation. Modules are the stations on an assembly line, where some operation takes place. Following Purnell et al. (forthcoming), I define a module as a 'distinct set of representations and computations that support a unique task,' in terms of how cognition works and how we can describe grammar as a formal system. Traditional models are strictly serial, with each step taking place in turn. Relationships are captured in terms of rules or constraints, of the type familiar from introductory exercises in phonology and elsewhere. A classic statement of how this works and how language change works in this model comes from Chomsky and Halle (1968: 249). In their focus on grammar as the linguistic competence of a speaker, they argue that:

> The rules that constitute the grammar of a particular speaker determine in detail the form of the sentences that the speaker will produce and understand. If two speakers differ in the phonetic (or semantic) interpretation they assign to sentences, this difference can only be due to some difference in the character or organization of the rules that make up their respective grammars. Consequently an observed linguistic change can have only one source – a change in the grammar that underlies the observed utterances.

That is, sound patterns are anchored in a system of phonology and sound changes reflect changes in the phonological grammar. Again, understanding sound change broadly requires attention to matters beyond just grammatical differences, as we've seen. For historical phonologists, the action is in the change in grammar but a holistic view also examines where and how those changes originate and bubble up, in phonetics and usage, and then move on to morphology and beyond.

Some today reject modularity, including some working in usage-based grammar and exemplar theory, as discussed in the previous chapter. These views often rest on evidence for frequency effects and how 'constructions' take on lives of their own in usage, storage and change. Using evidence from the ways that frequent collocations interact with phonemic categorization and phonetic processing, Hilpert (2008: 501) argues 'that syntactic and lexical knowledge are not stored in different mental modules, but rather form a continuum from heavily entrenched and conventionalized units to loosely connected elements.' These views are at odds with the highly modular views that are generally posited for human cognition, including vision (see Marr 1982). While it's beyond our immediate concern, I understand the patterns Hilpert is talking about as reflecting interactions across modules and more surface-oriented patterns rather than the deeper structures that a modular view treats in core syntax versus other modules. I suspect that these views can be reconciled.

A classic issue in the study of speech sounds comes to the center now, the 'lack of invariance' problem: The speech stream is incredibly variable – /t/ has many realizations in English, including but not limited to [t, tʰ, tˢ, tˀ, ɾ, ʔ] – yet, as speakers and listeners, we filter out that variability and overwhelmingly hear the intended /t/. Port and Leary (2005) deny that language is a discrete formal system, that there is invariance anywhere. 'Generative phonology, like any symbolic phonology theory, is based on the idea that linguistic structures are made by assembling small letter-like atoms into larger structures' (2005: 958). They dismiss formal approaches to language as 'something more like a religious commitment' (2005: 950), denying underlying cognitive invariance. Until such views are developed for sound change, I leave aside these rejections of phonology.

Following general views of biology and cognition, I adopt Purnell et al.'s 'hypermodular phonology' (forthcoming). The basic view is given here:

(7) Hypermodular phonology (Purnell et al. forthcoming)

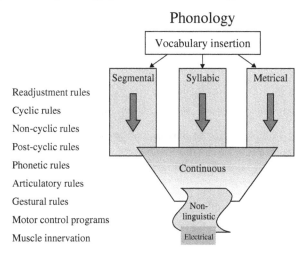

This model differs from earlier ones in a couple of ways. First, we assume some parallel processing, rather than strictly serial ordering. Traditional models were often like assembly lines, with operations happening at successive stages in ordered modules. Models like Optimality Theory explore doing phonology in a single pass, all at once (see below, §9.5). Second, these modules are not hermetically sealed off from one another, but can and do interact. Other models range from having no real distinction among modules to rigid separation. I again assume that abstract foundations for sound patterns must be integrated into the grammar without determining every piece of what happens in the grammar.

9.3 Contrast

The lack of invariance problem refers to the absence of simple and clear acoustic or perceptual correlates of contrasts, while contrasts are robust nonetheless. Historical phonologists focus on how those contrasts work as a system, generally treating contrasts as anchored in features. (Recall that whether phonological features are universal or not is under debate but not directly relevant.) Drawing on Modified Contrastive Specification (MCS, Dresher 2009; Dresher et al. 1994), we can treat two phonemes as contrasting based on a single feature, specified for one of the phonemes, but not the other (assuming privativity, §3.4). In Chapter 3, I argued that a contrast between sounds like those in English (or Somali or Cantonese) written as /t/ versus /d/ in the Roman alphabet involves a feature like [spread glottis] marking the /t/ and no marking on the /d/.

If we take specification literally – as an instruction from the brain to initiate some articulatory activity, such as opening the glottis – the absence of instructions allows freedom of variation. The most variable consonant by far in Germanic languages, /r/, has been argued to be completely unspecified. Dresher (2009: 45) reviews arguments by Trubetzkoy on this:

(8)   German consonants and the position of /r/ (Dresher 2009: 45, building on
       Trubetzkoy)

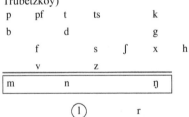

Dresher distinguishes /r/ from every other phoneme this way:

1. The horizontal line divides obstruents from sonorants, including /r/.
2. [Nasal] sets off the three consonants in the box.
3. This leaves only the liquids, of which /l/ is marked for lateral, leaving /r/ entirely unspecified.

That is, he introduces a feature [obstruent] to bracket off most of the inventory. From the remaining sounds, sonorants, the feature [nasal] captures all but the liquids, and [lateral] distinguishes those two, leaving /r/ unspecified for everything below [sonorant]. This 'Successive Division Algorithm' gives us a way of formalizing hypotheses about what information about particular segments is phonologically relevant within a system (Hall 2011: 15–16). The tree below in (9) is a graphic representation of the Successive Division Algorithm for German /r/:

(9) Contrastive hierarchy for German sonorants (adapted from Dresher 2009: 45)

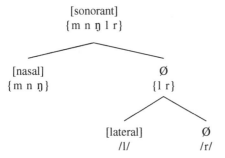

Trubetzkoy concludes that /r/'s phonological content is 'purely negative: it is not a vowel, not a specific obstruent, not a nasal, nor an l' (1969: 73, also in Dresher 2009: 44). Natvig and Salmons (2020) and Natvig (2020) show that West and North Germanic rhotics show stunning variation, with (1) places of articulation from apical or even labialized to velar and uvular and (2) manners from fricative to vowel, surfacing in dozens of variants in German, Dutch and English dialects (see Cruttenden 2001: 201 on English). The absence of specification, recognized since Trubetzkoy, licenses that variation. Natvig (2020, also Natvig and Salmons 2020) argues that such underspecification allows or promotes variability, yielding often dozens of rhotic variants. In a similar vein, Hall (2011: 42) hypothesizes that 'the contrastive absence of a privative feature is not subject to enhancement.'[2] At the same time, rhotics show what Chabot (2019) calls 'procedural stability' – where evidence from Polish palatalization and Brazilian Portuguese phonotactics shows a kind of 'phonological unity' – and 'diachronic stability.' Historically, Natvig (2020) argues that phonological representations remain stable, while phonetic completions and implementations may change. No single articulatory or acoustic characterization can unify the set of rhotics, though at an abstract level we see almost paradoxical unity.

Turning to how mergers and splits can change a phonological system, consider two kinds of cases we've already discussed – mergers and splits. Some mergers or splits can be described without changing the inventory of features used for the system – the merger of English /a/ with /ɔ/ removes a segment from the system by eliminating [round] in this pair but you may need it to mark [o] – but others can and do remove or introduce featural specifications, respectively. In terms of splits, pre-Old English only distinguished front from back vowels, as shown in (10), below.

The logic of the features and the tree is as above with /r/, though we fill in Ø values with unspecified features in parentheses. The feature hierarchies shown

---

2   This proposal is independent of but probably consistent with Eckert and Labov (2017: 491): 'change in the more abstract levels of phonological organization is not likely to generate meaning.'

in (10a) and (11a) show the ordering of features built into the trees, that [low] dominates [front] and so on.

(10) Pre i-umlaut Old English

    (a) [low] > [back] > [high] > [round]

    (b)

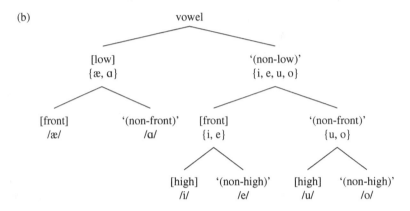

(11) Old English

    (a) [low] > [back] > [high]

    (b)

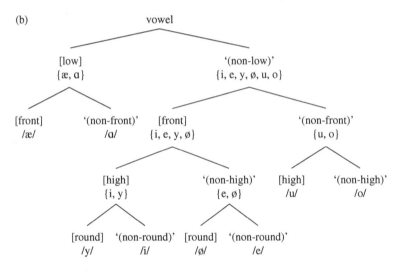

When umlaut vowels became contrastive that added featural complexity, a role for [round]. Building on the featural description of umlaut in §1.1, these figures are from Purnell et al. (2019), and we understand the relevant change this way:

> the front round vowels start as 'allophones' at the end of the phonology by way of dimensions being completed, and by some fill rules and some enhancement processes taking place. At that stage, /u/ and /o/ will be specified with [round] and the /y/ will have the [front] added by these latter rules which are necessary to account for the process, but unnecessary and even undesirable at earlier phonological stages.

Phonological contrasts often get enhanced phonetically; speakers provide additional phonetic cues to phonological contrasts. As Henton et al. (1992: 96) put it for laryngeal distinctions, 'some contrasts ... use a large number of cues for each distinctive feature.' (Features connect with phonetics but indirectly, and can't be reduced to simple phonetic realizations, see Salmons 2020.) Here, [back] was active in the grammar but [round] was surely present in an enhancing role, so a natural candidate for being added to the hierarchy. Phonetics plays a supporting role to phonology.

This theory provides a constrained model of changes. Oxford (2015: 317) proposes principles for change in hierarchies:

1. Contrastivist hypothesis: Only contrastive features are phonologically active.
2. Sisterhood merger hypothesis: Structural mergers apply to 'contrastive sisters.'
3. Contrast shift hypothesis: Contrastive hierarchies can change over time.
4. Segmental re-analysis hypothesis: A segment may be re-analyzed as having a different contrastive status.

The first is a statement about privativity, and I have just supplemented this with a prediction about unspecified material: It is prone to greater, freer variation. On the second, Oxford sees sisterhood merger as meaning that mergers of segments in diachronic change always occur in a 'sisterhood' relationship, eliminating parallel branches in a contrastive hierarchy. The addition of phonemes should follow the inverse hypothesis in appearing in the tree in a 'sisterhood' relationship with the segment they newly contrast with. In (11), with the addition of front rounded vowels to the system, [round] is included at the bottom of the tree. Later, when English lost front rounded vowels, this way of marking contrasts was no longer needed.

Oxford treats vowel changes in the history of Algic, Algonquian plus two distantly related languages, Yurok and Wiyot. Proto-Algonquian had four vowel qualities plus a length distinction, which I assume is structural, not featural, with Spahr (2016), Purnell et al. (2019) and Cudworth (2019). (That is, length is about a segment taking up two slots in a word rather than being a segment marked by a feature like [long], which he includes as [lng].)[3]

(12) Proto-Algic vowels

| i, iː | u, uː |
| ɛ, ɛː | a, aː |

Phonological activity is our guide to what is contrastive, as noted. *i palatalizes *t to [tʃ, ʃ], so [coronal] must be active. When an old sequence *wɛ becomes *o (or *u), the rounding is preserved on the vowel, so that [labial] must be active. Without working through the details, Oxford uses this analysis of features and including [lng]:

---

3   The traditional symbols don't match their positions in the vowel space. <ɛ> often patterns as a low vowel, as in the vowel space in (12). What is given as <u, uː> in (12) is usually written as <o, oː>.

(13) Contrastive hierarchy for Proto-Algonquian vowels
      [labial] > [coronal] > [low]

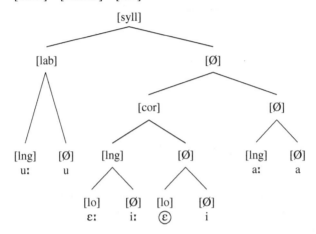

His [labial] and [coronal] capture frontness/backness and rounding. /a, aː/ are not specified at all, while [low] gets the contrast between /ɛ, ɛː/ and /i, iː/.

In one branch, Eastern Algonquian (which includes languages like Delaware, Mi'gmaq and Mahican), we see two major developments:

(14) Proto-Eastern Algonquian vowel changes and vowel system
      a. The length contrast in high vowels is lost, with short merging with long, leaving /iː, uː/
      b. /ɛ/ becomes shwa
         iː   uː
                 ə
         ɛː   a, aː

Because the length merger is shared by both high vowels, they must have been sisters, which requires adding [high] to the top of the hierarchy, as below.

(15) Contrastive hierarchy for Eastern Algonquian vowels
      [high] > [labial] > [coronal] > [low]

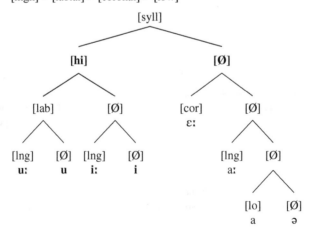

This is a relatively radical reorganization of the system in terms of contrast, more dramatic than it might appear from the surface inventories, but Oxford shows that different later developments in Eastern daughters follow naturally from this hierarchy. For example, Maliseet-Passamaquoddy and Mi'gmaq merge /a/ with /ə/, a straightforward result given that they are sisters in the tree above (Oxford 2015: 331–40).

Taking contrast seriously allows powerful generalizations about the abstract patterning of sounds. These are often hard to capture without abstract structure and are seldom the focus of work by those who don't posit (much) abstract structure.

9.4   Reversals[4]

Splits and mergers point to a role for an abstract system and the presence of features in sound change. In recent years, scholars have given important examples of another kind of support for this view – reversals – situations where features systematically flip between two classes, often involving tone. Let's look first at a flip that involves a vowel feature and then a case of tonal reversal.

To the first, Andersen (2006) compares two closely related Western Nilotic languages, Jumjum and Mayak. Both languages contrast vowels by the feature [ATR] (advanced tongue root, for present purposes much like a tense/lax distinction, also reflected in the transcriptions), but cognates show a featural reversal in high vowels: Jumjum [+ATR] vowels (/i, u/) correspond to Mayak [-ATR] vowels (/ɪ, ʊ/) and vice versa.

(16) ATR reversal in Jumjum

	Jumjum		**Mayak**	
/ii/	wìil	/ɪɪ/	wʊɪl	'tail'
/uu/	búuy	/ʊʊ/	bʊʊr	'shoulder'
/ɪɪ/	pɪ̂ɪk	/ii/	pii	'water'
/ʊʊ/	lòʊm	/uu/	luum	'grass'

Andersen accounts for this by carefully ordered steps (2006: 26, reformatted to signal stages):

- The reconstructed Proto-Western Nilotic vowel system consisted of the five [-ATR] vowel qualities /ɪ, ɛ, a, ɔ, ʊ/ and the five [+ATR] vowel qualities /i, e, ʌ, o, u/.
- Proto-Western Nilotic [+ATR] */i/ and */u/ shifted to and merged with [+ATR] */e/ and */o/, probably via diphthongization to */ie/ and */uo/.
- Next, Proto-Western Nilotic [-ATR] */ɪ/ and */ʊ/ changed to [+ATR] /i/ and /u/, thus filling up the space left by the lowering of */i/ and */u/. Finally, [+ATR] */e/ and */o/, now subsuming original */i/ and */u/, shifted to [-ATR] /ɪ/ and /ʊ/.

---

4   I benefitted greatly here from discussion with my fall 2018 class on Sound Change.

- As a result of this sequence of changes in pre-Jumjum, the high [-ATR] vowels of Proto-Western Nilotic have become high [+ATR] vowels in Jumjum, and high [+ATR] vowels of Proto-Western Nilotic have become high [-ATR] vowels in Jumjum.

This language showed familiar vowel mergers, losing a height distinction between high and mid vowels in the [+ATR] series. That gap was filled by [-ATR] vowels at the same places of articulation becoming [+ATR].

Our second example comes from Franconian languages spoken in Germany and the Low Countries which have evolved tone. One dialect, Arzbach, appears to have 'flipped' the tonal rules of closely related ones (though this reversal is not complete). Köhnlein (2015, and elsewhere) develops a story of how these tones arose and how the reversal took place. The patterns involve level versus contour tones, tones that maintain a consistent height over their duration and those that change from high to low or vice versa:

(17) Contour and level tones
        a. Contour Tone   b. Level Tone

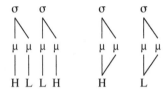

Köhnlein's project is not simply to understand how the tones arose (tonogenesis) but how they developed from there (2015: 232):

> in some languages, durational contrasts between level tones and contour tones can vary as a function of the 'linguistic age' of a tonal contrast, that is, the period of time since the contrast entered the language. In some systems with a 'younger' tone contrast, contour tones are phonetically longer than level tones. When such systems age, however, the durational differences can decrease or can even be reversed; there can even be cases where, in the present day system, originally longer contour tones are now shorter than originally shorter level tones.

Some sequences are phonetically longer than others, e.g. high vowels /i, y, u/ are somewhat shorter than low vowels, like /a/, or even mid vowels. These varieties also had durational differences between open and closed syllables, like the nominative singular of 'house' *haus versus the dative singular *hausə, where the diphthong was longer in the second word than the first. Like many other Germanic varieties, these underwent apocope, loss of the final schwa, leaving the length difference.

Köhnlein argues for a phonetic tonal contour over both types before contrastive tone arose. As shown in (18), the longer ones become Class 1, showing contour tones, while shorter ones become Class 2, with level tone. A longer syllable nucleus allows more time for the contour to be realized.

(18) Idealized tonal contours before accent genesis in Franconian

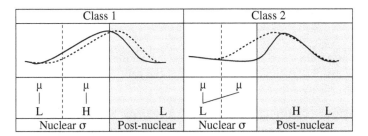

Pre-Class 1		Pre-Class 2	
μ μ		μ μ	
L	H L	L	H L
Nuclear σ	Post-nuclear	Nuclear σ	Post-nuclear

Learners and speakers eventually reinterpreted these patterns as tones, incorporating the contour in Class 1 but understanding Class 2 as level, so that they start to produce Class 2 as more level than it had been. This parallels the kind of small phonetic differences that lead to big, general sound changes we've seen in case after case.

(19) Idealized tonal contours after accent genesis in Franconian

Class 1		Class 2	
μ μ		μ μ	
L H	L	L	H L
Nuclear σ	Post-nuclear	Nuclear σ	Post-nuclear

Still later, in some dialects, the tones reverse their durational relationship. Köhnlein sees a couple of motivations for this effect of the phonology on the phonetics, perceptual and articulatory. For one, listeners need more time to recognize a level tone, to hear that non-movement, while we pick up on tonal change, contours, quickly. At the same time, he argues, it's not so easy to hold a level tone for a long time, motivating speakers to shorten.

(20) Durational reversal in Franconian

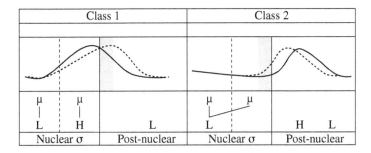

Class 1		Class 2	
μ μ		μ μ	
L H	L	L	H L
Nuclear σ	Post-nuclear	Nuclear σ	Post-nuclear

Here are Köhnlein's developmental stages:

(21) Five developmental stages in interactions between tone and duration on
two types of bimoraic sonorant units (Class 1 and Class 2), after Köhnlein
(2015)

Stage	Process	Description
1	Durational contrast	Bimoraic Class 1 has a phonetically longer duration than bimoraic Class 2
2	Pitch contrast	Longer Class 1 correlates with stronger pitch movements than shorter Class 2
3	Tonal contrast	Longer Class 1 develops a contour tone, shorter Class 2 a level tone
4	Durational adjustment	Weakening of the original durational contrast through shortening of Class 1 under the influence of the contour tone and/or lengthening of Class 2 under the influence of the level tone
5	Durational reversal	Originally longer Class 1 is phonetically shorter than originally shorter Class 2

He concludes this after drawing evidence for parallels from a set of languages
that have developed part of the way down this road:

> in such systems, tonal contrasts can arise as a consequence of the fact that
> phonetically longer units can host stronger pitch movements than shorter
> units. After such a pitch contrast has been phonologized (and is phonetically
> extended), there is a tendency to shorten the unit with the contour tone and to
> lengthen the unit with the level tone. It has been argued that in Franconian, this
> has led to durational reversals between two word classes, where the originally
> longer class, Class 1, is now shorter than its originally shorter counterpart,
> Class 2.

To summarize, then, the original relationship between tone and duration was
motivated by production – it takes time to create a tonal contour. The reversal,
Köhnlein argues, is driven by shortening by perception – you hear contour faster
than level tones. The phonologization of tone allows new phonetic effects. This
kind of tonal change is strikingly different from those we discussed earlier, and
shows particularly rich interactions between phonetics and the abstract system
it is part of, especially in reversal. In both these examples of reversal, the lower
level motivations are phonetic but lead to changes in representation and changes
to the features needed for representations.

9.5   Synchrony and diachrony

Labov (1989: 85) summarizes an old chestnut this way (emphasis added):

> One of the strongest arguments for the separation of synchronic and dia-
> chronic linguistics is *that children do not know the history of the language*

they are learning. As the grammar of the language must be the rule system that is learned and internalized by the language learner, and the child is ignorant of its history, it follows that historical linguistics is irrelevant for students of synchronic linguistics.

He shows that children acquire patterns of variation anchored in history, a point we explore now.

We have talked from the outset about how historical phonology and the study of sound change broadly have played major roles in synchronic phonological theory, including with the *Sound Pattern of English*. Some synchronic theories are explicitly and deeply rooted in sound change, like Evolutionary Phonology and Natural Phonology. Others, though, seem ill-suited to sound change. Optimality Theory (OT) made a splash in synchronic phonological theory when it arose in the early 1990s and continues to be used, but I have hardly mentioned it. The core of OT is seeing grammar as shaped not by the application of rules but rather by the evaluation of conflicting constraints, which allows the emergence only of an optimal form. Early OT rejected modularity (McCarthy and Prince 1995; Prince and Smolensky 1993), a position later abandoned (McCarthy 2008). While there were knife fights over this issue in synchronic phonology and allied areas, it never made much sense diachronically: Optimality Theory has made contributions to this area (Gess 1999 or Holt 2015), and, I argue, this work didn't go farther for a good reason: Synchronic phonology may well look monostratal but any reasonable historical record of complex sound changes shows patterns of layering of change, and accumulation of stepwise changes.

This is ameliorated by Kiparsky's 'Stratal OT' (2006, and elsewhere). But all these views require some kind of division of labor between synchronic phonology – what's happening in the speaker's or listener's head – and historical phonology – what is the product that history has handed us as learners and users. People can argue about whether complex synchronic phonological relationships require serial computations – widely discussed in regard to 'opacity' – but we see unfolding of sound change as layered developments over generations.

The problem of opacity in synchronic analyses is real. Take Idsardi's definition (2000: 338): 'An opaque generalization is a generalization that does crucial work in the analysis, but which does not hold of the output form.' That is, the steps in a derivational analysis can yield surface forms that do not directly reflect some rule that applied along the way. This book is filled with patterns that are historically related but synchronically opaque to speakers, often to the point that linguists don't connect them by rule today (though see the discussion of Lightner below). The relationships between *mouse/mice* and *foot/feet* or the palatalization of an old /k/ in 'choose' are utterly straightforward historically but we cannot see the /i/ that triggered umlaut (leaving aside other changes) or know that there was once a front vowel in *ceosan*. Opaque relationships like this are pervasive synchronically and have been difficult to capture without serial derivations. Diachronically, these layers are not something posited in the mind of a speaker but reflect historical processes which can and do layer in this way.

To see the value of knowing what's diachronic versus synchronic, consider the German velar nasal, /ŋ/ (Lass 1984; Vennemann 1970; the behavior of

English ŋ is similar to German). It participates in minimal pairs with other nasal consonants, such as *Sim* 'sim' (as in sim card), *Sinn* 'sense' and *sing* 'sing!'. Yet in other ways, it's an odd bird. Among other things, it doesn't occur initially: *mein* 'my', *nein* 'no' but *ngein. Even in codas, it occurs only after short vowels but not long vowels or diphthongs or other coda consonants, so that words like *Wurm* 'worm' are fine, but *wurng is impossible and sounds as weird to German ears as the English form would. (We have a few onomatopoeic forms like *boing*.) On views assuming much abstraction, these patterns are easily accounted for: There is no phoneme /ŋ/; where we find that surface form, it reflects an underlying /ng/ where the nasal assimilates to the velar /g/ and /g/ deletes. An alternative view treats these as historical processes – /ŋ/ exists in Germanic languages only where there was an /n/ followed by a velar consonant; /g/ was widely deleted in those positions. Because /ng/ was never a possible onset and because two coda consonants did not occur after long vowels, diphthongs or short vowel + consonant, those gaps are historical reflections of where /ng/ didn't occur, not part of synchronic derivations, parallel to tense vowel + /ʃ/ in §7.5. If phonology is about what's going in our minds, the question becomes whether we are engaging in assimilation and deletion each time we produce [ŋ]. (Productivity is one way that we gauge whether a process is synchronically active.)

As noted in §3.3 and since, both structuralist and generative traditions have tended to load these things into synchronic grammar. Lightner (1983, also Macaulay and Salmons 2017) pursues this program with vigor to its logical conclusion. English pairs like *long* and *length* or *foul* and *filth* are historically related, with the nouns derived from other words with a suffix *-th*, vowel shortening and umlaut. While not many speakers connect *foul* and *filth*, some are still recognizably related (*warm* and *warmth*). Lightner (1983: 203–6) insists that an 'analysis of *long, length* as separate lexical entries is not a rational possibility,' as it would represent a 'failure to grasp linguistically significant generalizations' (1983: 206). He does this for all recognizable relationships, even between native Germanic stock and Romance loanwords such as *father ~ paternal*, making Grimm's Law a synchronic alternation between native and borrowed words.

If you recall the premise of Evolutionary Phonology from Chapter 3 (Blevins 2004: 23) you see the counterpoint to these abstract synchronic analyses:

> Principled diachronic explanations for sound patterns have priority over competing synchronic explanations unless independent evidence demonstrates, beyond reasonable doubt, that a synchronic account is warranted.

Explanations for German velar nasal, for nouns derived with *-th* or Grimm-like alternations in the English lexicon are profoundly historical: They continue historical patterns and give history a clear role for understanding contemporary patterns and alternations. (What this means for explaining synchronic phonology is a step beyond our immediate interest.) Labov (1989: 85) argues that 'many stable linguistic variables with no synchronic motivation show historical continuity with little change over long periods of time.' This implies that synchronic phonology literally cannot capture parts of synchronic sound patterns. Whether you accept that, a lot of synchronic phonology makes more sense if you know the historical developments that led to it. Many of the most challenging issues in synchrony are straightforward in diachrony, including opacity.

9.6   Conclusion

We have shifted gears from an examination of low-level phonetics in the earliest stirrings of sound change to looking at the abstract structures and systems that learners and users fit fully developed changes into. Adopting a model that involves grammatical modules not only allows us to talk directly about an abstract sound system as a whole but to see patterns that do not straightforwardly align with the low-level phonetic motivations discussed in the previous chapter. This includes important changes to the system itself, like the features needed to represent contrasts, as they arise (in splits, for example) or disappear (in some mergers). Reversals illustrate another type of far-reaching change to the system *qua* system.

I have given evidence for 'phonological activity' in this chapter, but I have also given evidence for phonetic activity. They are different creatures with different character and impact. We've got phonetic and phonological motivations and mechanics and they are often distinct. In the view presented here, phonetics and phonology are connected, in synchrony and diachrony, but the relationship is a mediated one, as follows from a modular analysis. As my colleague Eric Raimy quips, phonetics presents a menu that phonology selects from.

Without venturing too far into the realm of synchrony, I have urged you to consider critically where and how we should be thinking about patterns in terms of what is going on in the speaker's mind versus what is inherited history.

While the obvious focus in the study of sound change falls on phonetics and phonology – the sound system itself – sound change reverberates far beyond that, with real effects in other parts of the grammar, especially morphology. Let us turn to those patterns.

Beyond this book

1.   Digging deeper: Data

If you've been engaging with these sections along the way, you now have a set of sound changes that you understand. The notion of 'phonological activity' used here is still new and hasn't been applied explicitly to many changes. Can you interpret any of the changes you've been looking at in terms of phonological activity? Do any of them raise potential questions or problems for how I've sketched phonological activity in sound change?

2.   Digging deeper: Theory

Read into the theory of contrast sketched here, drawing on Dresher, Hall, Purnell et al., and others. The principles proposed by Oxford (2015) especially show great promise for advancing our understanding of many sound changes.

3. Moving beyond what we know

- I've suggested above that the examples discussed are more easily captured by positing phonology in a robust and fairly traditional system. In some cases, like with rhotics or ATR reversal, I don't see how we would account for the patterns without phonology. Maybe you can?
- Many readers of this volume will find my dismissal of Optimality Theory too quick. If you're invested in OT, make the counter-case!
- Read Eckert and Labov (2017) and compare their proposal to how I've presented the relationship between specification and variation here. Are they compatible? Do they maybe even enhance one another?

10

Sound Change Beyond the Sound System

10.1 Introduction

Look at this Old English text and translation (from https://www.arts.gla.ac.uk/stella/readings/OE/anglo_chron.htm) and note the boldfaced bits.

Anno 449. Her Martianus and Valentinus onfeng**on** rice, and ricsod**on** seofon winter. And on hiera dag**um** Hengest and Horsa, fram Wyrtgeorne gelaþode, Bretta cyninge, gesoht**on** Bretene on **þæm stede** þe is genemned Ypwinesfleot, ærest Brett**um** to fultume, ac hie eft on hie fuht**on**.

Anno 449. In this year [lit. here] Martianus and Valentinus succeed**ed** to [lit. received] kingship, and rul**ed** seven years. And in their day**s** Hengest and Horsa, invit**ed** by Vortigern, king of [the] Britons, **came** to Britain **at the place** which is called Ebbsfleet, first as a help to [the] **Britons**, but they afterwards **fought** against them.

The Old versus Modern English passages illustrate easily the most famous example in historical linguistics of how sound change connects to morphology and syntax. We don't need a full analysis, but the bolded parts are inflections that English no longer has, -*on* for verbs with a plural subject, -*e* on a verb with a singular subject as well as -*um* to mark dative plurals and *þæm stede*, a dative singular form.

Two of the striking differences between Old English and the language you're reading now are in the marking of morphological categories, including case, and word order. In Old English, in a 'dog bites man' versus 'man bites dog' sentence, if you're using articles you distinguish for the relevant masculine nouns who is the biter (*se hund, se wer*, etc.) versus the bitee (*þone hund, þone wer*). While those examples involve more than unstressed vowels (an important point unto itself), Old English makes a good number of distinctions that are lost by Middle English, as these forms show:

(1) Homophony of Old English inflections in Middle English, Minkova (2014: 229)

Expected (Classical) Old English	Late Middle English		
<-e> for dat.sg. (masc., fem., neuter)	<-e>	[-(ə)]	
<-a> for gen.pl. (masc., fem., neuter)		<-e>	[-(ə)]
<-u> for nom./acc.sg. (fem., neuter)		<-e>	[-(ə)]
<-an> for weak nominal declensions		<-en>	[-(ə)n]
<-um> for dat.pl. (all nouns)		<-en>	[-(ə)n]
<-on> for pret.ind.pl.		<-en>	[-(ə)n]

The word order is not particularly surprising compared to the modern language, but earlier English allowed vastly greater flexibility than the modern language. In main clauses, for example, inflected verbs were typically in second position, with subjects after the inflected verb (example from van Gelderen 2018: 19):

(2) V2 in Old English

Ðes ilces geares **com** se abbot heanri of angeli æfter æsterne to burch.
This same year **came** the Abbot Henry of Anglia after Easter to Peterborough
The same year, the Abbot Henry of Anglia came after Easter to Peterborough.

Over time, English has basically lost case marking, aside from some pronouns (*she* ~ *her*, etc., but *it* ~ *it* and *you* ~ *you*) and word order has become vastly more fixed than it once was. These are widely thought to be closely interconnected. Today, the subject is generally before the verb and the direct object after. The traditional chain of thinking is that sound change – the reduction and loss of unstressed final syllables, called the Laws of Finals in Germanic scholarship – triggers the loss of morphology and that the loss of morphology drives the syntactic change, the fixing of word order. Sapir (1921; and Hawkins 1985; Willis 2017; and others) characterizes the development of English in terms of 'drift,' specifically a 'drift toward the invariant word,' where phonetic weakening leads to morphological and syntactic changes (1921: 168). Like others, Sapir sees 'language as a historical product' (that's the main title of his chapters on drift), arguing (1921: 171):

> Nothing is perfectly static. Every word, every grammatical element, every locution, every sound and accent is a slowly changing configuration, molded by the invisible and impersonal drift that is the life of language. The evidence is overwhelming that this drift has a certain consistent direction.

Alas, no one has conclusively shown the connections between phonetic, phonological, morphological and syntactic changes in the history of English, and Los (2015: 49) reasonably concludes that 'Loss of case does not immediately and automatically lead to less flexible word orders.' Likewise, as we saw above, reduction and loss of unstressed vowels cannot account for all the loss of morphology. The most famous story about how sound change connects to morphology and syntax is at best not so clear.

The rest of this chapter is organized around the relationship between sound change and other modules of grammar: Morphology, syntax and the lexicon. Since Chapter 1 I have shown that sound change is intertwined with morphology in rich ways. We'll flesh that out in §10.2 and treat grammaticalization separately in §10.3. I'll sketch some parallels in syntax in §10.4. Less often discussed but equally important is the relationship between sound change and the lexicon, whether sound change can be constrained by its potential effects on the lexicon, as in §10.5.

10.2   Sound change and morphology

The historical English patterns described above hold across Germanic, Romance, parts of Slavic, Hindi and so on: These languages have lost morphology over time, and even where it could not be proven in a court of law, people inevitably point their fingers at the same suspect: Sound change. Vennemann (1975: 293, cited in Willis 2017: 500) goes so far as to claim that 'Every morphological system is destroyed in time by phonological change.' Because 'in time' is potentially unrestricted, we cannot disprove the claim, but some languages with already complex morphology have increased rather than reduced the number of categories they mark. While Proto-Uralic nominal case could have been 'destroyed' over time, the Balto-Finnic branch has instead added more cases (Harris and Campbell 1995: 89–90).

Many human languages have been morphologically complex as far back as we can reconstruct, and even massive sound changes have not disturbed the core patterns. I've given numerous examples of sound changes in Algonquian. These languages spread across most of the breadth of North America and the diversification of the family is usually dated to 2,500–3,000 years ago (Pentland 1979: 329–31). Yet, all members of the family, even the most phonologically divergent ones, reshaped by restructuring of the vowel system, consonant system and basic prosody, have retained famously intricate morphology, with verbs often composed of three derivational pieces. Verbs are further divided into transitive and intransitive but also by whether the subject or object is animate versus inanimate, as in (3).

(3)   Algonquian verbs and animacy (from Macaulay forthcoming)

		Subject	**Object**
Animate Intransitive	AI	animate	
Inanimate Intransitive	II	inanimate	
Transitive Animate	TA		animate
Transitive Inanimate	TI		inanimate

Almost all Algonquian languages further retain complex morphological features such as one called 'Initial Change,' creating alternations where words with initial long vowels ('unchanged' CV:) change by inserting /ay/, yielding 'changed' CayV:, something which serves complex functions beyond our concern. And most fundamentally, they have extensive suffixing, with often eight distinct possible slots for suffixes on verbs. These examples, and it's easy to give more, challenge Vennemann's claim: Even over thousands of years, languages in some families undergo much sound change and little or no morphological reduction, sometimes even expansion. Maybe it just hasn't happened yet, but I'd be nervous predicting that it's coming.

Even in English, where sound change seems to have 'destroyed' a morphological system, careful analysis reveals that things are at least more complex than long assumed. 'Phonetic erosion' is argued to drive case loss elsewhere. Barðdal and Kulikov (2008: 471), in their apocalyptically titled 'Case in decline', write:

> In the simplest and most trivial cases, the (partial) merger of case morphemes and, eventually, the decay of case systems is due to certain phonological changes, foremost, to the erosion of inflection in word-final position (in languages with case suffixes) or, much more rarely, in word-initial position (in languages with case prefixes). Such a development may result in case syncretism, where case distinctions are erased in their entirety.

Their first example is Arabic, where they summarize a long tradition of scholarship this way:

> The evolution of the Arabic nominal inflection provides an instructive example. In the post-classical period, Arabic undergoes a strong reduction of case endings, resulting in the loss of the original three-case system. Phonologically, these processes essentially amount to the weakening, merger, and the subsequent loss of final vowels (in particular, Nom.Sg. -*u*, Gen.Sg. -*i* and Acc.Sg. -*a*).

What are interpreted as vestiges are found in various early varieties of Arabic, but lost in more recent ones. However, as reviewed in detail by Owens (2006: 79–118), there is some evidence that Proto-Arabic lacked these case forms. Owens argues for the co-existence of case-marked and caseless varieties. He suggests that the 'acquisition of many new native speakers of Arabic in the period following the Islamic diaspora' helped tip 'the advantage towards the caseless variety' (2006: 117–18). This parallels suggestions (including by Los) that language and dialect contact was central to case loss in the history of English, as throughout Germanic.

I am not implying that sound change cannot lead to collapse of morphological distinctions, but collapse is hardly inevitable and I give these examples as a reminder that we need careful, deep analysis to confirm such accounts.

10.3 Grammaticalization

The point of this section is simple: The inverse of sound change reducing morphology is that sound change can help create new morphological categories. This is often discussed from a distinct perspective, in the now massive body of work on grammaticalization. This development from more lexical to more grammatical forms, often from free word to affix, involves semantic 'bleaching' and phonetic/phonological reduction. A classic example is the new future auxiliary in English, *gonna* < *going to*, discussed in §4.2. We can use the older or newer form for the future but the reduced form only for the future, not for motion, *I'm gonna the store. For many speakers, including me, it can be far more reduced, basically to *I'ma*, even beyond that. This is part of a broader set of developing auxiliaries, including *finna* < *fixing to* for some African American speakers. (Southern white speakers use *fixing to* as an auxiliary but without that level of reduction, to my knowledge.) Such historical processes have become the object of intense study for American Sign Language and other sign languages, see Supalla and Clark (2014) and Wilcox and Occhino (2016).

Some of the earliest important work on this topic treated Swahili verbal morphology, such as that of Givón (1971a, 1971b). For example, the modal meaning 'want', *taka*, has become a future marker, *ta*, as shown in (4).

(4) Swahili grammaticalization
  (a) ni-na-taka cheza
       I-pres-want play
       'I am about to play'
  (b) ni-ta-cheza
       I-fut.-play
       'I will play'

Other markers developed from full verbs as well. Givón showed cross-linguistic parallel developments from old verbs to new affixes, such as Spanish *habere* and *ir* coming to mark past imperfect and future, respectively, as in *compraba* 'I used to buy' versus *compraré* 'I will buy.'

Phonetic-phonological reduction has hardly been a major focus in this area and early work was often vague about motivations for it. Givón (1971a) asks:

> why do bound morphemes atrophy, undergoing phonetic bleaching? One tentative answer is that in becoming bound morphemes they also undergo a parallel change of semantic bleaching, ridding themselves of many specific lexical-semantic features but retaining a few classificatory, generic ones.

Some go farther. Hopper and Traugott (1993: 145ff.) identify two tendencies of reduction: quantitative (forms get shorter) and qualitative (phonemes in the form come from a smaller set, often coronal consonants, §9.2). This correlates with lesser prominence (in some ways the opposite of prosodic skewing discussed in §5.3). Here again is a place where future work might bear fruit.

The bigger question in terms of understanding sound change is whether other elements of grammaticalization drive reduction in sounds or vice versa. They seem to go hand in hand and that may speak to the issue of whether grammaticalization is epiphenomenal – simply the co-occurrence of semantic bleaching and phonetic-phonological reduction with increasing grammatical function – or a 'thing' unto itself. That topic would take us too far afield, but see Norde (2009) for detailed discussion.

10.4 Sound change and syntax

Willis (2017: 499) writes that 'The impact of sound change on syntax is particularly profound,' and he's right. The chain of reasoning introduced at the beginning of this chapter implies that sound change can drive not just morphological but also syntactic change. Hawkins (1985: 5) makes this explicit in the goals of his book, which describes broad syntactic differences between Modern German and Modern English:

Diachronically, I shall appeal to an old idea in a new context: it will be argued that the phonological changes that destroyed the case system in the history of English were the ultimate trigger that set in motion the syntax changes leading to the present contrasts.

This depends on accepting that sound change 'destroyed' the case system, and that the connection to syntax is mediated by morphological change. But there are cases where sound change appears to more directly impact syntax, such as the loss of verb second (V2) in the history of Welsh. Middle Welsh had complex word order, including V2, where adverbials could appear before the inflected verb without counting as the first element. Two particles, *a* and *y*, marked structures that were part of the V2 system. In the examples below, *y* in (5a) shows that the adverbial takes first position, while in (5b) *a* indicates that the subject takes first position, and the adverbial does not count for word order.

(5)   Middle Welsh (Willis 2017: 501–2)
  (a)   Yn Hardlech y bydwch seith mlyned ar ginyaw ...
        In Harlech PRT be.FUT.2PL seven years at dinner
        'In Harlech you will be at dinner for seven years ...'
  (b)   Hir bylgeint Guydyon a gyuodes.
        early.morning Gwydion PRT get.up.PST.3SG
        'Early next morning, Gwydion got up.'

Willis (2017, and earlier work) shows that these two particles merge into schwa in the sixteenth century. Without these particles as cues to V2, learners were unable to acquire the system, interpreting a sentence like (5a) as verb-initial with an optional adverbial element. This merger drives other changes leading to Welsh as a verb-initial language.

10.5   Sound change and the lexicon

Under most theories, languages have a mental lexicon, a dictionary of forms connected with meanings and other information, including irregularities that can't be generated by rule, such as forms of the verb *to be* in English.

Hawkins (1985: 28ff., drawing on Sapir) extends drift down to the level of lexical semantics. German (and earlier English) generally has more precise word meanings than Modern English, where words have broader lexical semantics. For instance, in English we 'put on' or 'take off' clothes while German has a set of distinctions: *anziehen* for coats, gloves and such; *aufsetzen* for hats and wigs; *anlegen* for robes, armor and such; *umbinden* for ties and scarves; *umlegen* for necklaces; and *anstecken* for rings and brooches. Hawkins ties the 'collapse' of semantic distinctions back to drift, building on Sapir's comment that 'The English vocabulary is a rich medley because each English word wants its own castle' (1921: 170).

Other connections between sound change and the lexicon exist. We have already talked about lexical diffusion, which shifts sound change in a sense from phonology to something about the lexicon, where individual words change. We have also already dealt with one other kind of effect in the lexicon beyond the usual sense of morphology: umlaut in English was clearly once morphological but the traces we see today – such as a handful of irregular plurals and some derivational patterns, §1.1 – are easily captured in terms of forms stored in the lexicon rather than generated by morphological operations, on the view of grammar adopted here (recall Lightner's work in §9.5).

A core issue of sound change and the lexicon is the notion that there is pressure in language change to avoid creating homophony. The idea goes back earlier, but is widely associated with Martinet's notion of 'functional load' (*rendement fonctionel*, 1952, and elsewhere), how much 'work' a contrast does for creating distinctions. Blevins and Wedel (2009) explore the notion that sound change can be inhibited if it would create (too much) homophony. If sound change is 'blind' in the Neogrammarian sense (to use the traditional term quoted above) this shouldn't matter, and sound change can create massive homophony.

One good example of sound change that creates considerable homophony comes from Algonquian. As Goddard (1974, 1994), Pentland (1979) and many others show, Arapaho and Atsina have lost old *k entirely, while Cheyenne has partially lost it, illustrated in (6) from Goddard (1974: 107):

(6) Proto-Algonquian *k-loss in Arapaho and Atsina
     PA *mekwenta:kani throat > *mei?to:on   > Arapaho *béitóo*, Atsina *byíitóoo*
     PA *ki:šo?θwa sun   > *i:šo?š   > Arapaho *iisíís* Atsina *íisíis*

Pentland calculates the frequency of segments in Algonquian and finds that:

> Proto-Algonquian *k is by far the most common consonant: more than one-fifth of all stems begin with *k, and in texts *k occurs about 110 times in every thousand units (counting all single segments and consonant clusters as separate units).

This change seems unexpected on many fronts, including the loss of one of only three oral stops in the language, including initial position, a relatively uncommon environment for loss. But does homophony avoidance weigh against such a change?

Sampson (2013) takes the position that arguments for functional load have been so imprecisely formulated that they are not useful, ultimately not falsifiable. More importantly, he lays out the relevant history of Mandarin Chinese, maintaining that it has developed so much homophony that it challenges any notion of homophony avoidance by sound change. This language has undergone numerous sound changes creating new homophones, including loss of final *p, t, k*, merger of final *m, n*, simplification of the vowel system, and so on. He concludes: 'Far from Mandarin avoiding them, one is almost tempted to see this language as having selected homophony-creating changes' (2013: 590).

Tying back in to the work of Blevins and Wedel mentioned above, Kaplan (2015) directly takes up the challenge to provide a precise and falsifiable version of homophony avoidance and to test it, focusing on this: 'The more homophones a sound change would create, the less likely it is to occur' (2015: 269). She reviews several recent studies (including Wedel et al. 2013) that provide clear quantitative support for this hypothesis: 'on average, actual sound changes should result in few homophones relative to the space of possible sound changes. This is precisely the finding of several recent investigations' (Kaplan 2015: 274). She goes on to make a point that has not often been considered (2015: 274):

> although homophony avoidance by itself does not predict sound change perfectly, neither do other well-known tendencies. We know that [s] frequently changes to [h], and that one word may be rebuilt on analogy with a morphologically related word; what we do not know is exactly WHICH [s]s will debuccalize, or WHICH forms will be subject to analogy, or when. But we can make predictions about how likely it is that a given sound change will occur in a particular situation, and we can improve our predictions by basing them on the best information available. That information now includes the effect of functional load.

This is certainly in the spirit of this book: We need to understand not only the full set of factors that play a role in sound change but also how they interact, which factors play what roles at what point in change, in view of all the data.

10.6   Conclusion

It is easy, for some people almost inevitable, to see sound change as at the center of a bigger world, helping account for a lot of synchronic phonology and morphology. Sound change is situated in the broader context of language change and language structure.

In the complex and still controversial case of English, if sound change drives changes in morphology, syntax and the lexicon, it is an indirect chain of changes. In other examples, such as the loss of V2 in Welsh, the link appears more direct. The connections are more direct and immediate in the usual views of grammaticalization, where the reduction and neutralization of sounds goes hand in hand with changes in grammatical status and semantics. Discussed less commonly but still important is the relationship between sound change and our mental lexicon. The old notion of 'functional load' has come back, and even lexical semantics has been tied to sound change, if very indirectly.

As we focus more on connections and interactions across modules, there is much more to be done to understand how sound change – and synchronic sound patterns themselves – fit into grammar and language change. With that, let us step back to the bigger picture.

Beyond this book

1.   Digging deeper: Data

Some have argued that sound change can be morphologically conditioned. A search for claims of morphological conditioning of sound change will yield a lot, quite possibly for languages you're interested in. Find and probe a couple of those.

2. Digging deeper: Theory

I have laid out the bare bones of how I see grammar as it bears on sound change: Modular, with robust phonetic and phonological components, and so on. Many readers will be used to working with very different models of grammar. If you're one of those people, look for places where your views do or don't fit with what's presented here. Do you see good historical tests that would distinguish the two views?

3. Moving beyond what we know

If you have some background in a particular phonological theory (or more than one!), how does it handle sound change and connect to understanding sound change?

Part 5

The bigger picture

11

Conclusion: Toward a Synthesis

11.1 Introduction

It's time to close the circle that opened Chapter 1. This chapter revisits the wide-angle look at sound change over a broad span of time, returning to the example of umlaut and arguing for a life cycle, in the spirit of Kiparsky and others before and since, but in a restricted sense. A sound change can start in low-level phonetic processes, say assimilations in rapid speech, which then become phonologized in later generations, often moving through different levels of the phonology. The results can be encoded in morphological alternations, and changes to morphology lead to the loss of all but lexical remnants of those alternations. Umlaut in Germanic shows that full set of developments.

The history of West Germanic umlaut gives glimpses into two central issues that have been systematically developed throughout the book: (1) how sound change unfolds over time and (2) how we need to draw on a broad set of theories and analytical tools to understand sound change. Each chapter – albeit not in the order of a 'life cycle' – underpins that broader case in some particular arena, with case studies at less remote time depths, allowing us to see change closer up.

This closing chapter draws together some of those threads (§11.2) and notes some caveats and questions about the notion of a life cycle (§11.3).

11.2 Life cycles of change

Cycles of change and life cycles of sound change have been long discussed in linguistics. Van Gelderen (2011: 3) gives a list going back to the mid-eighteenth century, including Condillac, though often not in the specific sense at hand. In recent work, proposals for life cycles involving sound change include, among many others, Bermúdez-Otero (2007, 2015), Iverson and Salmons (2003, 2009), Kiparsky (2003) and Sen 2016, as well as Janda and Joseph's related 'Big Bang' (2003, and elsewhere). Bermúdez-Otero (2015) traces these ideas back to Kruszewski (1881). Consider two descriptions of the life cycle, the last long quotes of this book.

First, Kiparsky (2003: 330) describes the life cycle of phonological rules this way, within lexical phonology, boldfacing the big generalization:

> Sound change can be assumed to originate through synchronic variation in the production, perception, and acquisition of language, from where it is internalized by language learners as part of their phonological system. The changes enter the system as language-specific phonetic implementation rules, which are inherently gradient and may give rise to new segments or combinations of segments. These phonetic implementation rules may in turn become reinterpreted as phonological rules, either post-lexical or lexical, as the constraints of the theory require, at which point the appropriate structural conditions are imposed on them by the principles governing that module. In the phonologized stages of their life cycle, **rules tend to rise in the hierarchy of levels ....**

Second, Sen (2016: 6) gives this characterization, building especially on the life cycle developed by Bermúdez-Otero:

> Phonological processes start from language-independent, universal phonetic effects, becoming cognitively-controlled, language-specific phonetic implementation regularities (*phonologization*). They then become *stabilized* as categorical (synchronic) processes manipulating phonological units in linguistic computation; this occurs first in the context of full utterances, the *phrase level* (PL), then over time may come to affect word domains regardless of surrounding lexical context, the *word level* (WL), before applying within morphological stems regardless of surrounding morphological context (e.g. word-forming prefixes and suffixes), the *stem level* (SL). This gradual diminution in the domain of application of a process (*domain narrowing*) reflects the increasing sensitivity of a synchronic process to morphosyntax, absent from earlier historical stages of the sound change. Finally, the process might cease to be a dynamic aspect of linguistic computation; its surface effects are deemed to be intrinsic properties of lexical items (*lexicalization*), that is, the post-sound change form of the word is the stored version, not derived by online processing. Alternatively, the effect might be bound up with a morphological operation alone, and again no longer be a part of phonological computation (*morphologization*).

These views have important similarities and differences. Both use similar sets of modules – phonetic, phonological (lexical and post-lexical), and on to morphology/morphosyntax and the lexicon. Both make related generalizations – a rise through the levels of lexical phonology or 'domain narrowing.' I would suggest a couple of modest possible refinements or further considerations about the life cycle.

First, life cycles do not always stop at morphology or sets of lexical items. If – and it's a bigger 'if' for me than for many others – it is the case that sound change can help shape the basic structure of the lexicon and/or lexical semantics, as we saw with Hawkins in Chapter 10, sound change ends up having profound consequences on the entire lexicon. I would take seriously Kiparsky's conclusion that rules **tend** to go through this kind of cycle, a point to which we'll return.

Second, our discussions suggest adding another dimension – the spread of a change through society. Work on possible life cycles has generally, if not always, focused on directly structural change, but I argued (Chapters 6 and 7) that the progress of structural change through a community interacts profoundly with social factors all along the way, including constraints on language variation and change at different ages.

Third, Kiparsky stresses, as I have, the importance of variation. Yet variation is only now being deeply woven enough into sound change at every stage. Variation is the seed bed of change and everybody pays lip service to that today, but not all historical linguists seem to fully consider variation at each stage along the way.

With those notes, let's look at the nature of the life cycle.

11.3   Questions and caveats about life cycles

Starting from the issues raised in Bermúdez-Otero and Trousdale (2012) allows us to connect some important points. First I'll say a little about domain narrowing and then the related issue of modularity before turning to the matter of explaining sound change, beginning with teleology.

The quote from Sen above makes an important point: In at least many cases of cycle-like development, the path runs from morphologization to lexicalization. A concern of Sen's is with the 'domain narrowing' nature of life cycle changes, that changes move from the phrasal to the word to the stem level. (This is central to unidirectionality, see below.) For example, /ng/ forms in English once always included pronunciation of the [g], but this began to erode first in phrasal contexts where a word ended in this cluster but was followed by a word starting with a consonant ('sing that song'), but not when a following word began with a vowel ('sing it'). Umlaut clearly does not work that way – it begins, at least in Old High German where we can track this in documents, within adjacent syllables. It then extends to polysyllabic words and eventually, at least in the case of one author, Otfrid, comes to cross word boundaries, so not only *gasti* 'guest, inflected' umlauts to *gesti* but *drank ih* 'I drank' umlauts to *drenk ih*. (Boutilier 2019 provides detailed data on early umlaut by morphological category.)

Another issue is modularity (§9.2) – whether grammar involves distinct modules responsible for particular (sets of) distinct operations. While I, like Bermúdez-Otero, assume modularity, it is a contested question, reviewed broadly but succinctly by Robbins (2017). A full exposition of a 'hypermodular' approach to sound patterns will come in Purnell et al. (forthcoming), but note that much work in exemplar and usage-based linguistics does not adopt this view. An important question is how modules interact with one another. I asserted in §9.2 that modules can and do interact. Bermúdez-Otero (2015: 376, and elsewhere) draws on 'rule scattering,' that is, a situation where …

a process in one component of the grammar gives rise to a new rule at a higher level – fully in line with the life cycle – but without ceasing to apply at the lower level: as a special case, innovative phonological rules do not replace the phonetic rules from which they emerge, but typically coexist with them.

This is surely on the right track and helps account for many kinds of messiness that we find at various stages of sound change's unfolding. For example, we saw that voicing distinctions can lead to tonogenesis (§4.3). Often, though, voicing remains in the system as a cue, if no longer the primary one, to contrast, as in Wu languages (Gao 2015; Gao and Hallé 2015) and Tamang (Mazaudon and Michaud 2009). Such patterns are described for several languages in Haudricourt (1961) and in work since. The clean breaks we like to find in synchronic analysis – for example where a single phonological feature carries a contrast, maybe with some phonetic enhancement – differ from the underlying diachronic messiness of transphonologization.

I've mentioned the notion of teleology in sound change since §4.6, that is, the question of whether sound change serves a function or strives toward a goal in some sense. We saw in §9.2 that Ohala vehemently rejects this (2003), but many others see sound change as serving to 'improve' a system or serving some function, as with Vennemann's preference laws in §3.3 or Kaplan's arguments about homophony in §9.5. The very notion of a life cycle of sound change invites, or maybe implies, a teleological interpretation. I am inclined to reject that, at least in the usual sense of 'teleology' used in linguistics. (The philosophical and evolutionary biology discussions present a somewhat different picture.) Many links across modules in a life cycle present learners and users with possible generalizations that they may or may not pick up on. Low-level vowel-to-vowel assimilation of umlaut (§§1.2, 8.1) may invite hypocorrection, but it's not clear how having or not having umlaut is more functional or serves any purpose for early Germanic speakers, though one could argue that in morphology umlaut helps compensate for information once carried by final vowels. Much later, cues in input to learners (and probably users) had robust enough correlations of umlaut with plurality that German speakers generalized umlaut as one marker and kept it in the wide array of forms discussed in Chapter 1, while English speakers took the opposite route, leaving scattered remnants of a once-widespread morphological pattern.

One value of thinking of sound change in terms of a life cycle is that it facilitates seeing the roles of the dramatically different creatures that have been regarded as 'causes' of change – perception and ease of articulation, functionality of the whole system, social factors, and so on. That has been a major theme. Yes, understanding sound change involves some kind of 'multiple causation,' starting with the integration of 'internal' and 'external' factors urged by Dorian and others (see the Preface and §7.2) but including whole sets of different streams – phonetics, psycholinguistics, philology, sociolinguistics, and more. Often missing is an effort to put these pieces together. We all inevitably work on particular pieces of the cycle, but we can be aware that those are particular pieces that fit into a larger picture, of language structure, change and cognition. This book aims to be a first step.

To return to the bigger picture – the nature and ultimate status of a life cycle in sound change – I have argued, often gently, that the cross-module patterns connect easily in language acquisition and use. That is, phonetic changes in one generation can set the stage for phonological reinterpretation by learners, for one example, and that as broader morphological changes sweep through a language, lexical residues are left (like English umlaut plurals) for another. Bermúdez-Otero and Trousdale (2012) draw parallels to grammaticalization in §9.3. There, I noted discussion about whether grammaticalization represents a distinct process unto itself versus the tendency of certain changes to co-occur. (See van Gelderen 2011: 6–8 for strong arguments grounding grammaticalization in Universal Grammar.) For the life cycle, I see each stage as opening opportunities for the next, but without any inevitability or pre-determined directionality. At each juncture, there are structural biases in acquisition, along with changes in patterns of usage and so on that together nudge learners toward making certain kinds of generalizations. Where those come to fruition, we find life cycle effects, but there is nothing deterministic here. Even the matter of changes that stop rather than fully unfolding or that seem to ebb and flow (§4.6, and elsewhere) show how 'life cycle' is more helpful as a metaphor than a scientific principle or law. Still, it seems emphatically useful to me.

11.4   Conclusion

At the end of Chapter 1, I gave a statement attributed to Twain about hammers and nails. A decade ago I concluded a paper on sound change on a related note (2010: 104):

> Mark Twain quipped, 'To a man with a hammer, everything looks like a nail.' Most theories to date appear to be too tightfisted, attempting to account for (virtually) all sound change with one entity or process: ease of articulation, abstract phonological structure, prosodic structure, perception, or social motivations. What may be needed is a more nuanced understanding of the roles each plays and how they interact. This offers greater opportunities for progress than with pleading for any single-tool view.

In the meantime, I've learned that the attribution to Mark Twain is shaky at best and we have to be more inclusive about the gender of hammer swingers. But the point holds, with the big advances in corpus and other empirical resources, new theories of sounds and language change, and so on. Proposals of life cycles promise one way to link the various processes we've discussed throughout this book in a clear and logical way.

Something has come into clear focus for me in writing: When I'm working through arguments and evidence about some particular approach to sound change – say, those focused on the roles of perception, syllable structure, first language acquisition – I'm more or less awestruck by how tidy the playing field looks. Thinking in terms of hypo- versus hypercorrection or onsets as places for fortition and codas as places for weakening allows tight hypotheses and clear ways to test them. And that's how a lot of science works. I've argued vigorously for the value of these and other approaches and I deeply admire, maybe envy, the ingenious experimental designs and comprehensive typological surveys – I know how hard those are.

Still, at the end of the day, the bigger challenge seems to me to be how to integrate these pieces, approaches, tools into a single more or less coherent whole. It feels like asking people to think in an additional dimension and it probably is.

The rewards to understanding sound change in a holistic sense will match that challenge. It's a problem I hope will continue to grow over time – with more approaches to integrate and more data and kinds of data to draw on.

Beyond this book

I urge you to go out and test the claims and arguments in this book. I've worked to assemble a lot of pieces, using a lot of tools, but even as I write I know I've missed some, some of them important connections and tools. Find those missed connections. By the time you read this, there will be more, and some of the tools will be better and sharper … better than the stone ones I'm working with.

References

Adams, Douglas (1982), *Life, the Universe and Everything = 42*, New York: Del Ray.

Allan, Keith, ed. (2013), *The Oxford Handbook of the History of Linguistics*, Oxford: Oxford University Press.

Andersen, Torben (2006), '[ATR] reversal in Jumjum', *Diachronica* 23, 3–28.

Archibald, John (1996), 'The acquisition of Yucatec Maya prosody', in *Proceedings of the University of British Columbia International Conference on Phonological Acquisition*, ed. Barbara Bernhard, John Gilbert and David Ingram, Somerville, MA: Cascadilla Press, pp. 99–112.

Archibald, John (1997), 'The acquisition of English stress by speakers of non-accentual languages: Lexical storage versus computation of stress', *Linguistics* 35, 167–81.

Árnason, Kristján (2011), *The Phonology of Icelandic and Faroese*, Oxford: Oxford University Press.

Atkinson, Quentin D. (2011), 'Phonemic diversity supports a serial founder effect model of language expansion from Africa', *Science* 332(6027), 346–9.

Auer, Peter and Frans Hinskens (2005), 'The role of interpersonal accommodation in a theory of language change', in *Dialect Change: Convergence and Divergence in European Languages*, ed. Peter Auer, Frans Hinskens and Paul Kerswill, Cambridge: Cambridge University Press, pp. 335–57.

Auer, Peter, David Fertig, Paul J. Hopper and Robert W. Murray (2015), *Hermann Paul's Principles of Language History Revisited: Translations and Reflections*, Berlin: Walter de Gruyter.

Barðdal, Jóhanna and Leonid Kulikov (2008), 'Case in decline', in *The Oxford Handbook of Case*, ed. Andrej Malchukov and Andrew Spencer, Oxford: Oxford University Press, pp. 470–8.

Bat-El, Outi (1994), 'The optimal acronym word in Hebrew', *Proceedings of the 1994 Annual Conference of the Canadian Linguistic Association, Toronto Working Papers in Linguistics*, 23–37.

Bateman, Nicoletta (2011), 'On the typology of palatalization', *Language and Linguistics Compass* 5(8), 588–602.

Bauer, Matt (2009), 'Sound change and laryngeal height', *Proceedings from the Annual Meeting of the Chicago Linguistic Society* 45, Chicago: Chicago Linguistic Society, 29–38.

Baumann, Andreas (2018), 'Machine learning in diachronic corpus phonology: Mining verse data to infer trajectories in English phonotactics', *Papers in Historical Phonology* 3, 137–57.

Baxter, William H. and Laurent Sagart (2014), *Old Chinese: A New Reconstruction*, New York: Oxford University Press.

Beddor, Patrice Speeter, Andries W. Coetzee, Will Styler, Kevin B. McGowan and Julie E. Boland (2018), 'The time course of individuals' perception of coarticulatory information is linked to their production: Implications for sound change', *Language* 94, 931–68.

Bender, Margaret Clelland (2002), *Signs of Cherokee Culture: Sequoyah's Syllabary in Eastern Cherokee Life*, Chapel Hill: University of North Carolina Press.

Bermúdez-Otero, Ricardo (2006), 'Phonological change in Optimality Theory', in *Encyclopedia of Language and Linguistics*, ed. Keith Brown, 2nd edn, Oxford: Elsevier, pp. 497–505.

Bermúdez-Otero, Ricardo (2007), 'Diachronic phonology', in *The Cambridge Handbook of Phonology*, ed. Paul de Lacy, Cambridge: Cambridge University Press, pp. 497–517.

Bermúdez-Otero, Ricardo (2015), 'Amphichronic explanation and the life cycle of phonological processes', in *The Oxford Handbook of Historical Phonology*, ed. Patrick Honeybone and Joseph Salmons, Oxford: Oxford University Press, pp. 374–99.

Bermúdez-Otero, Ricardo and Graeme Trousdale (2012), 'Cycles and continua: On unidirectionality and gradualness in language change', in *The Oxford Handbook of the History of English*, ed. Terttu Nevalainen and Elizabeth Closs Traugott, New York: Oxford University Press, pp. 691–720.

Biedny, Jerome, Andrea Cudworth, Sarah Holmstrom, Monica Macaulay, Gabrielle Mistretta, Joseph Salmons, Charlotte Vanhecke and Bo Zhan (2019), 'Comparative Algonquian metrical phonology', University of Wisconsin – Madison, manuscript.

Blasi, Damián E., S. Moran, Scott R. Moisik, Paul Widmer, Dan Dediu and Balthasar Bickel (2019), 'Human sound systems are shaped by post-Neolithic changes in bite configuration', *Science* 363(6432), eaav3218.

Blevins, Juliette (2004), *Evolutionary Phonology: The Emergence of Sound Patterns*, Cambridge: Cambridge University Press.

Blevins, Juliette (2006a), 'A theoretical synopsis of Evolutionary Phonology', *Theoretical Linguistics* 32, 117–65.

Blevins, Juliette (2006b), 'New perspectives on English sound patterns: 'Natural' and 'unnatural' in Evolutionary Phonology', *Journal of English Linguistics* 34, 6–25.

Blevins, Juliette (2008), 'Natural and unnatural sound patterns: A pocket field guide', in *Naturalness and Iconicity in Language*, ed. Klaas Willems and Ludovic De Cuypere, Amsterdam: Benjamins, pp. 121–48.

Blevins, Juliette and Andrew Garrett (1998), 'The origins of consonant-vowel metathesis', *Language* 74, 508–56.

Blevins, Juliette and Andrew Garrett (2004), 'The evolution of metathesis', in *Phonetically-based Phonology*, ed. Bruce Hayes, Robert Kirchner and Donca Steriade, Cambridge: Cambridge University Press, pp. 117–56.

Blevins, Juliette and Andrew Wedel (2009), 'Inhibited sound change: An evolutionary approach to lexical competition', *Diachronica* 26, 143–83.

Blevins, Juliette, Ander Egurtzegi and Jan Ullrich (2020), 'Final obstruent voicing in Lakota: Phonetic evidence and phonological implications', *Language* 96, 294–337.

Bloomfield, Leonard (1933), *Language*, New York: Holt.

Blust, Robert (2005), 'Must sound change be phonetically motivated?', *Diachronica* 22, 219–69.

Bonfante, Giuliano (1947), 'The Neolinguistic position', *Language* 23, 344–75.

Boutilier, Matthew G. (2019), 'Phonological and morphological patterns in Old High German umlaut', PhD dissertation, University of Wisconsin – Madison.

Bowern, Claire (2018), 'Computational phylogenetics', *Annual Review of Linguistics* 4, 281–96.

Bowie, David and Malcah Yaeger-Dror (2015), 'Phonological change in real time', in *The Oxford Handbook of Historical Phonology*, ed. Patrick Honeybone and Joseph Salmons, Oxford: Oxford University Press, pp. 603–18.

Brentari, Diane (2019), *Sign Language Phonology*, Cambridge: Cambridge University Press.

Buckley, Eugene (1994), *Theoretical Aspects of Kashaya Phonology and Morphology*, Stanford, CA: CSLI.

Bybee, Joan (2001), *Phonology and Language Use*, Cambridge: Cambridge University Press.

Bybee, Joan, ed. (2011), 'The vanishing phonemes debate', *Linguistic Typology* 15, 147–53, special issue.

Campbell, Lyle and Mauricio J. Mixco (2007), *A Glossary of Historical Linguistics*, Edinburgh: Edinburgh University Press.

Campbell, Lyle and William J. Poser (2008), *Language Classification: History and Method*, Cambridge: Cambridge University Press.

Caplow, Nancy J. (2016a), 'Reconstructing stress in Proto-Tibetan', *Linguistics of the Tibeto-Burman Area* 39, 180–221.

Caplow, Nancy J. (2016b), 'Stress patterns and acoustic correlates of stress in Balti Tibetan', *Himalayan Linguistics* 15, 1–49.

Cassidy, Frederic G. and Joan Houston Hall, eds. (1985–2017), *The Dictionary of American Regional English*, Cambridge, MA: Harvard University Press.

Cedergren, Henrietta J. and David Sankoff (1974), 'Variable rules: Performance as a statistical reflection of competence', *Language* 50, 333–55.

Chabot, Alex (2019), 'What's wrong with being a rhotic?' *Glossa* 4(1), 38.

Chambers, J.K. (1992), 'Dialect acquisition', *Language* 68, 673–705.

Chambers, J.K. (2009), *Sociolinguistic Theory: Linguistic Variation and its Social Significance*, 3rd edn, Oxford: Blackwell.

Chen, Matthew and William S.-Y. Wang (1975), 'Sound change: Actuation and implementation', *Language* 51, 255–81.

Chomsky, Noam (1964), *Current Issues in Linguistic Theory*, The Hague: Mouton.

Chomsky, Noam (2005), 'Three factors in language design', *Linguistic Inquiry* 36, 1–22.

Chomsky, Noam and Morris Halle (1968), *The Sound Pattern of English*, New York: Harper & Row.

Coetzee, Andries W., Patrice Speeter Beddor, Kerby Shedden, Will Styler and Daan Wissing (2018), 'Plosive voicing in Afrikaans: Differential cue weighting and tonogenesis', *Journal of Phonetics* 66, 185–216.

Cohen Priva, Uriel and Emily Gleason (2020), 'The causal structure of lenition: A case for the causal precedence of durational shortening', *Language* 96, 413–48.

Collinge, N.E. (1985), *The Laws of Indo-European*, Amsterdam: Benjamins.

Coşeriu, Eugenio (1978), *Sincronía, diacronía e historia. El problema del cambio lingüístico*, 3rd edn, Madrid: Gredos. (First published 1957. German translation: *Synchronie, Diachronie und Geschichte. Das Problem des Sprachwandels*, München: Wilhelm Fink. 1984, 2nd edn.)

Cruttenden, Alan (2001), *Gimson's Pronunciation of English*, 6th edn, London: Arnold.

Cser, András (2015), 'Basic types of phonological change', in *The Oxford Handbook of Historical Phonology*, ed. Patrick Honeybone and Joseph Salmons, Oxford: Oxford University Press, pp. 193–204.

Cser, András (2016), 'Historical phonology and morphology in the nineteenth century: Abstractness versus empiricism', *Papers in Historical Phonology* 1, 37–49.

Cudworth, Andrea (2019), Menominee vowels: Quality, quantity, and a hierarchical model of representation', PhD dissertation, University of Wisconsin – Madison.

Cukor-Avila, Patricia and Guy Bailey (2013), 'Real and apparent time', in *The Handbook of Language Variation and Change*, ed. J.K. Chambers and Natalie Schilling, 2nd edn, Chichester: Wiley-Blackwell, pp. 239–62.

D'Arcy, Alexandra (2015), 'Variation, transmission, incrementation', in *The Oxford Handbook of Historical Phonology*, ed. Patrick Honeybone and Joseph Salmons, Oxford: Oxford University Press, pp. 583–602.

Dediu, Dan and Scott R. Moisik (2019), 'Pushes and pulls from below: Anatomical variation, articulation and sound change', *Glossa* 4, 1–33.

DeGraff, Michel (2003), 'Against creole exceptionalism', *Language* 79, 391–410.

Denes, Peter B. and Elliot N. Pinson (1963), *The Speech Chain: The Physics and Biology of Spoken Language*, New York: Anchor.

Donegan, Patricia J. and Geoffrey S. Nathan (2015), 'Natural Phonology and sound change', in *The Oxford Handbook of Historical Phonology*, ed. Patrick Honeybone and Joseph Salmons, Oxford: Oxford University Press, pp. 431–49.

Dorian, Nancy (1993), 'Internally and externally motivated change in language contact settings: Doubts about the dichotomy', in *Historical*

Linguistics: Problems and Perspectives, ed. Charles Jones, London: Longman, pp. 131–55.

Dresher, B. Elan (2009), *The Contrastive Hierarchy in Phonology*, Cambridge: Cambridge University Press.

Dresher, B. Elan, Glynn Piggott and Keren Rice (1994), 'Contrast in phonology: Overview', *Toronto Working Papers in Linguistics* 13, iii–xvii.

Dunkel, George (1981), 'Typology versus reconstruction', *Bono Homini Donum: Essays in Historical Linguistics in Memory of J. Alexander Kerns*, ed. Yoël Arbeitman and Allan Bomhard, Amsterdam: Benjamins, pp. 559–69.

Eckert, Penelope (1988), 'Sound change and adolescent social structure', *Language in Society* 17, 183–207.

Eckert, Penelope (1989), *Jocks and Burnouts: Social Categories and Identity in the High School*, New York: Teachers College Press.

Eckert, Penelope and William Labov (2017), 'Phonetics, phonology and social meaning', *Journal of Sociolinguistics* 21, 467–96.

Egurtzegi, Ander (2017), 'Phonetically conditioned sound change', *Diachronica* 34, 331–67.

Feagin, Crawford (2003), 'Vowel shifting in the southern states', in *English in the Southern United States*, ed. Stephen J. Nagle and Sara L. Sanders, Cambridge: Cambridge University Press, pp. 126–40.

Finazzi, Rosa Bianca and Paola Tornaghi (2013), 'Gothica Bononiensia: Analisi linguistica e filologica di un nuovo documento', *Aevum* 87(1), 113–55.

Foulkes, Paul and Gerard Docherty, (2006), 'The social life of phonetics and phonology', *Journal of Phonetics* 34(4), 409–38.

Foulkes, Paul and Marilyn Vihman (2015), 'First language acquisition and phonological change', in *The Oxford Handbook of Historical Phonology*, ed. Patrick Honeybone and Joseph Salmons, Oxford: Oxford University Press, pp. 289–312.

Foulkes, Paul, Gerard Docherty and Dominic Watt (2005), 'Phonological variation in child-directed speech', *Language* 81, 177–206.

Fruehwald, Josef (2017), 'The role of phonology in phonetic change', *Annual Review of Linguistics* 3, 25–42.

Fruehwald, Josef, Jonathan Gress-Wright and Joel Wallenberg (2013), 'Phonological rule change: The constant rate effect', in *NELS 40: Proceedings of the 40th Annual Meeting of the North East Linguistic Society*, vol. 1, ed. Robert Staubs, Seda Kan and Claire Moore-Cantwell, GLSA Publications, pp. 219–30.

Gamkrelidze, Thomas V. (1975), 'On the correlation of stops and fricatives in a phonological system', *Lingua* 35, 231–61.

Gamkrelidze, T'amaz V. and Vjačeslav V. Ivanov (1973), 'Sprachtypologie und die Rekonstruktion der gemeinindogermanischen Verschlüsse: Vorläufiger Bericht', *Phonetica* 27, 150–6.

Gao, Jiayin (2015), 'Interdependence between tones, segments and phonation types in Shanghai Chinese: Acoustics, articulation, perception and evolution', PhD dissertation, Université Sorbonne Nouvelle, Paris 3.

Gao, Jiayin and Pierre Hallé (2015), 'The role of voice quality in Shanghai tone perception', *Proceedings of the 18th International Congress of Phonetic Sciences*, Paper number 448, pp. 1–5.

van Gelderen, Elly (2006), *A History of the English Language*, Amsterdam: Benjamins.

van Gelderen, Elly (2011), *The Linguistic Cycle: Language Change and the Language Faculty*, Oxford: Oxford University Press.

van Gelderen, Elly (2018), *Analyzing Syntax through Texts: Old, Middle, and Early Modern English*, Edinburgh: Edinburgh University Press.

Gess, Randall (1999), 'Rethinking the dating of Old French syllable-final consonant loss', *Diachronica* 16, 261–96.

Givón, Talmy (1971a), 'Historical syntax and synchronic morphology: An archaeologist's field trip', *Chicago Linguistic Society* 7, 394–415.

Givón, Talmy (1971b), 'On the verbal origin of the Bantu verb suffixes', *Studies in African Linguistics* 2, 145–63.

Goddard, Ives (1974), 'An outline of the historical phonology of Arapaho and Atsina', *International Journal of American Linguistics* 40, 102–16.

Goddard, Ives (1994), 'The west-to-east cline in Algonquian dialectology', in *Actes du vingt-cinquième Congrès des algonquinistes*, ed. William Cowan, Ottawa: Carleton University, pp. 187–211.

Good, Jeff (2008), 'Introduction', in *Linguistic Universals and Language Change*, ed. Jeff Good, Oxford: Oxford University Press, pp. 1–19.

Gordon, Matthew (2001), *Small-Town Values and Big-City Vowels: A Study of the Northern Cities Shift in Michigan*, Durham, NC: Duke University Press.

Granovetter, M.S. (1973), 'The strength of weak ties', *American Journal of Sociology* 78, 1360–80.

Greenbaum, Sidney (1996), *The Oxford English Grammar*, Oxford: Oxford University Press.

Gütter, Adolf (2011), 'Frühe Belege für den Umlaut von ahd. /u/, /ō/, /ū/', *Beiträge zur Geschichte der deutschen Sprache und Literatur* 133, 1–13.

Hale, Mark (2003), 'Neogrammarian sound change', in *Handbook of Historical Linguistics*, ed. Richard D. Janda and Brian D. Joseph, Oxford: Blackwell, pp. 343–68.

Hale, Mark (2007), *Historical Linguistics: Theory and Method*, Oxford: Wiley-Blackwell.

Hall, Daniel Currie (2011), 'Phonological contrast and its phonetic enhancement: Dispersedness without dispersion,' *Phonology* 28(1), 1–54.

Hall, Tracy Alan (2014), 'The analysis of Westphalian German spirantization', *Diachronica* 31, 223–66.

Halle, Morris (1997), 'On stress and accent in Indo-European', *Language* 73, 275–313.

Harrington, Jonathan (2006), 'An acoustic analysis of "happy-tensing" in the Queen's annual Christmas broadcasts', *Journal of Phonetics* 34, 439–57.

Harrington, Jonathan (2007), 'Evidence for the relationship between synchronic variability and diachronic change in the Queen's annual Christmas broadcasts', in *Laboratory Phonology 9: Phonetics and Phonology*, ed. Jennifer Cole and José Hualde, Berlin: de Gruyter, pp. 125–44.

Harrington, Jonathan, Sallyanne Palethorpe and Catherine I. Watson (2000a), 'Does the Queen speak the Queen's English?', *Nature* 408, 927–8.

Harrington, Jonathan, Sallyanne Palethorpe and Catherine I. Watson (2000b), 'Monophthongal vowel changes in received pronunciation: An acoustic analysis of the Queen's Christmas broadcasts', *Journal of the International Phonetic Association* 30, 63–78.

Harris, Alice C. and Lyle Campbell (1995), *Historical Syntax in Cross-linguistic Perspective*, Cambridge: Cambridge University Press.

Harris, Randy Allen (1993), *The Linguistics Wars*, New York: Oxford University Press.

Haudricourt, André-Georges (1954), 'De l'origine des tons du vietnamien', *Journal Asiatique* 242, 69–82.

Haudricourt, André-Georges (1961), 'Bipartition et tripartition des systèmes de tons dans quelques langues d'Extrême-Orient', *Bulletin de la Société de Linguistique de Paris* 56, 163–80.

Hawkins, John A. (1985), *A Comparative Typology of German and English: Unifying the Contrasts*, Austin: University of Texas Press.

Hay, Jennifer and Laurie Bauer (2007), 'Phoneme inventory size and population size', *Language* 83, 388–400.

Hayes, Bruce (1995), *Metrical Stress Theory: Principles and Case Studies*, Chicago: University of Chicago Press.

Henton, Caroline, Peter Ladefoged and Ian Maddieson (1992), 'Stops in the world's languages', *Phonetica* 49, 65–101.

Hickey, Raymond (2002), 'Ebb and flow: A cautionary tale of language change', in *Sounds, Words, Texts, Change: Selected Papers from the Eleventh International Conference on English Historical Linguistics (11 ICEHL)*, ed. Teresa Fanego, Belén Mendez-Naya and Elena Seoane, Amsterdam: Benjamins, pp. 105–28.

Hickey, Raymond, ed. (2017a), *Listening to the Past: Audio Records of Accents of English*, Cambridge: Cambridge University Press.

Hickey, Raymond (2017b), 'Analyzing early audio recordings', in *Listening to the Past: Audio Records of Accents of English*, ed. Raymond Hickey, Cambridge: Cambridge University Press, pp. 1–12.

Hickey, Raymond (2017c), 'The development of recording technology', in *Listening to the Past: Audio Records of Accents of English*, ed. Raymond Hickey, Cambridge: Cambridge University Press, pp. 562–8.

Hilpert, Martin (2008), 'New evidence against the modularity of grammar: Constructions, collocations, and speech perception', *Cognitive Linguistics* 19, 491–511.

Hock, Hans Henrich (1991), *Principles of Historical Linguistics*, 2nd edn, Berlin: Mouton de Gruyter.

Hockett, Charles F. (1958), *A Course in Modern Linguistics*, New York: Macmillan.

Hockett, Charles F. (1985), 'Distinguished lecture: F', *American Anthropologist* 87, 263–81.

Hoenigswald, Henry M. (1960), *Language Change and Linguistic Reconstruction*, Chicago: University of Chicago Press.

Hoenigswald, Henry M. (1978), 'The annus mirabilis 1876 and posterity', *Transactions of the Philological Society (Commemorative Volume: The Neogrammarians)* 76, 17–35.

Holsinger, David J. (2000), 'Lenition in Germanic: Prosodic templates in sound change', PhD dissertation, The University of Wisconsin – Madison.

Holsinger, David (2008), 'Germanic prosody and consonantal strength', in *Lenition and Fortition*, ed. J. Brandão de Carvalho, T. Scheer and P. Ségéral, Berlin: Mouton de Gruyter, pp. 273–300.

Holt, D. Eric (2015), 'Historical sound change in Optimality Theory: Achievements and challenges', in *The Oxford Handbook of Historical Phonology*, ed. Patrick Honeybone and Joseph Salmons, Oxford: Oxford University Press, pp. 545–62.

Hombert, Jean-Marie, John J. Ohala and William G. Ewan (1979), 'Phonetic explanations for the development of tones', *Language* 55(1), 37–58.

Honeybone, Patrick (2001), 'Lenition inhibition in Liverpool English', *English Language and Linguistics* 5, 213–49.

Honeybone, Patrick (2005), 'Sharing makes us stronger: Process inhibition and segmental structure', in *Headhood, Elements, Specification and Contrastivity*, ed. P. Carr, J. Durand and C. Ewen, Amsterdam: Benjamins, pp. 167–92.

Honeybone, Patrick (2016), 'Are there impossible changes? θ > f but f ≯ θ', *Papers in Historical Phonology* 1, 316–58.

Honeybone, Patrick and Joseph Salmons, eds. (2015), *The Oxford Handbook of Historical Phonology*, Oxford: Oxford University Press.

Hopper, Paul (1973), 'Glottalized and murmured occlusives in Indo-European' *Glossa* 7, 141–66.

Hopper, Paul J. and Elizabeth Closs Traugott (1993), *Grammaticalization*, Cambridge: Cambridge University Press.

Howell, Robert B. (1993), 'German immigration and the development of regional variants of American English: Using contact theory to discover our roots', in *The German Language in America*, ed. Joseph Salmons, Madison: Max Kade Institute, pp. 190–212.

Howell, Robert B. (2007), 'Immigration and koineisation: The formation of early modern Dutch urban vernaculars', *Transactions of the Philological Society* 104, 207–27.

Howell, Robert B. (2012), 'Were the cities of Holland 1200–1650 "New Towns"? Urban demography and koineisation in the urban vernaculars of Holland', Invited Plenary at the Forum on Germanic Language Study, Sheffield, England, 6–7 January.

Howell, Robert B. and Joseph Salmons (1997), 'Umlautless residues in Germanic', *American Journal of Germanic Linguistics & Literatures* 9, 83–111.

Hualde, José Ignacio (2011), 'Sound change', in *The Blackwell Companion to Phonology*, vol. 4, ed. Marc van Oostendorp, Colin J. Ewen, Elizabeth Hume and Keren Rice, Malden, MA: Blackwell, pp. 2214–35.

Hualde, José Ignacio (2018), 'Aspiration in Basque', *Papers in Historical Phonology* 3, 1–27.

Hurford, James R. (2014), *The Origins of Language: A Slim Guide*, Oxford: Oxford University Press.

Hyman, Larry (2018), 'Why underlying representations?', *Journal of Linguistics* 54, 591–610.

Idsardi, William J. (2000), 'Clarifying opacity', *Linguistic Review* 17, 337–50.

Iverson, Gregory K. and Joseph Salmons (1995), 'Aspiration and laryngeal representation in Germanic', *Phonology* 12, 369–96.

Iverson, Gregory K. and Joseph Salmons (1996), 'The primacy of primary umlaut', *Beiträge zur Geschichte der deutschen Sprache und Literatur (PBB)* 118, 69–86.

Iverson, Gregory K. and Joseph Salmons (2003), 'The ingenerate motivation of sound change', in *Motives for Language Change*, ed. Raymond Hickey, Cambridge: Cambridge University Press, pp. 199–212.

Iverson, Gregory K. and Joseph Salmons (2005), 'Filling the gap: English tense vowel plus final /š/', *Journal of English Linguistics* 33, 207–21.

Iverson, Gregory K. and Joseph Salmons (2006a), 'On the typology of final laryngeal neutralization: Evolutionary phonology and laryngeal realism', *Theoretical Linguistics* 32, 205–16.

Iverson, Gregory K. and Joseph Salmons (2006b), 'Fundamental regularities in the Second Consonant Shift', *Journal of Germanic Linguistics* 18, 45–70.

Iverson, Gregory K. and Joseph Salmons (2008), 'Germanic aspiration: Phonetic enhancement and language contact', *Sprachwissenschaft* 33, 257–78.

Iverson, Gregory K. and Joseph Salmons (2009), 'Naturalness and the lifecycle of sound change', in *On Inflection: In Memory of Wolfgang U. Wurzel*, ed. Patrick Steinkrüger and Manfred Krifka, Berlin: Mouton de Gruyter, pp. 89–105.

Iverson, Gregory K. and Joseph Salmons (2011), 'Final devoicing and final laryngeal neutralization', in *Companion to Phonology*, vol. 3, ed. Marc van Oostendorp, Colin Ewen, Beth Hume and Keren Rice, Oxford: Wiley-Blackwell, pp. 1622–43.

Iverson, Gregory K. and Joseph Salmons (2012), 'Paradigm resolution in the life cycle of Norse umlaut', *Journal of Germanic Linguistics* 24, 101–31.

Jackendoff, Ray (2002), *Foundations of Language*, Oxford: Oxford University Press.

Jackendoff, Ray (2007), 'Linguistics in cognitive science: The state of the art', *The Linguistic Review* 24, 347–401.

Jacobs, Neil G. (2005), *Yiddish: A Linguistic Introduction*, Cambridge: Cambridge University Press.

Janda, Richard D. and Brian D. Joseph (2003), 'On language, change, and language change', in *Handbook of Historical Linguistics*, ed. Richard D. Janda and Brian D. Joseph, Oxford: Blackwell, pp. 3–180.

Janda, Richard D., Brian D. Joseph and Neil G. Jacobs (1994), 'Systematic hyperforeignisms as maximally external evidence for linguistic rules', in *The Reality of Linguistic Rules*, ed. Susan Lima, Roberta Corrigan and Gregory K. Iverson, Amsterdam: Benjamins, pp. 67–92.

Jatteau, Adèle and Michaela Hejná (2018), 'Gradient dissimilation in Mongolian: Implications for diachrony', *Papers in Historical Phonology* 3, 28–76.

Jespersen, Otto (1969), *Efficiency in Linguistic Change*, 3rd edn, Copenhagen: Munksgaard.

Josserand, Judy Kathryn (1983), 'Mixtec dialect history', PhD dissertation, Tulane University.

Justeson, John S. and Terrence Kaufman (1993), 'A decipherment of Epi-Olmec hieroglyphic writing', *Science* 259, 1703–11.

Kaplan, Abby (2015), 'The evidence for homophony avoidance in language change: Reply to Sampson (2013)', *Diachronica* 32, 268–76.

Kapović, Maté (2017), 'Proto-Indo-European phonology', in *The Indo-European Languages*, ed. Maté Kapović, London: Routledge, pp. 13–60.

Katz, Jonah (2016), 'Lenition, perception and neutralisation', *Phonology* 33(1), 43–85.

Kavitskaya, Darya (2002), *Compensatory Lengthening: Phonetics, Phonology, Diachrony*, New York: Garland.

Kiparsky, Paul (1965), 'Phonological change', PhD dissertation, MIT. (Reprinted Indiana University Linguistics Club, 1971.)

Kiparsky, Paul (2003), 'The phonological basis of sound change', in *Handbook of Historical Linguistics*, ed. Richard D. Janda and Brian D. Joseph, Oxford: Blackwell, pp. 313–42.

Kiparsky, Paul (2006), 'The Amphichronic Program versus Evolutionary Phonology', *Theoretical Linguistics* 32, 217–36.

Kiparsky, Paul (2008), 'Universals constrain change; change results in typological generalizations', in *Linguistic Universals and Language Change*, ed. Jeff Good, Oxford: Oxford University Press, pp. 3–53.

Kirby, James P. (2014a), 'Incipient tonogenesis in Phnom Penh Khmer: Computational studies', *Laboratory Phonology* 5, 195–230.

Kirby, James P. (2014b), 'Incipient tonogenesis in Phnom Penh Khmer: Acoustic and perceptual studies', *Journal of Phonetics* 43, 69–85.

Kirby, James and Marc Brunelle (2017), 'Southeast Asian tone in areal perspective', in *The Cambridge Handbook of Areal Linguistics*, ed. Raymond Hickey, Cambridge: Cambridge University Press, pp. 703–31.

Kloeke, Gesinus Gerhardus (1927), *De Hollandsche expansie in de zestiende en zeventiende eeuw en haar weerspiegeling in de hedendaagsche Nederlandsche dialecten*, The Hague: Nijhoff.

Koch, Harold (2004), 'The Arandic subgroup of Australian languages', *Australian Languages: Classification and the Comparative Method*, ed. Claire Bowern and Harold Koch, Amsterdam: Benjamins, pp. 127–50.

Köhnlein, Björn (2015), 'The complex durational relationship of contour tones and level tones: Evidence from diachrony', *Diachronica* 32, 231–67.

Kroch, Anthony S. (1989), 'Reflexes of grammar in patterns of language change', *Language Variation and Change* 1, 199–244.

Kruszewski, Mikołaj (1881), *Ueber die Lautabwechslung*, Kazan: Universitätsbuchdruckerei. (Trans. by Robert Austerlitz (1995), 'On sound alternation', in *Writings in General Linguistics*, ed. Konrad Koerner, Amsterdam: Benjamins, pp. 3–34.)

Kümmel, Martin (2015), 'The role of typology in historical phonology', in *The Oxford Handbook of Historical Phonology*, ed. Patrick Honeybone and Joseph Salmons, Oxford: Oxford University Press, pp. 121–32.

Kürsten, Otto and Otto Bremer (1910), *Lautlehre der Mundart von Buttelstedt bei Weimar*, Leipzig: Breitkopf & Härtel.

Labov, William (1966), *The Social Stratification of English in New York City*, Washington, DC: Center for Applied Linguistics.

Labov, William (1972), 'Some principles of linguistic methodology', *Language in Society* 1, 97–120.

Labov, William (1981), 'Resolving the Neogrammarian controversy', *Language* 57, 267–308.

Labov, William (1989), 'The child as linguistic historian', *Language Variation and Change* 1, 85–97.

Labov, William (1994), *Principles of Linguistic Change*. Vol. 1: *Internal Factors*, Oxford: Blackwell.

Labov, William (2001), *Principles of Linguistic Change*. Vol. 2: *Social Factors*, Malden, MA: Blackwell.

Labov, William (2007), 'Transmission and diffusion', *Language* 83, 344–87.

Labov, William (2010), *Principles of Linguistic Change*. Vol. 3: *Cognitive and Cultural Factors*, Oxford: Blackwell.

Labov, William (2020), 'The regularity of sound change', *Language* 96, 42–59.

Labov, William, Sharon Ash and Charles Boberg, (2006), *Atlas of North American English: Phonology and Sound Change*, Berlin: Mouton de Gruyter.

Language Files: Materials for an Introduction to Language and Linguistics (2016), Columbus: The Ohio State University Press.

Lass, Roger (1984), *Phonology: An Introduction to Basic Concepts*, Cambridge: Cambridge University Press.

Lass, Roger (1994), *Old English: A Historical Linguistic Companion*, Cambridge: Cambridge University Press.

Lass, Roger (2015), 'Interpreting alphabetic orthographies', in *The Oxford Handbook of Historical Phonology*, ed. Patrick Honeybone and Joseph Salmons, Oxford: Oxford University Press, pp. 100–20.

Lauersdorf, Mark Richard (2018), 'Historical (standard) language development and the writing of historical identities: A plaidoyer for a data-driven approach to the investigation of the sociolinguistic history of (not only) Slovak', in *V zeleni drželi zeleni breg: Studies in Honor of Marc L. Greenberg*, ed. Stephen M. Dickey and Mark Richard Lauersdorf, Bloomington, IN: Slavica Publishers, pp. 199–218.

Lehmann, Winfred P., ed. (1967), *A Reader in Nineteenth Century Historical Indo-European Linguistics*, Bloomington: Indiana University Press.

Lehmann, Winfred P. (1973), *Historical Linguistics: An Introduction*, 2nd edn, New York: Holt, Rinehart & Winston.

Le Page, Robert B. and Andrée Tabouret-Keller (1985), *Acts of Identity: Creole-based approaches to Language and Ethnicity*, Cambridge: Cambridge University Press.

Leskien, August (1876), *Die Declination im Slawisch-Litauischen und Germanischen*, Leipzig: Hirzel.

Lieber, Rochelle (1987), *An Integrated Theory of Autosegmental Processes*, Albany: SUNY Press.

Lightner, Theodore M. (1983), *Introduction to English Derivational Morphology*, Amsterdam: Benjamins.

Lippi-Green, Rosina (1989), 'Social network integration and language change in progress in a rural Alpine village', *Language in Society* 18, 213–34.

Lisker, Leigh and Arthur Abramson (1967), 'Some effects of context on voice-onset time in English stops', *Language and Speech* 10, 1–28.

Litty, Samantha (2017), 'We talk German now yet: The sociolinguistic development of voice onset time & final obstruent devoicing in Wisconsin German & English varieties, 1863–2013', PhD dissertation, University of Wisconsin – Madison.

Locke, John L. (1983), *Phonological Acquisition and Change*, New York: Academic Press.

Los, Bettelou (2015), *A Historical Syntax of English*, Edinburgh: Edinburgh University Press.

Macaulay, Monica (1996), *A Grammar of Chalcatongo Mixtec*, Berkeley: University of California Press.

Macaulay, Monica (forthcoming), *A Grammar of Menominee*.

Macaulay, Monica and Joseph Salmons (2017), 'Synchrony and diachrony in Menominee derivational morphology', *Morphology* 27, 179–215.

Macken, Marlys and Joseph Salmons (1997), 'Prosodic templates in sound change', *Diachronica* 14, 31–66.

Maguire, Warren (2015), 'Using corpora of recorded speech for historical phonology', in *The Oxford Handbook of Historical Phonology*, ed. Patrick Honeybone and Joseph Salmons, Oxford: Oxford University Press, pp. 164–172.

Malkiel, Yakov (1983), *From Particular to General Linguistics: Essays 1965–1978*, Amsterdam: Benjamins.

Marcus, Gary and Ernest Davis (2014), 'Eight (no, nine!) problems with big data', *New York Times* editorial, 6 April.

Marr, David (1982), *Vision*, San Francisco, CA: W.H. Freeman.

Martinet, André (1952), 'Function, structure, and sound change', *Word* 8, 1–32.

Martinet, André (1955), *Économie des changements phonétiques*, Berne: Francke.

Matisoff, James A. (1975), 'Rhinoglottophilia: The mysterious connection between nasality and glottality', in *Nasálfest: Papers from a Symposium on Nasals and Nasalization*, ed. Charles Ferguson, Larry Hyman and John Ohala, Stanford, CA: Language Universals Project, pp. 265–87.

Matras, Yaron (2009), *Language Contact*, Cambridge: Cambridge University Press.

Mazaudon, Martine and Alexis Michaud (2009), 'Tonal contrasts and initial consonants: A case study of Tamang, a "missing link" in tonogenesis', *Phonetica* 65, 231–56.

McCarthy, Corinne (2011), 'The Northern Cities Shift in Chicago', *Journal of English Linguistics* 39, 166–87.

McCarthy, John J. (2008), 'The serial interaction of stress and syncope', *Natural Language & Linguistic Theory* 26, 499–546.

McCarthy, John J. and Alan Prince (1995), 'Faithfulness and reduplicative identity', in *Papers in Optimality Theory*, ed. Jill Beckman, Laura Walsh Dickey and Suzanne Urbanczyk, Amherst, MA: GLSA, pp. 249–384.

Miller, D. Gary (2019), *The Oxford Gothic Grammar*, Oxford: Oxford University Press.

Milroy, James (1989), 'The concept of prestige in sociolinguistic argumentation', *York Papers in Linguistics* 13, 215–26.

Milroy, James (1992a), *Linguistic Variation & Change: On the Historical Sociolinguistics of English*, Oxford: Oxford University Press.

Milroy, James (1992b), 'Social network and prestige arguments in sociolinguistics', in *Sociolinguistics Today: International Perspectives*, ed. K. Bolton and H. Kwok, London: Kingsley Bolton, pp. 146–62.

Milroy, James and Lesley Milroy (1985), 'Linguistic change, social network and speaker innovation', *Journal of Linguistics* 21, 339–84.

Milroy, Lesley (1980), *Language and Social Networks*, Oxford: Blackwell.

Milroy, Lesley and Carmen Llamas (2013), 'Social networks', in *The Handbook of Language Variation and Change*, ed. J.K. Chambers and Natalie Schilling, 2nd edn, Chichester: Wiley-Blackwell, pp. 409–27.

Minkova, Donka (2014), *A Historical Phonology of English*, Edinburgh: Edinburgh University Press.

Minkova, Donka (2015), 'Establishing phonemic contrast in written sources', in *The Oxford Handbook of Historical Phonology*, ed. Patrick Honeybone and Joseph Salmons, Oxford: Oxford University Press, pp. 72–85.

Mithun, Marianne (1999), *The Languages of Native North America*, Cambridge: Cambridge University Press.

Mixdorff, Hansjörg, Patavee Charnvivit and Sudaporn Luksaneeyanawin (2006), 'Realization and perception of tones in mono- and polysyllabic words in Thai', Paper presented at the 7th International Seminar on Speech Production, 13–15 December.

Moran, Steven, Daniel McCloy and Richard Wright (2012), 'Revisiting population size versus phoneme inventory size', *Language* 88, 877–93.

Mortensen, David (2012), 'The emergence of obstruents after high vowels', *Diachronica* 29, 434–70.

Mufwene, Salikoko S. and Charles Gilman (1987), 'How African is Gullah, and why?', *American Speech* 62, 120–39.

Murray, Robert W. (2015), 'The early history of historical phonology', in *The Oxford Handbook of Historical Phonology*, ed. Patrick Honeybone and Joseph Salmons, Oxford: Oxford University Press, pp. 11–31.

Murray, Robert and Theo Vennemann (1983), 'Sound change and syllable structure in Germanic phonology', *Language* 59, 514–28.

Natvig, David (2017), 'A model of underspecified recognition for phonological integration: English loan vowels in American Norwegian', *Journal of Language Contact* 10, 22–55.

Natvig, David (2020), 'Rhotic underspecification: Deriving variability and arbitrariness through phonological representations', *Glossa* 5, 48.

Natvig, David and Joseph Salmons (2020), 'Fully accepting variation in (pre)history: The pervasive heterogeneity of Germanic rhotics', in *The Polymath Intellectual: A Festschrift in Honor of Professor Robert D. King*, ed. Patricia C. Sutcliffe, Dripping Springs, TX: Agarita Press, pp. 81–101.

Norde, Muriel (2009), *Degrammaticalization*, Oxford: Oxford University Press.

Norman, Jerry (1988), *Chinese*, Cambridge: Cambridge University Press.

Ohala, John J. (1981), 'The listener as a source of sound change', in *Papers from the Parasession on Language and Behavior* (Chicago Linguistic Society 17), ed. Carrie S. Masek, Roberta A. Hendrick and Mary Frances Miller, Chicago: Chicago Linguistics Society, pp. 178–203.

Ohala, John J. (1993), 'The phonetics of sound change', in *Historical Linguistics: Problems and Perspectives*, ed. Charles Jones, London: Longman, pp. 237–78.

Ohala, John J. (2003), 'Phonetics and historical phonology', in *Handbook of Historical Linguistics*, ed. Brian D. Joseph and Richard D. Janda, Oxford: Blackwell, pp. 669–86.

Öhman, Sven E.G. (1966), 'Coarticulation in VCV utterances: Spectrographic measurements', *The Journal of the Acoustical Society of America* 39, 151–68.

Osthoff, Hermann and Karl Brugmann (1878), *Morphologische Untersuchungen auf dem Gebiete der indogermanischen Sprachen*, Leipzig: Hirzel.

Owens, Jonathan (2006), *A Linguistic History of Arabic*, Oxford: Oxford University Press.

Oxford, Will (2015), 'Patterns of contrast in phonological change: Evidence from Algonquian vowel systems', *Language* 91, 308–58.

Paul, Hermann (1920 [1880]), *Prinzipien der Sprachgeschichte*, 5th edn, Halle: Max Niemeyer.

Payne, Arvilla C. (1980), 'Factors controlling the acquisition of the Philadelphia dialect by out-of-state children', in *Locating Language in Time and Space*, ed. William Labov, New York: Academic Press, pp. 143–78.

Penny, Ralph (1991), *A History of the Spanish Language*, Cambridge: Cambridge University Press.

Pentland, David (1979), 'Algonquian historical phonology', PhD dissertation, University of Toronto.

Phillips, Betty (2006), *Word Frequency and Lexical Diffusion*, New York: Palgrave Macmillan.

Pitts, Ann (1986), 'Flip-flop prestige in American *tune, duke, news*', *American Speech* 61, 130–8.

Podesva, Robert J. and Janneke Van Hofwegen (2014), 'How conservatism and normative gender constrain variation in inland California: The case of /s/', *University of Pennsylvania Working Papers in Linguistics* 20, 15.

Port, Robert and Adam Leary (2005), 'Against formal phonology', *Language* 81(4), 927–64.

Pouplier, Marianne (2012), 'The gaits of speech', in *The Initiation of Sound Change: Perception, Production, and Social Factors*, ed. Maria-Josep Solé and Daniel Recasens, Amsterdam: Benjamins, pp. 147–66.

Prince, Alan S. and Paul Smolensky (1993), *Optimality Theory: Constraint Interaction in Generative Grammar*, Rutgers: Technical Report 2, Rutgers Center for Cognitive Science. (Republished 2004, Malden: Blackwell.)

Purnell, Thomas C. (2008), 'Prevelar raising and phonetic conditioning: Role of labial and anterior tongue gestures', *American Speech* 83, 373–402.

Purnell, Thomas C. (2012), 'Dialect recordings from the Hanley Collection, 1931–1937', *American Speech* 87, 511–13.

Purnell, Thomas and Eric Raimy (2015), 'Distinctive features, levels of representation, and historical phonology', in *The Oxford Handbook of Historical Phonology*, ed. Patrick Honeybone and Joseph Salmons, Oxford: Oxford University Press, pp. 522–44.

Purnell, Thomas and Malcah Yaeger-Dror, eds. (2010), 'Accommodation to the locally dominant norm: A special issue', *American Speech* 85(2), 115–20.

Purnell, Thomas, Eric Raimy and Joseph Salmons (2017), 'Upper Midwestern English', in *Listening to the Past: Audio Records of Accents of English*, ed. Raymond Hickey, Cambridge: Cambridge University Press, pp. 298–324.

Purnell, Thomas, Eric Raimy and Joseph Salmons (2019), 'Old English vowels: Diachrony, privativity and phonological representations', *Language, Research Reports* 95(4), e447–e473.

Purnell, Thomas, Eric Raimy and Joseph Salmons (forthcoming), *Modularity in Phonology*.

Purnell, Thomas, Joseph Salmons, Dilara Tepeli and Jennifer Mercer (2005), 'Structured heterogeneity and change in laryngeal phonetics: Upper Midwestern final obstruents', *Journal of English Linguistics* 33, 307–38.

Purse, Ruaridh (2019), 'The articulatory reality of coronal stop "deletion"', *Proceedings of the 19th International Congress of Phonetic Sciences*, Melbourne, Australia, pp. 1595–9.

Rask, Rasmus (1818), *Undersøgelse om det gamle Nordiske eller Islandske Sprogs Oprindelse*, Copenhagen: Gyldensdalske Boghandling.

Ratliff, Martha (2015), 'Tonoexodus, tonogenesis, and tone change', in *The Oxford Handbook of Historical Phonology*, ed. Patrick Honeybone and Joseph Salmons, Oxford: Oxford University Press, pp. 245–61.

Recasens, Daniel (2014), *Coarticulation and Sound Change in Romance*, Amsterdam: Benjamins.

Rice, Keren (1994), 'Peripheral in Consonants', *Canadian Journal of Linguistics* 39, 191–216.

Rice, Keren (1996), 'Default variability: The coronal-velar relationship', *Natural Language and Linguistic Theory* 14, 493–543.

Rickford, John (1986), 'Social contact and linguistic diffusion', *Language* 62, 245–90.

Rimor, Mordechai, Judy Kegl, Harlan Lane and Trude Schermer (1984), 'Natural phonetic processes underlie historical change & register variation in American Sign Language', *Sign Language Studies* 43, 97–119.

Robbins, Philip (2017), 'Modularity of mind', in *The Stanford Encyclopedia of Philosophy*, ed. Edward N. Zalta, Stanford, CA: Center for the Study of Language and Information.

Robinson, Orrin W. (2001), *Whose German?: The* ich/ach *Alternation and Related Phenomena in 'Standard' and 'Colloquial'*, Amsterdam: Benjamins.

Rose, Sharon and Rachel Walker (2004), 'A typology of consonant agreement as correspondence', *Language* 80, 475–531.

Sakel, Jeanette (2007), 'Types of loan: Matter and pattern', in *Grammatical Borrowing in Cross-linguistic Perspective*, ed. Yaron Matras and Jeanette Sakel, Berlin: Mouton de Gruyter, pp. 15–29.

Salmons, Joseph (1990), 'The context of language change', *Research Guide on Language Change*, ed. Edgar C. Polomé, Berlin: Mouton de Gruyter, pp. 71–95.

Salmons, Joseph (1992), *Accentual Change and Language Contact: Comparative Survey and Case Study of Early Northern Europe*, Stanford, CA: Stanford University Press.

Salmons, Joseph (1993), *The Glottalic Theory: Survey and Synthesis*, Washington, DC: Institute for the Study of Man.

Salmons, Joseph (2010), 'Segmental phonological change', in *The Continuum Companion to Historical Linguistics*, ed. Vit Bubenik and Silvia Luraghi, London: Continuum, pp. 89–105.

Salmons, Joseph (2016), 'Review of *Frühmittelalterliche Glossen: Ein Beitrag zur Funktionalität und Kontextualität mittelalterlicher Schriftlichkeit* by Markus Schiegg', *Diachronica* 33, 417–22.

Salmons, Joseph (2018), *A History of German: What the Past Reveals about Today's Language*, 2nd edn, Oxford: Oxford University Press.

Salmons, Joseph (2020), 'Laryngeal phonetics, phonology, assimilation and final neutralization', in *The Cambridge Handbook of Germanic Linguistics*, ed. B. Richard Page and Michael T. Putnam, Cambridge: Cambridge University Press, pp. 119–42.

Salmons, Joseph (forthcoming a), 'Contributions to phonology of nineteenth century historical linguistics', in *Oxford Handbook of the History of Phonology*, ed. B. Elan Dresher and Harry van der Hulst, Oxford: Oxford University Press.

Salmons, Joseph (forthcoming b), *Dialect*, Oxford: Oxford University Press.

Salmons, Joseph and Huibin Zhuang (2018), 'The diachrony of East Asian prosodic templates', *Linguistics* 56, 549–80.

Salmons, Joseph, Robert Fox and Ewa Jacewicz (2012), 'Prosodic skewing of input and the initiation of cross-generational sound change', in *The Initiation of Sound Change: Production, Perception and Social Factors*, ed. Maria-Josep Solé and Daniel Recasens, Amsterdam: Benjamins, pp. 167–84.

Sampson, Geoffrey (2013), 'A counterexample to homophony avoidance', *Diachronica* 30, 579–91.

Sankoff, Gillian (2006), 'Age: Apparent time and real time', in *Elsevier Encyclopedia of Language and Linguistics*, 2nd edn, ed. Keith Brown, Amsterdam: Elsevier, pp. 110–16.

Sankoff, Gillian and Hélène Blondeau (2007), 'Language change across the lifespan: /r/ in Montreal French', *Language* 83, 560–88.

Sanstedt, Jade Jørgen Michael (2018), 'Feature specifications and contrast in vowel harmony: The orthography and phonology of Old Norwegian height harmony', PhD dissertation, University of Edinburgh.

Sanz-Sánchez, Israel (2013), 'Dialect contact as the cause for dialect change: Evidence from a phonemic merger in colonial New Mexican Spanish', *Diachronica* 30, 61–94.

Sapir, Edward (1921), *Language: An Introduction to the Study of Speech*, New York: Harcourt Brace.

Saussure, Ferninand de (1986), *Cours de linguistique générale*, Édition préparée par Tullio de Mauro, Paris: Payot.

Schiegg, Markus (2015), *Frühmittelalterliche Glossen: Ein Beitrag zur Funktionalität und Kontextualität mittelalterlicher Schriftlichkeit*, Heidelberg: Winter.

Schmidt, Karl Horst (1962), *Studien zur Rekonstruktion des Lautstandes der südkaukasischen Grundsprache*, Wiesbaden: Steiner.

Schuchardt, Hugo (1972), 'On sound laws: Against the neogrammarians', in *Schuchardt, the Neogrammarians and the Transformational Theory of Phonological Change*, ed. Theo Vennemann and Terence Wilbur, Frankfurt: Athenäum, pp. 1–72. (Published 1885 as *Über die Lautgesetze—Gegen die Junggrammatiker*, Berlin: Oppenheim.)

Schuessler, Axel (2015), 'New Old Chinese', *Diachronica* 32, 571–98.

Seiler, Annina (2014), *The Scripting of the Germanic Languages: A Comparative Study of 'Spelling Difficulties' in Old English, Old High German and Old Saxon*, Zürich: Chronos.

Sen, Ranjan (2016), 'Examining the life cycle of phonological processes: Considerations for historical research', *Papers in Historical Phonology* 1, 5–36.

Sievers, Eduard (1881 [1876]), *Grundzüge der Phonetik*, 2nd edn, Leipzig: Breitkopf & Härtel.

Smalley, William A., Chia Koua Vang and Gnia Yee Yang (1990), *Mother of Writing: The Origin and Development of a Hmong Messianic Script*, Chicago: University of Chicago Press.

Smith, Laura Catharine and Joseph Salmons (2008), 'Historical phonology and evolutionary phonology', *Diachronica* 25, 411–30.

Smith, Laura Catharine and Adam Ussishkin (2015), 'The role of prosodic templates in diachrony', in *The Oxford Handbook of Historical Phonology*, ed. Patrick Honeybone and Joseph Salmons, Oxford: Oxford University Press, pp. 262–85.

Sonderegger, Morgan, Jane Stuart-Smith, Thea Knowles, Rachel Macdonald and Tamara Rathcke (2020), 'Structured heterogeneity in Scottish stops over the twentieth century', *Language* 96, 94–125.

Sonderegger, Stefan (2003), *Althochdeutsche Sprache und Literatur*, 3rd edn, Berlin: Walter de Gruyter.

Spahr, Christopher (2016), 'Contrastive representations in non-segmental phonology', PhD dissertation, University of Toronto.

Stacy, Elizabeth (2004), 'Phonological aspects of Blackfoot prominence', Master's thesis, University of Calgary.

Stampe, David (1969), 'How I spent my summer vacation: A dissertation on natural phonology', PhD dissertation, University of Chicago.

Stanford, James N. (2015), 'Language acquisition and language change', in *The Routledge Handbook of Historical Linguistics*, ed. Claire Bowern and Bethwyn Evans, London: Routledge, pp. 466–83.

Stockwell, Robert P. (1978), 'Perseverance in the English vowel shift', in *Recent Developments in Historical Phonology*, ed. Jacek Fisiak, The Hague: Mouton, pp. 337–48.

Stroop, Jan (1981), 'Diffuse diftongering', *Nieuwe taalgids* 74(1), 1–16.

Sturtevant, Edgar Howard (1917), *Linguistic Change: An Introduction to the Historical Study of Language*, Chicago: University of Chicago Press.

Supalla, Ted and Patricia Clark (2014), *Sign Language Archaeology: Understanding the Historical Roots of American Sign Language*, Washington, DC: Gallaudet University Press.

Sweet, Henry (1900), *The Practical Study of Languages: A Guide for Teachers and Learners*, New York: Henry Holt and Sons.

Tagliamonte, Sali A. (2012), 'The elephant and the pendulum: Variationist perspectives', Plenary presentation at NWAV 41, Bloomington, IN, USA, 25–8 October.

Teil-Dautrey, Gisèle (2008), 'Et si le proto-bantu était aussi une langue … avec ses contraintes et ses déséquilibres', *Diachronica* 25, 54–110.

Tiersma, Pieter Meijes (1985), *Frisian Reference Grammar*, Dordrecht: Foris.

Todd, Simon, Janet B. Pierrehumbert and Jennifer Hay (2019), 'Word frequency effects in sound change as a consequence of perceptual asymmetries: An exemplar-based model', *Cognition* 185, 1–20.

Trubetzkoy, Nikolai (1969), *Principles of Phonology*, translation by Christine A.M. Baltaxe, Berkeley: University of California Press.

Trudgill, Peter (2010), *Investigations in Sociohistorical Linguistics: Stories of Colonization and Contact*, Cambridge: Cambridge University Press.

Tuite, Kevin (1997), *Svan*, München: Lincom Europa.

Unger, Marshall (2015), 'Interpreting diffuse orthographies and orthographic change', in *The Oxford Handbook of Historical Phonology*, ed. Patrick Honeybone and Joseph Salmons, Oxford: Oxford University Press, pp. 86–99.

Van Coetsem, Frans (1988), *Loan Phonology and the Two Transfer Types in Language Contact*, Dordrecht: Foris.

Van Coetsem, Frans (2000), *A General and Unified Theory of the Transmission Process in Language Contact*, Heidelberg: Winter.

Vaught, George Mason (1977), 'A study of "auslautsverhärtung" in Old High German', PhD dissertation, University of Massachusetts, Amherst.

Vennemann, Theo (1970), 'The German velar nasal', *Phonetica* 22, 65–81.

Vennemann, Theo (1975), 'An explanation of drift', in *Word Order and Word Order Change*, ed. Charles N. Li, Austin: University of Texas Press, pp. 269–305.

Vennemann, Theo (1988), *Preference Laws for Syllable Structure and the Explanation of Sound Change – With Special Reference to German, Germanic, Italian, and Latin*, Berlin: Mouton de Gruyter.

Verner, Karl (1875), 'Eine Ausnahme der ersten Lautverschiebung', *Zeitschrift für vergleichende Sprachforschung* 23, 97–130.

Walkden, George (2019), 'The many faces of uniformitarianism in linguistics', *Glossa* 4(1) 52, 1–17.

Wang, William S.-Y. (1969), 'Competing changes as a cause of residue', *Language* 45, 9–25.

Wedel, Andrew (2015), 'Simulation as an investigative tool in historical phonology', *The Oxford Handbook of Historical Phonology*, ed. Patrick Honeybone and Joseph Salmons, Oxford: Oxford University Press, pp. 149–63.

Wedel, Andrew, Abby Kaplan and Scott Jackson (2013), 'High functional load inhibits phonological contrast loss: A corpus study', *Cognition* 128(2), 179–86.

Weinreich, Uriel, William Labov and Marvin I. Herzog (1968), 'Empirical foundations for a theory of language change', in *Directions for Historical Linguistics: A Symposium*, ed. Winfred P. Lehmann and Yakov Malkiel, Austin: University of Texas Press, pp. 97–195.

Weismer, Gary (1979), 'Sensitivity of Voice Onset Time (VOT) measures to certain segmental features in speech production', *Journal of Phonetics* 7, 197–204.

Wiese, Richard (1996), 'Phonological versus morphological rules: On German umlaut and ablaut', *Journal of Linguistics* 32, 113–35.

Wiese, Richard (2000), *The Phonology of German*, 2nd edn, Oxford: Clarendon Press.

Wilcox, Sherman and Corrine Occhino (2016), 'Historical change in signed languages', in Oxford Handbooks Online, New York: Oxford University Press.

Willis, David (2017), 'Endogenous and exogenous theories of syntactic change', in *The Cambridge Handbook of Historical Syntax*, ed. Adam Ledgeway and Ian Roberts, Cambridge: Cambridge University Press, pp. 491–514.

Winford, Donald (2005), 'Contact-induced changes: Classification and processes', *Diachronica* 22, 373–427.

Yang, Gangyuan and Dongmei He (2012), 'Disyllabic phenomenon of Thai words', *Journal of Yunnan Nationalities University* (*Social Sciences*) 2, 134–7.

Yip, Moira (2006a), 'Is there such a thing as animal phonology?' in *Wondering at the Natural Fecundity of Things: Studies in Honor of Alan Prince*, ed. Eric Baković, Junko Ito and John J. McCarthy, Santa Cruz, CA: Department of Linguistics, University of California.

Yip, Moira (2006b), 'The search for phonology in other species', *Trends in Cognitive Sciences* 10, 442–5.

Yu, Alan C.L. (2010), 'Perceptual compensation is correlated with individuals' "autistic" traits: Implications for models of sound change', *PLOS ONE* 5(8), e11950.

Yu, Alan C.L. (2015), 'The role of experimental investigation in understanding sound change', in *The Oxford Handbook of Historical Phonology*, ed. Patrick Honeybone and Joseph Salmons, Oxford: Oxford University Press, pp. 410–28.

Yu, Alan C.L., Julian Grove, Martina Martinovic and Morgan Sonderegger (2011), 'Effects of working memory capacity and "autistic" traits on phonotactic effects in speech perception', in *Proceedings of the International Congress of the Phonetic Sciences XVII, Hong Kong: International Congress of the Phonetic Sciences*, pp. 2236–9.

Yule, George (2017), *The Study of Language*, 6th edn, Cambridge: Cambridge University Press.

Zimmer, Benjamins and Charles E. Carson (2011), 'Among the new words', *American Speech* 86, 454–79.

Ziolkowski, Jan, ed. (1990), 'What is Philology?', *Comparative Literature Studies* 27(1), 1–12, special issue.

Index of Languages and Families

Index of Subjects

Index of Names

CPSIA information can be obtained
at www.ICGtesting.com
Printed in the USA
JSHW032350120421
13462JS00001BB/1